Law in the Domains of Culture

The Amherst Series in Law, Jurisprudence, and Social Thought

Each work included in The Amherst Series in Law, Jurisprudence, and Social Thought explores a theme crucial to an understanding of law as it confronts the changing social and intellectual currents of the late twentieth century.

The Fate of Law, edited by Austin Sarat and Thomas R. Kearns

Law's Violence, edited by Austin Sarat and Thomas R. Kearns

Law in Everyday Life, edited by Austin Sarat and Thomas R. Kearns

The Rhetoric of Law, edited by Austin Sarat and Thomas R. Kearns

Identities, Politics, and Rights, edited by Austin Sarat and
Thomas R. Kearns

Legal Rights: Historical and Philosophical Perspectives, edited by
Austin Sarat and Thomas R. Kearns

Justice and Injustice in Law and Legal Theory, edited by Austin Sarat
and Thomas R. Kearns

Law in the Domains of Culture, edited by Austin Sarat and
Thomas R. Kearns

Cultural Pluralism, Identity Politics, and the Law, edited by
Austin Sarat and Thomas R. Kearns

History, Memory, and the Law, edited by Austin Sarat and
Thomas R. Kearns

Law in the Domains of Culture

Edited by
AUSTIN SARAT
and
THOMAS R. KEARNS

Ann Arbor
THE UNIVERSITY OF MICHIGAN PRESS

First paperback edition 2000
Copyright © by the University of Michigan 1998
All rights reserved
Published in the United States of America by
The University of Michigan Press
Manufactured in the United States of America
⊗ Printed on acid-free paper

2003   2002   2001   2000   5   4   3   2

A CIP catalog record for this book is available from the British Library

Library of Congress Cataloging-in-Publication Data

Law in the domains of culture / edited by Austin Sarat and Thomas R.
   Kearns.
      p.   cm. — (Amherst series in law, jurisprudence, and social
   thought)
   Includes bibliographical references and index.
   ISBN 0-472-10862-X (cloth : acid-free paper)
      1. Culture and law.   2. Popular culture.   3. Mass media.
   I. Sarat, Austin.   II. Kearns, Thomas R.   III. Series.
   K487.C8L394   1997
   340'.115—dc21   97-21205
                                                                  CIP

ISBN 0-472-08701-0 (pbk. : alk. paper)

Acknowledgments

The conception of this book emerged as part of the intellectual venture that we share with our colleagues Lawrence Douglas and Martha Umphrey. We are grateful to them. We are also grateful to Amherst College for the support that has been shown for our efforts to develop legal study in the liberal arts.

Contents

The Cultural Lives of Law

Austin Sarat and Thomas R. Kearns

The concept of culture is troublingly vague and, at the same time, hotly contested, and law's relation to culture is as complex, varied, and disputed as the concept itself. Against this background, *Law in the Domains of Culture* brings the insights and approaches of cultural studies to law and tries to secure for law a place in cultural analysis.[1] This book is, however, neither a comprehensive overview of the ways law shapes culture and culture shapes law nor a history of the role of ideas of law and culture in promoting particular political projects. Instead it provides a sampling of significant theoretical issues in the cultural analysis of law and illustrates some of those issues in provocative examples of that genre. *Law in the Domains of Culture* is designed as an encouragement in the still tentative efforts to forge a new interdisciplinary synthesis, a cultural studies of law.[2]

To talk about culture is, in the first instance, to venture into a field where there are almost as many definitions of the term as there are discussions of it,[3] and where inside as well as outside the academy argu-

---

1. For general examples or overviews of cultural studies, see Raymond Williams, *The Sociology of Culture* (New York: Schocken Books, 1981). Also Fred Inglis, *Cultural Studies* (Oxford: Blackwell Publishers, 1993) and Lawrence Grossberg et al., eds., *Cultural Studies* (New York: Routledge, 1992).

2. Such a synthesis is described by Steve Redhead, *Unpopular Cultures: The Birth of Law and Popular Culture* (Manchester: Manchester University Press, 1995).

3. While we acknowledge the difficulty of disciplining the concept of culture, we do not agree with those who believe it to be analytically useless. Exemplifying such claims are the following: "Like 'ideology' (to which, as a concept, it is closely allied) 'culture' is a term that is repeatedly used without meaning much of anything at all, a vague gesture toward a dimly perceived ethos . . . ." Stephen Greenblatt, "Culture," in *Critical Terms for Literary Study*, ed. Frank Lentricchia and Thomas McLaughlin (Chicago: University of Chicago Press, 1990), 225. Or, as Mary Douglas has said about the concept of culture, "[N]ever was such a fluffy notion at large . . . since singing angels blew the planets across

ments rage.[4] In recent years these arguments have come to play a progressively more visible role in our national life. Identity politics has merged with cultural politics so that to have an identity, one must have a culture.[5] As a result, it seems as if almost every ethnic, religious, or social group seeks to have its "culture" recognized. Yet advocates of multiculturalism and cultural pluralism acknowledge a danger in politicizing the taken-for-granted assumptions of shared values and common identities.[6] It is the danger that the possession of culture will mark social groups as "exotic" or that it will become the consolation prize of the marginal and the disadvantaged. As Rosaldo puts it, "in 'our' own eyes, 'we' appear to be 'people without culture.' . . . [F]ull citizenship and cultural visibility appear to be inversely related. When one increases, the other decreases. Full citizens lack culture, and the most culturally endowed lack full citizenship."[7]

Nonetheless, the backlash against the proliferation of cultures and identities, and what is called the "politics of recognition,"[8] has been vehement. Politicians proclaim "culture wars" in an effort to reassert both the meaning and the centrality of certain allegedly transcendent human values.[9] Debates about the meaning and significance of culture become arguments about "civilization" itself in which acknowledgment of cultural pluralism and its accompanying decanonization of the "sacred" texts of the Western tradition are treated as undermining national unity, national purpose, and the meaning of being "American."[10]

---

the medieval sky or ether filled in the gaps of Newton's universe." Mary Douglas, "The Self-Completing Animal," *Times Literary Supplement,* 8 August 1975, 886.

4. As Renato Rosaldo puts it, "These days questions of culture seem to touch a nerve" (*Culture and Truth: The Remaking of Social Analysis* [Boston: Beacon Press, 1989], ix).

5. Ibid. "[Q]uestions of culture . . . quickly become anguished questions of identity." Joan Scott, "Multiculturalism and the Politics of Identity," in *The Identity in Question,* ed. John Rajchman (New York: Routledge, 1995), 3.

6. "[D]oes it makes any sense," Etienne Balibar asks, "to speak of identity in the field of culture when . . . the suspicion can be raised that the very notion of 'culture' designates less a definite object than a place or a function that remains indeterminate?" Etienne Balibar, "Culture and Identity (Working Notes)," trans. J. Swenson, in *The Identity in Question,* ed. John Rajchman (New York: Routledge, 1995), 182.

7. Rosaldo, *Culture and Truth,* 198.

8. Charles Taylor, *Multiculturalism: Examining the Politics of Recognition* (Princeton: Princeton University Press, 1994).

9. See Fred Whitehead, ed., *Culture Wars: Opposing Viewpoints* (San Diego: Green Haven Press, 1994).

10. For a discussion of these debates, see James Hunter, *Culture Wars: The Struggle to Define America* (New York: Basic Books, 1991).

These culture wars are also being fought within universities.[11] There the history, meaning, and utility of culture as a category of analysis in the humanities and social sciences are all up for grabs.[12] Where once the analysis of culture could neatly be assigned to the respective disciplines of anthropology or literature, today, fueled by the growing popularity of cultural studies, the study of culture is pervasive; it refuses disciplinary cabining and forges new interdisciplinary connections.[13]

Traditionally the study of culture was the study of " 'that complex whole which includes knowledge, belief, art, morals, law, custom, and any other capabilities and habits acquired by man as a member of society.' "[14] This definition, in addition to being hopelessly vague and inclusive, treats culture as a thing existing outside of ongoing local practices and social relations. In addition, by treating culture as "capabilities and habits acquired," culture was made into a set of timeless resources to be internalized in the "civilizing" process through which persons were made social. Finally, culture was identified as containing a kind of inclusive integrity, parts combining into a "whole."

Today this conception no longer has pride of place within the academy. Critiques of the traditional, unified, reified, civilizing idea of culture abound.[15] It is now indeed almost imperative to write, to quote Lila Abu-Lughod's influential essay, "against culture,"[16] or, in the face of these critiques, to "forget culture."[17] Thus, during the course of a suit filed by the Mashpee Indians of Cape Cod in 1977, James Clifford exam-

---

11. See Gerald Graff, *Professing Literature: An Institutional History* (Chicago: University of Chicago Press, 1987).

12. "The recent critics of culture in no respect comprise an internally homogeneous block, and the objections currently in play represent a complex skein of partially discrete, partially convergent influences from political economy, modernist and postmodernist anthropologies, varieties of feminist writing, cultural studies, and diverse other sources." Robert Brightman, "Forget Culture: Replacement, Transcendence, Reflexification," *Cultural Anthropology* 10 (1995): 509.

13. Annette Weiner notes about the discipline of anthropology and its relation to the idea of culture that "Today . . . 'culture' is increasingly a prized intellectual commodity, aggressively appropriated by other disciplines as an organizing principle." Annette Weiner, "Culture and Our Discontents," *American Anthropologist* 97 (1995): 15.

14. Edward Tylor, cited by Greenblatt, "Culture," 225.

15. For a particularly useful summary of these critiques, see Brightman, "Forget Culture," 509.

16. Lila Abu-Lughod, "Writing Against Culture," in *Recapturing Anthropology: Working in the Present* (Santa Fe: School of American Research Press, 1991), 137.

17. See Brightman, "Forget Culture," 509.

ined the way culture stood up in a context where the very idea of cultural authenticity was on trial. Culture, he said,

> was too closely tied to assumptions of organic form and development. In the eighteenth century culture meant simply "a tending toward natural growth." By the end of the nineteenth century the word could be applied not only to gardens and well-developed individuals but to whole societies. . . . [T]he term culture retained its bias toward wholeness, continuity, and growth. Indian culture in Mashpee might be made of unexpected everyday elements, but it had in the last analysis to cohere, its elements fitting together like parts of a body. The culture concept accommodates internal diversity and an "organic" division of roles but not sharp contradictions, mutations, or emergences. . . . This cornerstone of the anthropological discipline proved to be vulnerable under cross-examination.[18]

Culture, Clifford concluded, is "a deeply compromised idea. . . . Twentieth-century identities no longer presuppose continuous cultures or traditions."[19] Or, as Luhrmann observed, the concept of culture is "more unsettled than it has been for forty years."[20]

Yet in this unsettled moment in the life of the concept of culture, efforts are under way to rehabilitate and reform it. In such efforts, contemporary cultural studies has played an especially important role.[21] Cultural studies has had a bracing impact in giving new energy and life to the study of culture, freeing it from its homogenizing and reifying tendencies. It has done so by radically extending what counts in the analysis of culture beyond the realm of "high culture."[22] It invites study of the quotidian world. Film, advertising, pop art, and contemporary music—these and other products of "popular culture" have been legitimized as objects of study.[23]

But, in addition to this liberating expansion in the objects of study,

---

18. James Clifford, *The Predicament of Culture: Twentieth-Century Ethnography, Literature, and Art.* (Cambridge: Harvard University Press, 1988), 338, 323.

19. Ibid., 10, 14.

20. T. M. Luhrmann, "Review of Hermes' Dilemma and Hamlet's Desire: On the Epistemology of Interpretation," *American Anthropologist* 95 (1993): 1058.

21. See Grossberg et al., *Cultural Studies.*

22. Herbert Gans, *Popular Culture and High Culture: An Analysis and Evaluation of Taste* (New York: Basic Books, 1974).

23. See Redhead, *Unpopular Cultures.*

cultural studies has also linked the study of culture to questions of social stratification, power, and social conflict. "[C]ultural processes," as Richard Johnson notes, "are intimately linked with social relations, especially with class relations and class formations, with sexual division, with the racial structuring of social relations. . . . [C]ulture involves power and helps produce asymmetries in the abilities of individuals and social groups to define and realize their needs. And . . . culture is neither an autonomous nor externally determined field, but a site of social differences and struggles." Thus culture, Johnson continues, can be understood as "historical forms of consciousness or subjectivity, or the subjective forms we live by, or, . . . the subjective side of social relations."[24]

Law and legal studies are relative latecomers to cultural studies.[25] To examine *Law in the Domains of Culture* has been, until recently, a kind of scholarly transgression. As Robert Post explains,

> We have long been accustomed to think of law as something apart. The grand ideals of justice, of impartiality and fairness, have seemed to remove law from the ordinary, disordered paths of life. For this reason efforts to unearth connections between law and culture have appeared vaguely tinged with expose, as though the idol were revealed to have merely human feet. In recent years, with a firmer sense of the encompassing inevitability of culture, the scandal has diminished, and the enterprise of actually tracing the uneasy relationship of law to culture has begun in earnest.[26]

In the last fifteen years, however, first with the development of critical legal studies, and then with the growth of the law and literature movement, and finally with the growing attention to legal consciousness and legal ideology in sociolegal studies, legal scholars have come regularly to attend to the cultural lives of law and the ways law lives in the domains of culture.[27]

---

24. Richard Johnson, "What Is Cultural Studies Anyway?" *Social Text* 16 (1986): 39, 43.

25. But see Stuart Hall et. al., *Policing the Crisis: Mugging, the State, and Law and Order* (New York: Holmes and Meier Publishers, 1978).

26. Robert Post, ed., *Law and the Order of Culture* (Berkeley: University of California Press, 1991), vii.

27. See Susan Silbey, "Making a Place for a Cultural Analysis of Law," *Law and Social Inquiry* 17 (1992): 39. Also Stewart Macaulay, "Images of Law in Everyday Life: The

Fueled in part by Clifford Geertz's description of law as "a distinctive manner of imagining the real," they have begun to be attentive to the imaginative life of the law and the way law lives in our imagination. Law, as Geertz suggested, is not "a mere technical add-on to a morally (or immorally) finished society, it is, along of course with a whole range of other *cultural realities*, . . . an active part of it. . . ."[28] Treating law as a cultural reality means looking at the material structure of law to see it in play and at play, as signs and symbols, fantasies and phantasms.[29] In the tradition of cultural studies, cultural analysis of law rejects "the dichotomy between agency and structure. . . . Treating consciousness as historical and situational, cultural analyses also shift attention to the constitution and operation of social structure in historically specific situations . . ."[30] It insists on examining the ways that the cultural lives of law contribute to what Johnson calls "asymmetries in the abilities of individuals and social groups to define and realize their needs."[31]

Meaning is perhaps the key term in the vocabulary of those who speak about the cultural lives of law, of those who seek to connect the word and the world.[32] "Our gaze," Geertz observed, "focuses on meaning, on the ways . . . (people) make sense of what they do—practically, morally, expressively, . . . juridically—by setting it within larger frames of signification, and how they keep those larger frames in place or try to, by organizing what they do in terms of them."[33] Focusing on the production, interpretation, consumption, and circulation of legal meaning suggests that law is inseparable from the interests, goals, and understandings that deeply shape or comprise social life. "[L]aw does more than reflect or encode what is otherwise normatively constructed; . . . law is part of the cultural processes that actively contribute in the

---

Lessons of School, Entertainment, and Spectator Sports," *Law and Society Review* 21 (1987): 185; Anthony Chase, "Toward a Legal Theory of Popular Culture," *Wisconsin Law Review* (1986): 527; Anthony Chase, "Historical Reconstruction in Popular Legal and Political Culture," *Seton Hall Law Review* 24 (1994): 1969; "Symposium: Popular Legal Culture," *Yale Law Journal* 98 (1989): 1545.

28. Clifford Geertz, *Local Knowledge: Further Essays in Interpretive Anthropology* (New York: Basic Books, 1983), 184, 218.

29. For a general discussion of the materiality of cultural life, see Raymond Williams, *Problems in Materialism and Culture: Selected Essays* (London: Verso, 1980).

30. Silbey, "Making a Place," 47.

31. Johnson, "What Is Cultural Studies Anyway?" 39.

32. Culture, Rosaldo suggests, "refers broadly to the forms through which people make sense of their lives" (*Culture and Truth*, 26).

33. Geertz, *Local Knowledge*, 232.

composition of social relations."[34] Law is part of the everyday world, contributing powerfully to the apparently "stable, taken-for-granted quality of that world and to the generally shared sense that as things *are*, so *must* they be."[35]

The power exerted by a legal regime "consists less in the force that it can bring to bear against violators of its rules," as Robert Gordon recently put it, "than in its capacity to persuade people that the world described in its images and categories is the only attainable world in which a sane person would want to live."[36] From the perspective of law's cultural lives, law operates largely by influencing modes of thought rather than by determining conduct in any specific case. It enters social practices and is, indeed, "imbricated" in them, by shaping consciousness, by making law's concepts and commands seem, if not invisible, then perfectly natural and benign. Law is, in this sense, constitutive of culture.[37]

Legal thought and legal relations influence self-understanding and understanding of one's relations to others. Legal forms provide ways of knowing, and seeing. And so powerful is their presence in our cultural life that their distinctly legal attributes become almost imperceptible. Thus part of the work of cultural analysis of law of the kind represented in *Law in the Domains of Culture* is to read the legal dimensions of cultural productions and the cultural meanings encoded in the popular representation of legal processes and events.[38]

We are not, however, merely pushed and pulled by laws that exert power over us from the "outside."[39] Rather, we come, in uncertain and contingent ways, to see ourselves as law sees us; we participate in the construction of law's "meanings" and its representations of us even as we internalize them, so much so that our own purposes and under-

---

34. Silbey, "Making A Place," 41.

35. Austin Sarat and Thomas R. Kearns, "Across the Great Divide: Forms of Legal Scholarship and Everyday Life," in *Law in Everyday Life*, ed. Austin Sarat and Thomas R. Kearns (Ann Arbor: University of Michigan Press, 1993), 30.

36. Robert Gordon, "Critical Legal Histories," *Stanford Law Review* 36 (1984): 108.

37. Silbey, "Making a Place," 41.

38. Lawrence Friedman, "Law, Lawyers, and Popular Culture," *Yale Law Journal* 98 (1989): 1579. "[L]egal and popular culture," Friedman claims, "as images of each other, help explicate and illuminate their respective contents."

39. "Cultural analyses challenge the notion that something is added from the outside. Power does not insert itself . . . .The constitutive perspective insists instead that the assertion of externality itself is integral to the effects of power" (Silbey, "Making a Place," 48).

standings can no longer be extricated from those meanings. We are not merely the inert recipients of law's external pressures; rather, law's "demands" tend to seem natural and necessary, hardly like demands at all. In this way the cultural lives of law, Peter Fitzpatrick contends, have been central "in the scaffolding of the modern-nation state" with its construction of the rights-bearing subject, imagined social contract, and insistence on boundary and boundedness.[40]

Yet law and legal ideas do not just colonize consciousness and provide the superstructure for modernist sensibilities. Legal meanings are not invented and communicated in a unidirectional process. Because they are produced in concrete and particular social relations, the meaning and the materiality of law are inseparable. Litigants, clients, consumers of culture, and others bring their own understandings to bear;[41] they deploy and use meanings strategically to advance interests and goals. They press their understandings in and on law and, in so doing, invite adaptation and change in the practices of law. Law thus exists as what Raymond Williams called "moving hegemony."[42] This concept, Barbara Yngvesson explains, allows us to recognize the "coexistence of discipline and struggle, of subjection and subversion and directs attention toward a dynamic analysis of what it means to be caught up in power."[43]

Law's cultural lives and its power in and over cultural production are continually renewed, re-created, defended, and modified. But they are also continually resisted, limited, altered, challenged. Law's cultural lives are, as a result, not placid and calm. They are alive with the push and pull of contestation that always marks what Johnson has called "the subjective side of social relations."[44] Meanings are advanced and resisted strategically, though neither the meanings advanced nor

---

40. Peter Fitzpatrick, *The Mythology of Modern Law* (London: Routledge, 1992), 202.

41. Austin Sarat, "'. . . The Law Is All Over': Power, Resistance, and the Legal Consciousness of the Welfare Poor," *Yale Journal of Law and the Humanities* 2 (1990): 343; Michel de Certeau, *The Practice of Everyday Life*, trans. Steven Rendell (Berkeley: University of California Press, 1984), 37; Jon Cruz and Justin Lewis, *Viewing, Reading, Listening: Audiences and Cultural Reception* (Boulder, CO: Westview Press, 1994).

42. Williams defines hegemony as "a complex interlocking of political, social, and cultural forces" that sustains particular forms of inequality and domination. Raymond Williams, *Marxism and Literature* (Oxford: Oxford University Press, 1977), 112.

43. Barbara Yngvesson, "Inventing Law in Local Settings: Rethinking Popular Legal Culture," *Yale Law Journal* 98 (1989): 1693.

44. Johnson, "What Is Cultural Studies Anyway?" 43.

the goals purportedly served in advancing those meanings exist independent of one another. Power is seen in the effort to negotiate shared understandings and in the evasions, resistances, and inventions that inevitably accompany such negotiations.

But law also plays and has played a large role in regulating the terms and conditions of cultural production.[45] The regime of copyright, to take a prominent example, has protected and promoted certain kinds of expression and discouraged others; it has tethered the life of signs to the fortunes of capital and contributed importantly to the linkage of artistic value with ideas of originality, authenticity, and "ownership of the image."[46] Through doctrines of "personality rights," law "authors the celebrity" and, in so doing, gives a particular shape to the practices of "popular culture."[47]

Law's cultural lives cannot escape the forces that, at the end of the twentieth century, afflict and transform cultural life everywhere. The cultural lives of law are located in the emergent crisis of representation as well as contemporary changes in the organization of symbols and the rhythms of symbolic construction.[48] Postmodernity and postcoloniality present new challenges to the cultural lives of law as boundaries collapse and the circulation of legal meanings becomes more fluid.[49] As

45. See Jane Gaines, *Contested Culture: The Image, the Voice, and the Law* (Chapel Hill: University of North Carolina Press, 1991).

46. See Melville Nimmer and David Nimmer, *Nimmer on Copyright: A Treatise on the Law of Literary, Musical, and Artistic Property and the Protection of Ideas*, 8th ed., 4 vols. (Albany, NY: Matthew Bender, 1989); Bernard Edelman, *Ownership of the Image: Elements for a Marxist Theory of Law*, trans. Elizabeth Kingdom (London: Routledge and Kegan Paul, 1979). Also Peter Jaszi, "Toward a Theory of Copyright: The Metamorphoses of 'Authorship,'" *Duke Law Journal* (1991): 455.

47. Rosemary Coombe, "Author/izing the Celebrity: Publicity Rights, Postmodern Politics, and Unauthorized Genders," in *The Construction of Authorship: Textual Appropriation in Law and Literature*, ed. Martha Woodmansee and Peter Jaszi (Durham, NC: Duke University Press, 1994), 101. Also Harold Gordon, "Right of Property in Name, Likeness, Personality, and History," *Northwestern University Law Review* 55 (1960): 553; Joan Gross, "The Right of Publicity Revisited: Reconciling Fame, Fortune, and Constitutional Rights," *Boston University Law Review* 62 (1982): 986.

48. See Michael Rolph Trouillot, *Silencing the Past: Power and the Production of History* (Boston: Beacon Press, 1995), 21. Trouillot says, "The acknowledgement that there is indeed a crisis of representation, that there is indeed an ongoing set of qualitative changes in the international organization of symbols . . . does not require a postmortem . . . the postmortem inherent in the postmodern mood implies a previous world of universals. It implies a specific view of culture and of cultural change. It implies, at least in part, the Enlightenment and nineteenth-century Europe."

49. Steven Connor, *Postmodernist Culture: An Introduction to Theories of the Contemporary* (London: Basil Blackwell, 1989).

a result, attending to the cultural lives of law requires that we attend to complex cultural borrowings, importations of new meanings, and new points of resistance.

Thinking about *Law in the Domains of Culture* requires attention to networks of cultural practices. It requires us to read and interpret those practices to understand how their form and content are constituted by law and also for what they reveal about the meanings of law itself. Attention to *Law in the Domains of Culture* is important as a way of unpacking what Rosemary Coombe calls "the signifying power of law and law's power over signification."[50] It invites us to acknowledge that legal meaning is found and invented in the variety of locations and practices that comprise the domains of culture and that those locations and practices are themselves encapsulated, though always incompletely, in legal forms, regulations, and legal symbols. Thus, the interpretive task for the cultural analyst is quite challenging as she or he seeks to read everyday cultural forms. To recognize that law has meaning-making power, then, is to see that social practices are not logically separable from the laws that shape them and that social practices are unintelligible apart from the legal norms that give rise to them. But studying *Law in the Domains of Culture* also highlights the limits of law's ability to constitute, regulate, or contain the imagination, invention, creativity, and improvisation that are culture itself.

Law in the Domains of Culture brings together essays by six scholars who are either at the forefront of cultural studies or who have already made significant contributions to the study of the cultural lives of law. Two of these essays (by Coombe and Ross) raise broad theoretical issues that will have to be addressed in the development of a cultural studies of law. The remaining four furnish compelling case studies in that genre. They present rich readings of the regulative power of law and its constitutive role in cultural production (Woodmansee), of the presence of legal forms in the episteme of popular culture (Clover), and of the way political and moral issues are played out in popular culture representations of law (Garber and Miller). Each essay, in its own distinctive way, reads the "subjective in social relations" and speaks to issues of social stratification, social power, and social difference.

---

50. See Rosemary J. Coombe, "Contingent Articulations: A Critical Cultural Studies of Law," this volume.

We begin with Rosemary Coombe's broad, theoretical overview of what she calls a "Critical Cultural Studies of Law." In this essay she inquires into the history of the ideas of law and culture, and her inquiry reveals that these ideas are not merely empty academic constructs, but that they "share a parallel trajectory in ideologies that legitimate and naturalize bourgeois power and global European hegemonies." Here following Edward Said,[51] Coombe argues that a *critical* cultural studies of law must expose the historical contingency of the concepts of law and culture as well as their complicity in particular political projects. Law and culture, she claims, traditionally have been used to mark distinctions between the civilized and the savage, the enlightened Self and the Other; they have played key roles in the establishment of a racialized hierarchy of states and societies.

A critical cultural studies of law must not only expose the history and political complicity of ideas of law and culture, but, according to Coombe, it must also de-reify them. Doing so means ending the divorce of law and culture from "creative practice and human agency." Coombe endorses Abu-Lhugod's suggestion that we should write "against culture" and also focus on "practices and problems of interpretation, exploring contradiction, misunderstanding, and misrecognition, aware of interests, inclinations, motivations, and agendas." Moreover, because law and culture express and reproduce social difference and inequality, both must be thought of as arenas of conflict and contestation rather than "integrated systems of meaning." Law and culture provide signifying forms around which conflicting political and social forces mobilize and about which pitched political battles are regularly fought.

A critical cultural studies of law needs also to be attentive to law's regulatory role in the realm of cultural production and consumption. What Coombe calls "cultural flows" have always been subject to the rules and regulations of nation-states, but today, in an era of globalization, the intensification of the regulatory regime is quite remarkable. Nonetheless, global restructuring continues to challenge the idea that we can maintain discrete cultures with self-contained systems of meaning and autonomous legal orders capable of policing and maintaining cultural boundaries. In this regard Coombe calls our attention to the

---

51. Edward Said, *Orientalism* (New York: Vintage Books, 1979). Also Edward Said, *Culture and Imperialism* (New York: Knopf, 1993).

importance of examining laws of copyright and other rules that shape "the direction and tempo of cultural flows" as well as the production of textualized meanings, the basis of their authority, and their interaction with "existing ensembles of cultural meanings."

In various ways, the next four essays take up these tasks. The first of these essays, by Martha Woodmansee, looks at a moment in the history of copyright law to assess its impact on the construction of the meaning of authorship. The following essays by Carol Clover, Marjorie Garber, and William Miller all attend to one medium—film—and take up questions of production, authority, and generativity in the representation of law and legal forms.

Woodmansee's essay focuses on Great Britain in the year 1842 and on a particularly important episode in the development of law's regulatory role in the domain of culture. This episode illustrates ways that law has, throughout the modern period, been used to foster the "enclosure of the public domain" in terms of the production and use of literary works. Woodmansee wants to debunk the notion that law's role has been simply a matter of protecting preexisting entitlements of "authors" and show how copyright helped constitute the author. Copyright law pretends to protect that which it helps to bring into being while effecting a powerful denigration of the public interest in widespread circulation of imaginative productions and literary works.

Woodmansee looks to the legislative debates in Parliament concerning a proposed revision in the then existing laws of copyright. That legislation, she claims, is "extraordinary in having been largely the work of authors." Its purpose was to secure fair compensation for what were perceived to be the important contributions of literary genius to the framing of English national identity. The debate surrounding the reform of copyright consisted largely of the "telling and retelling of the *lives* of authors living and dead." The result of both the debate and the legislation it produced was to attach to the idea of authorship a powerful emotional and symbolic charge.

The ostensible purpose of those who introduced the Copyright Act of 1842 was to extend the period during which literary works were protected against unauthorized reprinting from twenty-eight years after the date of *publication* to the period of the author's life plus sixty years *after his (or her) death*. While the length of protection was eventually reduced to a term of forty-two years or the author's life plus seven years, the legislation "represented a substantial victory for [its] proponents." It conferred considerable respectability on the profession of authorship, a respectability that continues even today to provide the touchstone for legal regulation and protection of cultural production.[52]

That the act was ultimately passed, in even its compromised form, Woodmansee attributes to the powerful mythologizing of authorship as well as to the behind-the-scenes presence of a great literary figure, William Wordsworth. Wordsworth's conceptions of genius and originality carried the day and provided the energizing force for increasing the legal protection for the prerogatives of authors. That conception, Woodmansee argues, is still present in the legal regime of copyright, which even as it faces the reality of mass culture and the global circulation of cultural products, on the one hand, and the increasingly corporate and collaborative nature of cultural production, on the other, clings to romantic ideas about authorship, genius, and originality that first surfaced in the Copyright Act of 1842.

Woodmansee's work provides precisely the kind of historical work that Coombe sees as central to a critical cultural studies of law. It provocatively links law and culture with notions of class privilege and the reproduction of nationalism and national identity. And it shows law to be both a terrain of contest over culture and cultural value and, at the same time, a powerful force in establishing or maintaining hegemonic cultural conceptions.

The presence and power of law in the domains of culture can, however, also be seen in its more subtle imbrication in ways of knowing, seeing, and understanding that are transmitted in and through popular culture. This point is powerfully made in Carol Clover's essay about trial films and trials as models for reading film itself. Clover begins her essay by noting the Anglo-American fascination with legal trials, a fascination not characteristic of other societies. This fascination is both a response to and a source of the "fantastic generativity of the [trial] form in Anglo-American popular narrative." Books, television programs, and films about trials abound. Focusing her attention on

---

52. Arguments in support of the Copyright Act were driven by a highly romantic conception of the role of the author in British national life. Britain's authors, proponents of the act argued, "have replaced her admirals and British dominance . . . depend(s) upon direct, or pure dissemination of the Authorial word," purity that would be lost if their works fell too quickly into the public domain where entrepreneurs would reprint, edit, or abridge—and, in so doing, vulgarize—them. Opponents attacked the legislation on the one hand as monopolistic and on the other hand as vesting too great a power in the authors' heirs, who themselves might suppress or mutilate the work.

film, Clover argues that "trials are already movielike to begin with and movies are already trial-like to begin with." There is, she notes, a fundamental likeness, an affinity at the level of structure, between the two forms, trials and popular film or television drama.[53]

It is to the trial-like quality of movies that Clover's essay addresses itself. Clover reviews the experience of watching trials and notes that there is a regular structure to that experience. In that structure, closure is seldom easily reached. Closure is commonly said to be one of the great virtues of the trial as a form, but the whole structure of the Anglo-American trial works *against* clear closure. Thus, reasonable doubt is a mechanism for bringing an end to something you can't decide—but the end so arrived at is not closure in the classic sense.[54]

So pervasive is the trial-like quality of movies that even movies in which there are no trials are, nonetheless, structured by the trial form. Clover advances this claim through a close reading of one film—*Basic Instinct*—a thriller or suspense drama. This whodunit works by engendering doubt about what we know even as it introduces new bits of evidence in every scene and each piece of dialogue. This film and lots of others "normally classified as thrillers" depend on narratives that are "fragmented, evidence-examining, forensically visualized, backstory-driven, X-not-X-structured, polygraphically photographed, intricately plotted, doubt-cultivating, and jury-directed."

Though there is no trial in *Basic Instinct*, there is "a trial underneath and behind it; the movie mimics the phases, the logic, and the narrative texture of the trial." It and other movies "follow the trial recipe even though they never set foot in the courtroom." The experience of watching, then, is an experience of the trial as it unfolds, as a textual process, over time. The trial form is present, though not readily discernible. It is this affinity at the level of structure as much as the kind of overt regulatory program discussed by Woodmansee that accounts for the hegemonic power of law in shaping popular consciousness.

The next essay, Marjorie Garber's "Cinema Scopes: Evolution, Media, and the Law," focuses on one famous trial—the so-called Scopes

---

53. Clover discusses several aspects of legal trials—in particular, the role of the jury and the adversary system—that are crucially important to their importance in popular culture. Following Tocqueville, Clover contends that the jury is a pervasive influence on the way Americans watch and the adversary system on the way we know.

54. For a rich example of the problem of closure in law, see William Finnegan, "Doubt," *New Yorker*, 31 January 1994, 48.

trial, which involved a 1925 Tennessee law prohibiting the teaching of evolution. The trial was, right from the start, a media event. "'My gavel,'" Garber quotes the judge as saying, "'will be heard around the world.'" The media and the popular culture audience it cultivated turned the space of law into a particular kind of performative space.[55] Thus the convergence of "radio, movie camera, still photography, print reporting, and commercial advertising" took control of law in the same way that law itself tries to take control of the cultural flows in which such media are located. The Scopes trial was, however, also a major moment in the articulation of a recurring crisis in American culture in which the question was whether the injunction to avoid evil would become indistinguishable from the injunction to avoid knowledge.

Garber discusses what she calls "three moments in the trial's reception . . . 1925, the date of the actual court case . . . ; 1960, the date of the Stanley Kramer film *Inherit the Wind* . . . ; and the mid-1990s, when . . . the Scopes trial, Darwinism, and evolution returned to public attention and concern." The trial itself was, Garber contends, at several levels about what could be heard, for example, whether the children of Tennessee could hear the doctrine of evolution in the classroom and whether the nation would hear, over the radio, the great debate about evil and knowledge that was played out in the courthouse of one small Tennessee town. It was about the nature of meaning and whether anything, even the Bible, could be said to have literal meaning.[56]

These themes get renarrated as the legal event is put on film. But film lives in many different time periods all at once. Garber suggests that when we see *Inherit the Wind,* the 1960 movie about the Scopes trial, now, more than thirty-five years later, and seventy years after the trial itself, history presents itself as a "set of nested boxes." We see many points in time at once, coming together to help give meaning to each other.

How do we read the film, Garber asks? Is it "unreflectively liberal"? Though set in the South of 1925, the film seems, at first glance, to have little to say about race. There are, in fact, no black characters. Yet Garber notes that the film is deeply anxious about race, an anxiety

---

55. For a general treatment of such spaces, see Andrew Parker and Eve Sedgwick, eds., *Performativity and Performance* (New York: Routledge, 1995).

56. Garber shows that even the word *evolution* could be said to betray the illusory quality of literal meanings as it has evolved from its roots in theology, deriving from a word meaning to "roll out."

revealed in its "repeated mention of lynching and of the Ku Klux Klan" and in the presence of the figure of the monkey as the trope for evolution itself. Thus the film suggests that the effort to stop talk about evolution was a way of carrying on a racialized war on behalf of whiteness. *Inherit the Wind* also captured a key cultural event in American history that was itself made into a media event, namely, the civil rights movement.

But Garber claims that the legal scene contains cultural meanings that cannot be so singularly labeled and contained. Thus *Inherit the Wind* can also be seen as an allegory for the Army–McCarthy hearings of the early 1950s. And with its repeated scenes of protesters outside the courtroom with their "contorted faces, intemperate signs, and biblical quotations," is it not also a signifier for today's "pro-life" protest? The power of the legal scene is not in the singularity and hegemonic heaviness of the readings that it enables, but of their proliferation, of the quick movements and multiple associates that they sponsor.

And, at another level, *Inherit the Wind* helps us see the scrambling of political categories that is now all too characteristic of our times. The liberal, pro-evolution bias of the film slips away in light of today's liberal critique of the kind of Darwinism and evolutionary psychology seen in books like *The Bell Curve*.[57] This phenomenon is also exemplified in the reemergence of creationism in the program of the New Right and in contemporary revisitations of the Scopes trial and the antievolution movement. Here the refusal to provide equal time to creationism in public schools is attacked by ardent conservatives like Supreme Court justice Antonin Scalia as " 'repressive' and 'illiberal,' " and creationists now present themselves as defenders of the very academic freedom that the original Tennessee ordinance was designed to limit. "Academic freedom, local option, religion in the schools, prayer in the courtroom. The events of 1925 seem uncannily familiar. . . . Are these 'liberal' or 'conservative' issues?"

Garber warns that "ideas and events are read differently in different cultural domains" and that, just as there are no Archimedean points in debate about the meanings of texts, there are no Archimedean points to which anyone can, with confidence, attach themselves in the search for timeless answers to legal and political issues. "Repetition and repression" are the "twin mechanisms" through which legal and cul-

---

57. Richard Herrnstein and Charles Murray, *The Bell Curve: Intelligence and Class Structure in American Life* (New York: Free Press, 1994).

tural meaning lives in history. Thus while trials like the Scopes trial have "an enduring impact upon the law," Garber contends that they have "an even greater immediate effect in the cultural imaginary . . ."

Repetition and repression also turn out to play a key role in the analysis of Clint Eastwood's film *Unforgiven* that provides the centerpiece of William Miller's contribution to this volume. Yet unlike Garber, who directs our attention to the impact of law on the cultural imaginary, Miller directs it to the way certain legal themes are worked out in popular culture. Culture, his analysis reminds us, shapes law just as law shapes culture.

Miller takes the legal and cultural status of revenge as his subject. Miller notes that American culture is deeply conflicted about the moral status of revenge. This conflict manifests itself as a deep ambivalence about law. Revenge is thought to be antithetical to law itself.[58] Thus law seeks to quell and control our vengeful instincts. Nonetheless, throughout our culture, revenge retains its appeal; it is a pervasive theme in the movies most people pay to see, the TV they watch, or the novels they read.

Revenge, Miller argues, is neither primitive nor primordial. It is alive as an aspiration to justice, an aspiration all too frequently frustrated in and by the legal process. In popular culture this type of justice takes the form of an exchange in which injury is paid back for injury. Thus the popularity of revenge in film stands as a countertheme to its suppression and frustration in law. As Miller puts it, "The position of popular culture is not just that wild justice is real justice. It doesn't stop there. Implicit in stories of revenge is that revenge is a criticism of state-delivered justice." This criticism is directed at law's technicality and its preoccupation with procedure. What is left unsatisfied in the representations of law and vengeance in popular culture is the need to assuage the victim's sense of violation.

But Miller warns that we should not be fooled; the revenge genre does not fantasize the end of law. Quite the contrary, revenge functions in the popular imagination as a complement to law; it fulfills an equitable function. Avenging heroes kill only those who "deserve" to be killed; they defend the weak against the strong; they respect community norms about good and evil. The avenger must always be able to

---

58. Austin Sarat, "The Return of Revenge: Hearing the Voice of the Victim in Capital Trials," *Social and Legal Studies: An International Journal* 6 (1997): 163.

garner the sympathies of the audience. To do so he must act in accordance with values we hold dear, with our sense of justice.

Unforgiven, Miller argues, puts at issue and complicates these themes even as it plays them out. This film, which is set in the Old West, depicts the quest of a group of prostitutes to buy justice for one of their number who was attacked by a customer. Clint Eastwood plays the reluctant hero who heeds their call. Yet throughout the film, while vengeance is presented as justified, as an equitable complement to law, it is not simply heroic. The film shows the ways that the call to heroism, the call to be at the center of a heroic narrative, may compromise the demands of justice. *Unforgiven* is at once then a praise of revenge, but also a caution about it, an invitation to do justice justly, to do it humbly, to do it no more than absolutely needs to be done. Thus at the moment of his vengeful triumph, Eastwood's character woefully explains that "'deserve's got nothing to do with it.'"

Popular culture both invents the avenger and creates our image of "the avenger's straw men: the legal system . . ." While legal forms like the trial may provide the narrative structure for movies, they cannot dictate their content. Yet it is true, as Miller contends, that "an overly formal, inept law, blind to the substantive demands of justice" is just what "enables a certain style of good story." Popular culture draws our attention to the failings and inadequacy of a legal order that we cannot live without.[59] Law is thus always called to account by narratives that it cannot fully contain or control. Those narratives provide powerful reminders of the gap between the justice that law regularly provides and the justice that resonates most powerfully throughout our culture.

Andrew Ross's "Components of Cultural Justice" concludes this volume by carrying forward the conversation about justice, but by locating it in a broader terrain of theory. He is in particular interested in what he calls "cultural rights" for social and ethnic groups, and he uses his inquiry into cultural rights to suggest the distance between cultural and legal justice. He warns at the outset that cultural justice entails more than the recognition of formal legal rights. "[E]veryday concepts of justice," Ross tells us, "are much broader and deeper than what is ordinarily understood as the rule of law."

Cultural justice demands respect for difference and that we see the

---

59. Friedman, "Law, Lawyers, and Popular Culture," 1599. Also Anthony Chase, "On Teaching Law and Popular Culture," *Focus on Legal Studies* 3 (1988): 9. Chase notes that Americans have a "split image" of law that is fostered in popular culture portrayals.

limitations of the reigning formal justice model that, for example, treats color blindness as the only road to cultural justice. Opponents of affirmative action, Ross contends, foster a return to the previously discredited idea of culture as uniform, undifferentiated, homogenizing, and civilizing. As he puts it, "appeals to some simple and common . . . tradition . . . [are] a ludicrous proposition." The resolution of a vexing legal issue depends critically on an image of culture and of cultural justice.

Cultural justice, Ross believes, is what is also at stake in the culture wars that are being waged by conservative politicians. Those politicians seek to discredit cultural politics and contestation and promote a return to *"the ordinary principles of our culture"* (emphasis in original). This, Ross says, is yet another example of the way hegemony works: dominant interests "masquerade informally as a background, default condition."

Cultural fundamentalism of the kind represented in the debate on affirmative action and by the advocates of the culture wars is, in part, a response to new transnational formations that have liberalized what Ross calls the "circulation and reception of cultural and information products." Like Coombe, Ross sees the transformation of culture through its globalization as setting the agenda for thinking about the contemporary legal and political dimensions of culture. Like her, he sees the globalization-fundamentalism dynamic as defining the terrain on which struggles for cultural justice will occur well into the next century. As he puts it, "It is not by happenstance that this macaronic image of a hybrid near future has emerged at the same moment as a fierce rekindling of nativist sentiment . . ."

This desire to produce sameness in the face of the assertion of cultural difference is also seen in efforts to use law to repress particular styles of expression and representation. Ross compares the repressive response to "gangsta" rap with the warm reception of violent films like Arnold Schwartzenegger's *True Lies*. Outlawing the former while condoning the latter amounts, Ross notes, to an attack on "the only form of cultural expression with experiential links to the life of poor minorities" while tolerating racist and misogynistic representations that serve to promote a "militarized public consciousness." Where is cultural justice in this choice?

Ross concludes his essay by reminding us that the effort to pursue cultural justice can neither be certainly aided nor definitively hindered by law. Law's regulatory power is important but not, in the end, deci-

sive. The struggle for cultural justice is a struggle to legitimate improvisation and experimentation, which struggle law can only incompletely understand.

Here then may be perhaps the most important lesson about *Law in the
Domains of Culture*. As powerful as are law's regulatory devices and its
hold on the "subjective side of social relations," as powerful as is the
colonization of popular culture by legal forms, as powerful as is the
pull of legality, nevertheless culture overflows, if not overpowers, law.
It refuses containment. Examining *Law in the Domains of Culture* puts us
in touch both with the pervasive power of law and, at the same time,
with the precariousness of its hold on our identities and imaginations.

Contingent Articulations: A Critical Cultural Studies of Law

Rosemary J. Coombe

The relationship between law and culture should not be defined. Law and culture(s) emerge conceptually as autonomous realms in Enlightenment and Romantic imaginaries; they share a parallel trajectory in ideologies that legitimate and naturalize bourgeois class power and global European hegemonies. Historical recognitions of the Eurocentric, racial, and colonialist roots of these terms do, however, suggest new avenues of inquiry. Whether this interdisciplinary opportunity is deemed a cultural studies of law, a critical legal anthropology, or a subgenre of cultural studies matters less than the rejection of reified concepts of law and culture.

An exploration of the nexus between law and culture will not be fruitful unless it can transcend and transform its initial categories. To ask under what conditions it became conceivable to comprehend law as something that regulates culture or culture as something that helps us understand law is to inquire into a history that reveals mutual implications in European modes of domination. To make this point, I will delineate a genealogy of these concepts as they developed in European modernity. From this genealogy we discover points of departure from which to effect a displacement of law and culture as discrete and naturalized domains of social life. An ongoing and mutual rupturing—the undoing of one term by the other—may be a more productive figuration than the image of relationship or joinder.

Recent discussions about culture—its heuristic value and political limitations as a term of analysis—reveal a pervasive unease. Scholars in both contemporary cultural anthropology and the emergent field of cultural studies tend to write "against culture." As anthropologists acknowledged the orientalizing tendencies of a concept of culture that delineated cultures as discrete formations, to be studied in their own terms, they became cognizant of the complex relations between power and meaning in everyday life. In reaction to the Eurocentrism and elitism of the humanities that privileged Culture as a canon of discrete works of European art and literature, a body of critical cultural studies was similarly and simultaneously forged. Rejecting modern aesthetic tenets that insisted that Culture be approached as a field of self-contained texts to be studied in terms of their own formal relations, those who practiced cultural studies focused on the social power of popular forms of textuality. These disciplinary developments share a recognition of the historical contingency of the culture construct and its political provenance. Such developments have parallels in recent directions in law and social inquiry. Many law and society scholars have turned away from positivist, formalist (doctrinalist or structuralist) and institutionally centered accounts of law to explore law as a diffuse and pervasive force shaping social consciousness and behavior. Although sociolegal studies has not developed an explicit agenda of writing "against law," such tendencies are nascent, if not fully realized, in a growing body of scholarship.[1] Throughout this survey of the tendencies and tensions, propensities and potentials in the scholarly literature, I will show how the challenges of transnationalism and the politics of global capital restructuring make a cultural studies of law and juridical understandings of cultural production, dissemination, and reception ever more pressing. The articulation of this contingent relationship—law/culture—will increasingly engage our critical attention as it is rhetorically developed in new political struggles for identity, recognition, and legitimacy.

Modernity's Misrecognitions

Law and culture emerge and develop into autonomous social fields from the mid-eighteenth through the late nineteenth centuries in Euro-

---

1. Most scholars of law and society write against law as a body of self-sufficient doctrine, or law as an autonomous set of institutions, and most also reject the abstractions of structuralist analyses of law or of liberal legal discourse, even when such practices are allegedly critical, as they are in critical legal studies and critical race theory. These might be seen, then, as propensities to write against law in the sense that these scholars are writing against its dominant self-representations.

pean Enlightenment, Romantic, and social science thought. They share parallel trajectories and are mutually implicated in the articulation of an occidental being, the West, and in evolutionary visions of human civilization and its development. Law develops conceptually as the antithesis of culture, anthropologically defined (albeit glossed as tradition, myth, or custom), but as constitutive of civilization and thus of Culture as the preserve of European nation-states. Peter Fitzpatrick points to a narrative of law—its modern mythology—that has law emerging as the constitutive feature of a European civilization defined in opposition to a savage other characterized by a lack of law and an excess of culture.[2] As we shall see, traces of this historical development continue to haunt contemporary anthropological debates and controversies within the field of cultural studies.

Robert Young argues that the concept of culture itself has origins in European anxieties about racial difference and racial amalgamation emergent in colonial encounters and forced migrations. Culture was understood to be "symptomatic of the racial group that produced it."[3] It became a commonplace of Romantic thinking that each language embodied a distinct worldview; although distinguished from nature, cultures were conceived of as themselves organic, unified, and whole. The culture concept, however, is always defined antithetically. Whether differentiated from nature or anarchy, or distinguished as a lesser state of being from the higher state of civilization (cultures as opposed to Culture), culture develops, Young suggests, as "a dialectical process, inscribing and expelling its own alterity" (30). Culture derives its modern meaning in processes of colonization, even in its meaning as the tilling of soil, which emphasizes the physicality of territory to be occupied, cultivated, and possessed to the exclusion of tribal others (31).

Culture's original reference was an organic process. Drawing upon Raymond Williams's genealogy of the term,[4] Young finds the concept and related ideas of cultivation and civilization increasingly deployed by European elites to mark social distinctions of class, race, and gender:

> From the sixteenth century this sense of culture as cultivation, the tending of natural growth, extended to human development: the

---

2. Peter Fitzpatrick, *The Mythology of Modern Law* (London: Routledge, 1992).

3. Robert J. C. Young, *Colonial Desire: Hybridity in Theory, Culture, and Race* (London: Routledge, 1995), 4.

4. See Raymond Williams, *Keywords* (New York: Oxford University Press, 1983) and *Culture and Society: 1780–1950* (New York: Columbia University Press, 1983).

cultivation of the mind. In the eighteenth century it came to represent also the intellectual side of civilization, the intelligible as against the material. With this it gradually included a more abstract, general social process, and in "cultivated" took on a class-fix . . . The OED cites 1764 as the date that "cultured" was first used in the sense of "refined." The social reference of cultivation was allied to the earlier distinction between the civil and the savage . . . operat[ing] within the later ideological polarity of the country and the city, for the inhabitants of the city contrasted themselves to the savages outside by appropriating, metaphorically, an agricultural identity. The city people became the cultivated ones, and the hunters defined by their lack of culture—agricultural, civil, and intellectual. This refined culture of the city was first named as "civilization" in English by the Scot James Boswell . . . in 1772.[5]

Such an understanding of *civilization* was metaphorically extended on a global sphere in Enlightenment ideologies, which used the term to express the "sense of the achieved but still progressive secular development of modern society . . . the end-point in an historical view of the advancement of humanity."[6] Societies could be judged more or less civilized and placed upon a universal trajectory upon which their arts and institutions could be measured. By the nineteenth century, stages of civilization—reduced now "to the cultural-racial categories of savagery, barbarism and civilization" (35)—were increasingly identified with racial difference. Influenced by German Romanticism and nationalism, dominant meanings for the concept of culture subdivided during this period. No longer merely the equivalent of civilization, and that which savage others lacked, nascent tendencies within Enlightenment thought were elaborated to differentiate *between* cultures. In Romantic reactions against the disenchanted realities of a grim modernity, primitive or popular cultures could be called upon as resources for an ideological critique of civilized society:

This is the mark of the decisive change initiated . . . by Herder: a Romantic reaction against the grand claims for civilization, in which the word "culture" was used as an alternative word to express other kinds of human development, other criteria for

5. Young, *Colonial Desire*, 31.
6. Ibid., 32.

human well-being and, crucially, in the plural, "the specific and variable cultures of different nations and periods." (37)

Differentiations in race theory emerge simultaneously with this differentiation within the culture concept, and both are brought into congruence with the naturalization of the nation as the constitutive unit of human society. Herder believed that the character of a nation was intimately related to land and climate and the popular traditions generated from such conditions. Cultural achievements, then, were invariably local and tied to their native places of origin. Every place had its culture and every culture its place; the nation is the embodiment of a people, their language, and their land. As Young explains, "This Romantic passion for ethnicity, associated with the purity of a people, language and folk-art still in intimate relation with the soil from which they sprang, was also closely related to the development of racial ideologies and the idea of the permanent difference of national-racial types" (42). A homogeneous, uniform basis for a polity, culture is the natural foundation for the nation. Each people, from barbarians and savages through the ancient civilizations, had its own culture and formed its own distinct national character. National cultures, moreover, could be judged in terms of their degree of civilization. Thus, Young suggests, there were already two "anthropological" usages of culture current throughout the nineteenth century; the first "referring to the particular degree of civilization achieved by individual societies within a general notion of the culture of humanity" (44), and the second deploying a concept of culture that was often indistinguishable from race and promulgated absolute forms of difference. A nonracialized concept of culture developed only in the twentieth century and "was inextricably linked with the cultural re-evaluation of primitivism associated with early Modernism. Indeed the idea of the culture of a society worth studying in itself reflects early twentieth-century modernist aesthetic practices" (37). I will return to modern anthropology's modernist aesthetic in my discussion of contemporary controversies over the culture concept. For now, it is important to note that a people's culture, in both its racialized and ethnographic senses, was a complex of forms in which law was understood to be at least as significant as the arts in defining national character and the degree of civilization a society had achieved.

According to Fitzpatrick, it is one of modernity's myths that others live in worlds of static, uniform, and closed systems of meaning, whereas "we" (a European, literate, and propertied male "we" in any case) occupy a world of progress, differentiation, and openness. This "white mythology" assumes that the West has law, order, rule, and reflective reason, whereas others have only violence, chaos, arbitrary tradition (mindless habit), or coercive despotism to govern social life. The mythic, cultural worlds in which others were said to live were constructed, he suggests, as "the mute ground which enables 'us' to have a unified 'law.'"[7] This is modernity's myth, in the sense that it was forged without regard for historical evidence and served to resolve tensions and contradictions in domestic and colonial social relationships and ideologies. Law was one indication of civilization, a potentially universal evolutionary pinnacle, which only the European had thus far achieved. Civilization, moreover, was equated with private property, a state of cultivated being that allegedly required an explicit and permanent set of ordering principles. Legal orders were seen as unified, harmonious, autonomous, and self-sustaining; uniform legal systems had conquered the irrational forces of custom and tradition and subsumed local differences. Such legal unities were themselves indicative of the qualities of national cultures and their level of civilization. Distinct kinds of law were tied to distinct nations, depending upon their place in a predetermined and universal teleology. A civilized human being had one king, one law, one faith, whereas the savage state admitted of no singular sovereignty, no law, and no singular deity but a multiplicity of disordered forms of authority demanding deference. The idea of law as singular integrated order, ever more differentiated and refined to meet the needs of ever more developed nations, was always already fully realized only in bourgeois society. Others were undifferentiated but indelibly different; they occupied the space of a uniform difference, whereas European societies were characterized by complex differentiations. Models of legal evolution (from Maine through Durkheim and Weber) confirmed these imaginary contrasts between the West and the rest.

The so-called study of primitive society, from which contemporary anthropology derives, has its origins in larger questions of comparative law:

As [Adam] Kuper tells us, "the study of primitive society was not generally regarded as a branch of natural history. Rather, it was

7. Fitzpatrick, *Mythology*, 3.

treated initially as a branch of legal studies." Primitive society itself was "a fantasy . . . constructed by speculative lawyers in the late nineteenth century." Furthermore, "the issues investigated—the development of marriage, the family, private property, and the state—were conceived of as legal questions."[8]

Such studies, of course, were integrally related to contemporaneous debates about colonial governance. Henry Maine's work *Ancient Law,* heralded as producing "the common currency of legal thought," was an entirely speculative evolutionary narrative, but one that implicitly addressed the governing of India.

The social lives and modes of power enjoyed diverse peoples could not, Fitzpatrick notes, be seen merely to be different, but had to be related historically to a trajectory in which European law saw its own past in the jural forms of others. "Such difference is accommodated as precursor to what inexorably and universally has to come about."[9] From the internal colonialisms of the sixteenth and seventeenth centuries to the overseas colonialism of the late eighteenth through nineteenth centuries, this fully evolved unitary law was both the justification for and the instrument of imperialism. It was the gift of civilization to be brought to others; as an incomparable vehicle for establishing peace and order, it was simultaneously the vehicle through which forces of violence and disordering were legitimated (107–9). In this experience, the small static, kin-based social group, governed by habitual and indolent custom (by culture, in short), "was created both in fantastic inversion of European identity and by colonial regulation" (111). Local customs and "customary law" were both fabricated and repudiated by regimes of colonial governance. Stagnant, superstitious, uniform, fixed, and self-reproducing, this colonially generated image of non-European cultures establishes the racial foundation for law's modern identity (111).

This identity was also forged with particular models of nationhood and subjectivity, Fitzpatrick suggests. Just as the residues of a colonially produced concept of culture continue to attract controversy in anthropological circles, so too, modernist understandings of the nation and subjectivity continue to inhabit the discipline's central precepts. The

---

8. Ibid., 102, citing Adam Kuper, *The Invention of Primitive Society: Transformation of an Illusion* (London: Routledge, 1988), 3–8.
9. Fitzpatrick, *Mythology,* 107.

birth of European nationalism in the nineteenth century provided new momentum for the creation and imposition of homogeneous and exclusive national cultures unified by language, law, and tradition. National literatures, musical traditions, and dance forms were discerned and their distinctions reified. Canons of discrete literary and artistic works defined a national culture and its contributions to a larger human civilization. Each nation exhibited unique examples of progress in the arts and sciences and thus could be measured by the level of its contributions to Culture, the realm of human perfection in creative endeavor.

Ideas of race were central to national identities and their presumed integrity. The self-elevation of European nations was legitimated by judicial nationalisms in which the nation's legal culture was seen to be uniquely reflective of its character as a national community and, simultaneously, evidence of the nation's place in a universal trajectory of progress toward civilization. A uniform law, encompassing and subordinating other forms of regulation and social ordering distinguished an evolved nation from those lesser races without the law, "still" ruled by custom and habit. The laws of developed nations demanded a particular form of sovereign subject—self-directing, reflexive, no longer bound by the constraints of community and tradition that so tied racial others. This self—the modern individual—is connected to other individuals, not by traditional, ritual bonds, but by modern legal forms, among which the contract was preeminent.[10] As Fitzpatrick notes, this European subject was the product of disciplinary powers, as power itself became misrecognized as a negative restraint upon free individuals (129). Others, by contrast, were incapable of self-determination, lived in societies of "inert mindless uniformity" (137), and were regulated by rigid custom. The tacit worldviews of such others were never explicit and could be made explicit only by the Western individual's rendering of "tribal" custom and the colonial administrator's determination of "customary law." Anthropology, of course, has its origins in precisely this ideology, of which the mythology of modern law is constitutive:

> placing Hart's concept of law within the European mythology of origin can help explain the silent suppression of linguistic philosophy along with the popular creation of meaning. All the inhabitants of the primal scene, from the savages of North America to the colonized of Africa, shared a convenient characteristic which pre-

---

10. Ibid., 118–29.

vented their contributing to linguistic use: they could not speak and thus had to be spoken for. In the imperial mentality which informs Hart's account and its sources, true knowledge is brought by the European to the mute and inglorious savages. Their reality is thereby known for the first time—known properly and fully both in itself and in the universal nature of things. Inadequate local knowledges are infinitely encompassed and given adequacy by European knowledge which is, in turn, elevated in its relation to them. (202)

Against culture(s)

It is now critical orthodoxy that in the dominant functionalist, structuralist, and interpretive (or hermeneutical) variants of modern anthropology, cultures were depicted as holistic, integrated, and coherent systems of shared meaning.[11] This depiction of cultures enabled (and was enabled by) the elision of the social and political practices whereby meanings and texts were produced. Social relations of production and interpretation were emptied of specificity so that those who produce and interpret meanings were without class, gender, race, or age and thus did not occupy social positions that might incline them toward alternative interpretations. Interpretive processes were represented without reference to cultural differences, social inequalities, and conflicts within communities.[12] The dialogic, contested dimensions of social life were evaded by a focus on *dominant* interpretations as the univocal voice of *legitimate* meanings and values. The interpretive approach engaged scholars in the discovery and description of the distinct lifeworlds in which phenomena had significance—as Clifford Geertz put it, the task involved "placing things in local frames of awareness."[13]

In its classical modern form, cultural anthropology recognized and

11. See Robert Brightman, "Forget Culture: Replacement, Transcendence, Relexification," *Cultural Anthropology* 10 (1995): 509 for a recent overview of critical attitudes toward the concept of culture in the discipline of anthropology over the last two decades. My argument here is derived from Rosemary Coombe, "Beyond Modernity's Meanings," *Culture* 11 (1991): 111.

12. John Brenkman, *Culture and Domination* (Ithaca, NY: Cornell University Press, 1987), 30–38. I explore this proposition in a critical consideration of legal interpretation and interpretive communities in Rosemary Coombe, "Same as It Ever Was: Rethinking the Politics of Legal Interpretation," McGill Law Journal 34 (1989): 603.

13. Clifford Geertz, *Local Knowledge: Further Essays in Interpretive Anthropology* (New York: Basic Books, 1983), 6.

respected differences between cultures but effaced differences within cultures. Defining culture as shared, zones of difference—where alternative interpretations are generated and dominant meanings contested—appeared to be areas of deviance and marginality, not central to the culture under study.[14] Anthropologists divorced culture from creative practice and human agency. Cultural theories, Lila Abu-Lhugod suggests, tend to overemphasize coherence and tend to project an image of communities as bounded and discrete.[15] Failing to represent contradictions, conflicts of interest, doubts, or changing motivations and circumstance serves to essentialize difference between societies while denying differences within them and, in so doing, effects a recognition (and legitimation) of certain regimes of power by giving priority to dominant representations and interpretations. Anthropologists maintained a modernist aesthetic sensibility. The art museum, suggested Rosaldo, was an apt figure for a field of intellectual endeavor that privileged classic ethnographies—creative works that represented cultures as autonomous, integrated, and formally patterned:

> Cultures stand as sacred images; they have an integrity and coherence that enables them to be studied as they say, on their own terms, from within, from the "native" point of view . . . [Like the work in an art museum] each culture stands alone as an aesthetic object . . . Once canonized all cultures appear to be equally great . . . Just as [one] does not argue whether Shakespeare is greater than Dante [one] does not debate the relative merits of the Kwakiutl . . . versus the Trobriand Islanders . . .[16]

Feminist anthropologists demonstrated that the representation of culture as a unified system of meaning was achieved primarily by excluding the cultural meanings that women and other subordinate groups in society attributed to their own experiences. They suggested

---

14. See Renato Rosaldo, *Culture and Truth: Remaking Social Analysis* (Boston: Beacon Press, 1989), 27–30; William Roseberry, *Anthropologies and Histories: Essays in Culture, History, and Political Economy* (New Brunswick and London: Rutgers University Press, 1989), 24–25.

15. Lila Abu-Lughod, "Writing against Culture," in *Recapturing Anthropology*, ed. Richard J. Fox (Santa Fe: School of American Research Press, 1991), 137, 146.

16. Rosaldo, *Culture and Truth*, 43.

that cultural truths were partial and often based upon institutional and contestable exclusions.[17] Ethnographers too often interpreted native elite male assertions and activities to metonymically represent social reality. Instead, feminists proposed an analytical attitude that "treats culture as contested rather than shared, and therefore represents social practice more as an argument than as a conversation."[18] Moreover, they drew attention to the multiple orders of difference existing in any social arena and their intersection in shaping human experience.[19] Drawing upon this work, Nicholas Thomas proposes that anthropologists explore cultural difference or local meaning through works that convey the politics of producing and maintaining structures of meaning "so as to disclose other registers of cultural difference," replacing "cultural systems with less stable and more derivative discourses and practices."[20]

Theorists of postmodernism reiterate several of these assertions, arguing that all totalizing accounts of (a) society, (a) tradition, or (a) culture are exclusionary and enact a social violence by suppressing continuing and continually emergent differences. One form of cultural critique (which both feminist and reflexive anthropologists endeavor to realize) is "to deconstruct modernism . . . in order to rewrite it, to open its closed systems . . . to the 'heterogeneity' of texts"—to challenge its purportedly universal narratives with the 'discourses of others.'"[21] According to Steven Connor, a postmodern consideration of power and value "identif[ies] centralizing principles—of self, gender, race, nation,

---

17. J. Clifford, introduction to *Writing Culture: The Poetics and Politics of Ethnography,* by J. Clifford and George Marcus, eds. (Berkeley: University of California Press, 1986).

18. Rena Lederman, "Contested Order: Gender and Society in the Southern New Guinea Highlands," *American Ethnologist* 16 (1989): 230. Lederman criticizes a dominant tendency in ethnographic work on the New Guinea Highlands that represents these societies in terms of male-dominated clan relationships, giving the exchange networks in which women are prominently involved secondary or negligible significance. Such an emphasis does not represent these societies as effectively as it echoes and gives legitimacy to a specific, interested indigenous perspective—an ideology of male dominance—that is contested by women and disputable even between men.

19. Henrietta Moore, *A Passion for Difference: Anthropology and Gender* (Bloomington: Indiana University Press, 1994).

20. Nicholas Thomas, "Against Ethnography," *Cultural Anthropology* 6 (1991): 306, 312.

21. Hal Foster, ed., *The Anti-Aesthetic: Essays on Postmodern Culture* (Port Townsend, WA: Bay Press, 1983), ix, x.

aesthetic form—in order to determine what those centres push to their silent or invisible peripheries."[22]

If differences within cultures became more apparent, or were finally articulated by anthropologists with new agendas, differences between cultures were simultaneously scrutinized on both political and empirical grounds. Culture, it seemed, operated conceptually to enable us to separate so-called discrete others from ourselves and to ignore the regimes of power and circuits of exchange that both connect and divide us. Abu-Lhugod suggests that culture served to reify differences that inevitably carry a sense of hierarchy; as a discipline built upon the historically constructed divide between the West and the non-West, anthropology "has been and continues to be primarily the study of the non-Western other by the Western self."[23] Culture is the concept that consolidates and naturalizes distinctions between self and other, but it also *makes* others other. It constructs, produces, and maintains the differences it purports merely to explain.[24] Modern cultural anthropology rests on an unstated assumption that others *must* be different, from us and from each other, even though those groups of people that anthropologists referred to as having "cultures" were bounded, created, named, and reified in nineteenth-century European colonial struggles and their consequent administrative hegemonies.[25] Even in its more progressive guise as a cultural critique of Western assumptions, anthropology "depended upon the fabrication of alterity, upon a showcase approach to other cultures that is now politically unacceptable."[26]

Writing against culture(s)

To write "against culture" is to focus upon practices and problems of interpretation, exploring contradiction, misunderstanding, and misrecognition, aware of interests, inclinations, motivations, and agendas.[27] Building upon Bourdieu's insight "that culture commits anthropology to a legalist perspective on conduct,"[28] Abu-Lhugod asserted

---

22. Steven Connor, *Postmodernist Culture: An Introduction to Theories of the Contemporary* (London: Basil Blackwell, 1989), 228.

23. Abu-Lhugod,"Writing against Culture," 139.

24. Ibid., 143.

25. Thomas, "Against Ethnography."

26. Ibid., 310.

27. Abu-Lhugod, "Writing against Culture," 147.

28. Discussion of Pierre Bourdieu, *Outline of a Theory of Practice* (Cambridge: Cambridge University Press, 1977) in Brightman, "Forget Culture," 513.

that juridical tropes like rules and models, regimes and structures need to be replaced with less static configurations that might account for the more creative and improvisational ways in which meaning is produced in everyday life.[29] Refusing distinctions between ideas and practices, or text and world, a contramodernist anthropology might emphasize individuals' usages of signifying resources and the reinforcements and transformations of dominant meanings thereby accomplished. Refusing to accept the modern predilection to avoid questions of political economy when addressing issues of culture, contemporary ethnographers seek to articulate the complex interrelationships between cultural meanings and social and material inequalities.

Culture is both the medium and the consequence of social differences, inequalities, dominations, and exploitations, the form of their inscription and the means of their collective and individual imbrication. An emphasis upon shared meanings evades (and is complicit with) those historical processes through which some meanings are privileged while others are delegitimated or denied voice—practices in which unity is forged from difference by the exclusion, marginalization, and silencing of alternative visions and oppositional understandings. Culture must be reconceptualized as an activity of struggle rather than a thing, as conflictual signifying practices rather than integrated systems of meaning.[30] To write against culture is to reject modernity's meanings, shifting focus from structures and systems to the signifying practices that construct, maintain, and transform multiple hegemonies.

Scholars of law and society have also argued for new paradigms with which to model relationships between law and society (including the necessity to stop conceiving these terms as separate entities that require the exposition of *relationship* as the adequate term of address). As disillusionment with instrumentalist, functionalist, and structuralist paradigms set in, concerns with law's legitimation functions—its cultural role in *constituting* the social realities we recognize—were emphasized. Constitutive theories of law recognize law's *productive* capacities as well as its prohibitions and sanctions—shifting attention to the workings of law in ever more improbable settings.[31] Focusing less

---

29. Abu-Lhugod, "Writing against Culture," 147.

30. For other examples from the field of Mediterranean ethnography, see Rosemary Coombe, "Barren Ground: Honour and Shame in Mediterranean Ethnography," *Anthropologica* 32 (1990): 221.

31. Frank Munger, "Sociology of Law for a Postliberal Society," *Loyola of Los Angeles Law Review* 27 (1993): 89. See also Alan Hunt, *Explorations in Law and Society: Toward a Con-*

exclusively upon formal institutions, law-and-society scholarship has begun to look more closely at law in everyday life,[32] in quotidian practices of struggle, and in consciousness itself.[33] Austin Sarat and Tom Kearns suggest that "a focus on law in everyday life can help to bridge the gap between so called 'constitutive' and 'instrumentalist' views of the law, providing a powerful means by which the everyday is understood and experienced, but also a tool that enables people to imagine and effect social change."[34]

Legal forums are obviously significant sites for practices in which hegemony is constructed and contested—providing institutional venues for struggles to establish and legitimate authoritative meanings. The adoption of legal strategies may give meanings the force of material enforcement. Law is constitutive of social realities, generating positivities as well as prohibitions, legitimations, and opposition to the subjects and objects it recognizes.[35] As John Comaroff remarks, the revitalization of scholarly interest in the anthropology of law has con-

---

stitutive Theory of Law (New York: Routledge, 1993) and Sue Lees, "Lawyers' Work as Constitutive of Gender Relations," in *Lawyers in a Postmodern World: Translation and Transgression,* ed. Christine Harrington and Maureen Cain (New York: New York University Press, 1994), 124. For a discussion of the constitutive perspective, see Austin Sarat and Thomas R. Kearns, "Beyond the Great Divide: Forms of Legal Scholarship and Everyday Life," in *Law in Everyday Life,* ed. Austin Sarat and Thomas R. Kearns (Ann Arbor: University of Michigan Press, 1993), 21.

32. See Austin Sarat and Thomas R. Kearns, eds., *Law in Everyday Life* (Ann Arbor: University of Michigan Press, 1993). Also Craig McEwen, Lynn Mather, and Richard Maiman, "Lawyers in Everyday Life: Mediation in Divorce Practice," *Law and Society Review* 28 (1994): 149.

33. Sally Merry, *Getting Justice and Getting Even: Legal Consciousness among Working-Class Americans* (Chicago: University of Chicago Press, 1990), Austin Sarat, "'. . . The Law All Over': Power, Resistance, and the Welfare Poor," *Yale Journal of Law and Humanities* 2 (1990): 243; Susan Silbey and Patricia Ewick, "Conformity, Contestation, and Resistance: An Account of Legal Consciousness," *New England Law Review* 26 (1992): 731.

34. Sarat and Kearns, "Beyond the Great Divide," 21.

35. These processes are explored in relation to legal regimes of intellectual property in my following works: "Publicity Rights and Political Aspiration: Mass Culture, Gender Identity and Democracy," *New England Law Review* 26 (1992): 1221; "Tactics of Appropriation and the Politics of Recognition in Late Modern Democracies," *Political Theory: An International Journal of Political Philosophy* 21 (1993): 411; "The Properties of Culture and the Politics of Possessing Identity: Native Claims in the Cultural Appropriation Controversy," *Canadian Journal of Law and Jurisprudence* 6 (1993): 249; "Embodied Trademarks: Mimesis and Alterity on American Commercial Frontiers," *Cultural Anthropology* 11 (1996): 202; and the studies collected in *Cultural Appropriations: Authorship, Alterity and the Law* (Durham, NC: Duke University Press, 1998).

tributed to our theoretical understandings of power, hegemony, and resistance.[36] Legal discourses are spaces of resistance as well as regulation, possibility as well as prohibition, subversion as well as sanction. Beth Mertz also draws attention to the complexities of legal relations of power:

> By contrast with accounts that discuss law as the one-way imposition of power, where lawmakers simply mold social actors and groups like clay, the social constructionist approach . . . understands the subjects of law as agents, actors with at least some ability and power to shape and respond to legal innovations . . . law becomes a form of social mediation, a locus of social contest and construction. And yet, because of its social character, legal mediation does not operate on a level playing field; . . . [we must be] mindful of the effects of differential power and access to resources on the struggle and its outcomes.[37]

If law is central to hegemonic processes, it is also a key resource in counterhegemonic struggles. When it shapes the realities we recognize, it is not surprising that its spaces should be seized by those who would have other versions of social relations ratified and other cultural meanings mandated. Law, then, is culturally explored "as discourse, process, practice, and system of domination and resistance"[38] to be connected to larger historical movements, while remaining sensitive to the nuances of "the ontological and epistemological categories of meaning on which the discourse of law is based."[39] Historically structured and locally interpreted, law provides means and forums both for legitimating and contesting dominant meanings and the social hierarchies they support. Hegemony is an ongoing articulatory practice that is performatively enacted in juridical spaces, where, as Susan Hirsch and Mindie Lazarus-Black put it, "webs of dominant signification enmesh at one

36. John Comaroff, foreword to *Contested States: Law, Hegemony and Resistance,* by Susan Hirsch and Mindie Lazarus-Black, eds. (New York: Routledge, 1994).

37. Elizabeth Mertz, "A New Social Constructionism for Sociolegal Studies," *Law and Society Review* 28 (1994): 1243, 1246.

38. Susan Hirsch and Mindie Lazarus-Black, eds., *Contested States: Law, Hegemony and Resistance* (New York: Routledge, 1994), 1–2.

39. Peter Just, "History, Power, Ideology, and Culture: Current Directions in the Anthropology of Law," *Law and Society Review* 26 (1992): 373.

level even those who would resist at another" and "hegemonic and oppositional strategies both constitute and reconfigure each other."[40]

Elsewhere I have argued that the law is simultaneously a generative condition and a prohibitive boundary for hegemonic articulations.[41] With such an assertion I want to move beyond the constitutivist claim that law both enables and constrains by attending to the cultural dimensions of power (as embedded in and expressed by processes of signification) and the politics of signifying practices in which distinction and difference are constructed and contested. Law is understood as the authoritative means and medium of a cultural politics in which the social is articulated. By recognizing that the social world must itself be represented, performatively expressed, and institutionally inscribed, we can avoid a metaphysics of political presence. This perspective draws upon poststructuralist, deconstructionist, and psychoanalytic insights[42] to reject any vision of a social world in which differences exist before the law and law is merely called upon to resolve and legitimate social claims generated elsewhere. Instead, I suggest we see law as providing the very signifying forms that constitute socially salient distinctions, adjudicating their meanings, and provoking the shape of those practices through which meanings are disrupted. Rather than assert the positivity of social identity, I suggest we see identities as merely temporary and uncertain resting points in quests for recognition, legitimation, and identification.

The actual engagement of the political is a historical moment in which particular signifiers in particular discourses become meaningful for particular agents. Situations of subordination are transformed into

---

40. Hirsch and Lazarus-Black, *Contested States*, 8, 9.

41. Coombe, "Tactics of Appropriation," 412.

42. Theoretical underpinnings for this approach may be discerned in Aryeh Botwinick, *Postmodernism and Democratic Theory* (Philadelphia: Temple University Press, 1993); David Caroll, "Community after Devestation: Culture, Politics, and the 'Public Space,'" in *Politics, Theory, and Contemporary Culture*, ed. Mark Poster (New York: Columbia University Press, 1993); Costas Douzinas, Peter Goodrich, and Yifat Hachamovitich, eds., *Politics, Postmodernity and Critical Legal Studies: The Legality of the Contingent* (London: Routledge, 1994); Ernesto Laclau, "Power and Representation," in *Politics, Theory, and Contemporary Culture*, ed. Mark Poster (New York: Columbia University Press, 1993), 277, and the essays in Ernesto Laclau, ed., *The Making of Political Identities* (London: Verso, 1994); Miami Theory Collective, *Community at Loose Ends* (Minneapolis: University of Minnesota Press, 1991); David Scott, "A Note on the Demand of Criticism," *Public Culture* 8 (1995): 41; and Jean-Luc Nancy, *La Communaute Desoeuvree* (Paris: Cristian Bourgeois, 1986).

spaces for articulation through identifications with specific signifiers that hold promise for new forms of political recognition. Because meanings expressed through systems of signification are, by definition, perpetually unstable, they are always capable of being deployed against the grain. The ambiguities and traces of cultural forms may be seized upon by those who may well repeat, imitate, and appropriate elements of a dominant cultural order while critically marking differences in social experience. Legal means and forums may legitimate or undermine such deployments.

The law must be understood not simply as an institutional forum or legitimating discourse to which social groups turn to have preexisting differences recognized, but, more crucially, as a central locus for the control and dissemination of those signifying forms with which difference is made and remade. The signifying forms around which political action mobilizes and with which social rearticulations are accomplished are attractive and compelling precisely because of the qualities of the powers legally bestowed upon them. Such mobilizations and new articulations may have political consequence when they "provoke a crisis within the process of signification and discursive address."[43] The enabling power of law, then, is not simply that it provides instruments and discursive resources through which social groups may seek to have their differences legitimated or their needs addressed (although it may be experienced in this fashion), but also that law generates the signs and symbols—the signifying forms—with which difference is constituted and given meaning. It provides those unstable signifiers whose meanings may be historically transformed by those who "wish to inscribe their own authorial signature on the people, the nation, the state—the official social text."[44] It invites and shapes (although it does not determine) activities that legitimate, resist, and potentially rework the meanings that accrue to these forms in public spheres. Such processes of institutionalization and intervention are both ongoing and unstable. The mutual rupturing and destabilization effected by this interchange provide significant sites for considerations of the relation between law and culture.

---

43. Coombe, "Tactics of Appropriation," 419, citing Homi Bhabha. Similar insights into law and politics may be found in Michael McCann, *Rights at Work: Pay Equity Reform and the Politics of Legal Mobilization* (Chicago: University of Chicago Press, 1994) and in Lisa Bower, "Queer Acts and the Politics of Direct Address: Rethinking Law, Culture and Community," *Law and Society Review* 28 (1994): 1009.

44. Coombe, "Tactics of Appropriation," 420.

Cultures of Legality

Hegemonic struggles take place in ever more expansive terrain as communications, transportations, and migrations assume global dimen-
sion. Global capital restructuring multiplies and complicates the legal
venues and idioms through which processes of institutionalization and
intervention take place and form. Changing configurations of power
and new dimensions of representation demand new forms of attention;
the relationship between law and culture, politically understood,
assumes a new urgency.

The anthropological concept of culture (or the sociological preoccupation with "society," for that matter) arguably presupposed the
European nation-state as a naturalized form of power rather than a
nineteenth-century political artifact.[45] The contemporary decline in the
significance of state power may be partially responsible for our current
uneasiness with the culture concept. Comaroff asserts that the so-called
crisis in representation is related to the fact that our received categories
of analysis are so closely linked with the rise of the European nation-
state:

> The very idea of "society" has always been tied to modernist imag-
> inings of political community (the nation in complex societies,
> tribes, chiefdoms and the like in simple societies—with scare
> quotes); likewise culture, which in its anthropological connotation,
> has always referred to the collective consciousness of those who
> live within a territorially defined polity.[46]

As "national" workforces disperse around the globe, national gov-
ernments struggle to regulate flows of people, goods, representations,
and capital that threaten their administrative capacities and resources,
challenges to the jurisdiction of nation-states multiply. The new global

---

45. See James Ferguson and Akhil Gupta, eds., *Culture, Power, Place: Critical
Explorations in Anthropology* (Durham, NC: Duke University Press, 1997) for elabora-
tions of this argument and examples of scholarship critical of the discipline's traditional relationship to bounded spaces as the locus of community and social relationships of significance.

46. John L. Comaroff, "Ethnicity, Nationalism and the Politics of Difference in an
Age of Revolution," in *The Politics of Difference: Ethnic Premises in a World of Power*, ed. E.
Wilmsen and P. McAllister (Chicago: University of Chicago Press, 1996).

cultural order will take shape in many forums, and in both traditional and emergent legal venues. Nations have limited (but still significant) roles in global cultural flows of representation:

> Much of the traffic in culture is transnational rather than international . . . Indeed, a corollary of the development of the postcolonial world is the growing irrelevance of old imperial centres and capitals. A few global cities may have become powerful foci for the flow of money, media, and migration. But taken over all, the emerging global order is much more dispersed: its borders are *virtual* frontiers which exist as much in electronic as in geophysical space, and its centres are the pulse points of complex networks rather than the capitals of nation-states.[47]

Cultural flows are legally regulated, imagined, managed, and contested. Let me provide some examples of this to suggest new areas of sociolegal inquiry. Legal regimes regulating the flow of imagery—telecommunications policies, regional broadcasting agreements, criminal laws in digital environments, and customs and import restrictions—are only a few that spring to mind. Empirically, we might ask, just how overwhelmed are nation-states by such invasions of textuality? How effective are such laws, and what are their unintended consequences? Do such old-fashioned notions as cultural imperialism continue to influence decision makers, and in what legal contexts? Given the international tendency to treat the flow of texts as a matter of trade, what social difference does it make when what we used to call culture is transformed into commodified information? How are "culture industries" legally defined, and how are they administratively formulated as national bastions against the effects of free trade? How are local resistances generated in relation to so-called global harmonizations—GATT rounds, Dunkel Drafts, and TRIPS Agreements, for example? What is the relation between legal and religious authorities in legislating this influx and circulation of cultural forms?

More genealogical inquiries are also invited. If, as Fitzpatrick suggested, the rise of the idea of an autonomous and integrated law was simultaneous with the rise of the European nation-state and its distinctive culture of civilization, then perhaps

---

47. Ibid.

we need to understand the centrality of the culture of law in the scaffolding of the modernist nation-state; of the significance, in its architecture, of the rights-bearing subject, of constitutionality and citizenship, of private property and an imagined social contract. What exactly are the invisible components of the cultures of legality that underpin modernist sensibilities in the West . . . How exactly are they constructed and connected to one another? How and when do they come to be taken for granted? When and why do they become objects of struggle?[48]

One scholarly initiative has been a renewed interrogation of the nation as a social construct—an exploration of the forms in which it has been naturalized[49] and the forms of power it legitimates. Law may well be central to the unique culture that nations imagine they possess. Bill Maurer, for example, explores the significance of "law and order" as a rhetorical form that contains British Virgin Islanders' sense of their distinctiveness as a nation and how this collective sense of pride and attachment to juridical regimes precludes any social movement to achieve self-determination.[50]

Cultural anthropology's modernist heritage—the desire to project cultures as bounded, coherent fields of shared meaning that have an autonomous integrity—no longer commands respect in the complex cultural contexts of a postcolonial era in which global economic forces have provoked unprecedented migrations and displacements. The disappearance of any territorial boundaries between those colonial entities once identified as "cultures" is a sufficient and compelling reason for rethinking the concept. Arjun Appadurai suggests that in the late twentieth century,

the landscapes of group identity—the ethnoscapes—around the world are no longer familiar anthropological objects, insofar as groups are no longer tightly territorialized, spatially bounded, his-

---

48. Comaroff, foreword to *Contested States*, xi.

49. See, for example, Homi Bhabha, ed., *Nation and Narration* (London: Routledge, 1990) and Andrew Parker et al., eds., *Nationalism and Sexualities* (New York: Routledge, 1992) for studies of the nation's cultural articulation.

50. Bill Maurer, "Writing Law, Making a 'Nation': History, Modernity, and Paradoxes of Self-Rule in the British Virgin Islands," *Law and Society Review* 29 (1995): 255. See also Peter Goodrich, "Poor Illiterate Reason: History, Nationalism and the Common Law," *Social and Legal Studies* 1 (1992): 7.

torically unselfconscious, or culturally homogeneous. We have fewer cultures in the world and more internal cultural debates.[51]

Similarly, James Clifford asserts, "culture is contested, temporal, and emergent . . . [one cannot] occupy, unambiguously, a bounded cultural world from which to journey out and analyze other cultures. Human ways of life increasingly influence, dominate, parody, translate, and subvert one another."[52] This implies a change of scholarly direction:

> While anthropology has dealt effectively with implicit meanings that can be situated in the coherence of one culture, contemporary global processes of cultural circulation and reification demand an interest in meanings that are explicit and derivative . . . We cannot understand cultural borrowings, accretions, or locally distinctive variants of cosmopolitan movements, while we privilege the local- ized conversation and the stable ethnography that captures it. . . . Derivative lingua franca have always offended those preoccupied with boundaries and authenticity, but they offer a resonant model for the uncontained transpositions and transcultural meanings which cultural inquiry must now deal with.[53]

Anthropologists are ever more aware of the significance of local sys- tems of meaning in determining world capital's impact in non-Western societies. Indigenous cultural values shape the transformations that external forces engender and the ironies and resistances they generate. Jean Comaroff,[54] for example, shows that advancing capitalist systems interact with indigenous cultural forms to produce dialectically recip- rocal transformations; "indigenous trajectories of desire and fear inter- act with global flows of people and things."[55]

The global restructuring of capitalism, and new media, informa- tion, and communications technologies further challenge the idea of

51. Arjun Appadurai, "Global Ethnoscapes: Notes and Queries for a Transnational Anthropology," in *Recapturing Anthropology*, ed. Richard J. Fox (Santa Fe: School of Amer- ican Research Press, 1991), 191.

52. James Clifford, *The Predicament of Culture* (Cambridge: Harvard University Press, 1988), 19, 22.

53. Thomas, "Against Ethnography," 317.

54. Jean Comaroff, *Body of Power, Spirit of Resistance* (Chicago: University of Chicago Press, 1985).

55. Arjun Appadurai, "Disjunctures and Difference in the Global Cultural Econ- omy," *Public Culture* 2 (1990): 1, 3.

discrete cultures that can be studied simply in terms of their internal system of meanings. Political communities must increasingly be forged, and to be forged they must first be imagined, given the heterogeneity of peoples and the mobility of populations to which political leaders must appeal. Benedict Anderson's influential definition of nationalism as "imagined community" suggests that communities must be constructed through images of communion[56] and that polities of any scale must be created through cultures of representation. Moreover, mass media communications enable people to participate in communities of others with whom they share neither geographical proximity nor a common history, but a shared access to legally regulated signs, symbols, images, narratives, and other signifying resources with which they construct identity and convey solidarity, social challenges, and aspirational ideals. Appadurai suggests that ethnographic strategy now requires an understanding of the deterritorialized world that many persons inhabit and the possible lives that many persons are now able to envision:

> . . . we live in a world of many kinds of realism, some magical, some socialist, some capitalist . . . the latter in the visual and verbal rhetoric of contemporary American advertising . . . imagination has now acquired a singular power in social life . . . many persons throughout the world see their lives through the prisms of possible lives offered by mass media. These complex, partly imagined lives must now form the bedrock of ethnography, at least of the sort of ethnography that wishes to retain a special voice in a transnational, deterritorialized world. For the new power of imagination in the fabrication of social lives is inescapably tied up with images, ideas, and opportunities that come from elsewhere, often moved around by the vehicles of mass media . . .[57]

The ordinary, the everyday, the local life of meaning is often fueled with media forms and possibilities and their imaginative appropriations. Legal ideas and the equitable envisionings they may evoke are significant here, for it is in the juxtapositions of old juridical sensibilities and new ideas of equity, traditional senses of obligation and new conceptions of rights, that new imaginaries of justice may be forged and new

---

56. Benedict Anderson, *Imagined Communities* (London: Verso: 1983), 115.
57. Appadurai, "Global Ethnoscapes," 197, 199.

demands upon traditional laws and legal elites made. We need to consider the possibility that multiple, overlapping, and conflicting "juridiscapes" exist simultaneously in places characterized by transnational flows of information, representation, and imagery. Certainly one question that sociolegal scholars must address is the ways in which Western legal terms are given new meanings when deployed in new contexts or in new social structurations, not just as law is globalized "over there," but as "others" within all societies give new meanings to old terms based on their particular historical trajectories. Scholars of law and society have some distance to go in representing the complexity of such global processes and their local legal consequence.[58]

How are revitalized fundamentalisms of various sorts interacting with the legal architecture of the modern nation-state, and how is legal authority imagined in situations where separations between religious and secular power are foreign impositions?[59] How are Enlightenment imaginaries accommodating or being transformed by indigenous regimes of value? How are the impacts of global investment policies locally imagined in social worlds devastated by World Bank structural adjustment policies? How is the withdrawal of regulation and legal form represented and understood in areas of the world where the nation-state commands neither resources nor legitimacy?[60] What are the cultural means by which law's absence—the withdrawal or disappearance of modern state apparatuses—is experienced or expressed in regions suffering rapid and profound economic decline?[61] For those concerned with the social study of law, the time could not be more ripe to investigate just how influential (and in what ways) law is in shaping the nature of the cultural worlds we occupy.

In globalized conditions, modern disciplinary heritages are increasingly inadequate, as this brief genealogy of the culture construct

---

58. See further discussion in Rosemary Coombe, "The Cultural Life of Things: Anthropological Approaches to Law and Society in Conditions of Globalization," *American University Journal of International Law and Policy* 10 (1995): 791.

59. This question is suggested by a reading of Partha Chaterjee, "Religious Minorities and the Secular State: Reflections on an Indian Impasse," *Public Culture* 8 (1995): 11.

60. See, for example, Michael J. Shapiro, "Moral Geographies and the Ethics of Post-Sovereignty," *Public Culture* 6 (1994): 479. For a recent consideration of fraud in the Nigerian political imagination, see Andrew Apter, "IBB = 419: Nigerian Democracy and the Politics of Illusion," in John and Jean Comaroff, eds., *The Struggle for Civil Society in Postcolonial Africa* (Chicago: University of Chicago Press, forthcoming).

61. This question is addressed (albeit enigmatically) in "Figures of the Subject in Times of Crisis," *Public Culture* 7 (1995): 323.

has revealed. Anthropologists now find themselves engaged in a new cultural materialism concerned with "the everyday life of persons, not the cultural life of a people."[62] Exploring a diversity of cultural forms in fields of significance and power, they consider the way these forms shape people's desires and motivations and how they are deployed to express experiences of self and community, senses of identity, and practices of identification. The forms of signification that provide the cultural resources for these ongoing activities of self-definition do not come from any singular system, nor are they contained by any singular structure of power: "twentieth-century identities no longer presuppose continuous cultures or traditions. Everywhere individuals and groups improvise local performances from (re)collected pasts, drawing on foreign media, symbols, and languages."[63] Forces of global capitalism have created a situation of late modernity that is "decentered, fragmented, compressed, flexible, refractive,"[64] and meanings are fashioned with materials from diverse cultural lifeworlds.

Understanding intersections of power and meaning, however, does not limit critical inquiry to individual performatives. We must regard the worlds of trade and investment, migration and production, no less than worlds of regulation and consumption—as proper fields for a culturally materialist inquiry. The Comaroffs, for example, call upon anthropologists to "ground subjective, culturally configured action in society and history."[65] They urge the promotion of anthropological practices capable of addressing larger and more complex fields—international armed forces and arbitrations, refugee camps and enterprise zones, diasporas and development banks (my examples).

> Such systems only seem impersonal and unethnographic to those who would separate the subjective from the objective world, claiming the former for anthropology while leaving the latter to global theories. In fact, systems appear impersonal, and holistic analyses stultifying, *only* when we exclude from them all room for human manoeuvre, for ambivalence and historical indeterminacy—when we fail to acknowledge that meaning is always, to

62. Richard Fox, introduction to *Recapturing Anthropology: Working in the Present* (Santa Fe: School of American Research Press, 1991), 12.

63. Clifford, *Predicament of Culture*, 14.

64. Fox, introduction to *Recapturing Anthropology*, 14.

65. Jean Comaroff and John Comaroff, *Ethnography and the Historical Imagination* (Boulder, CO: Westview Press, 1992), 11.

some extent, arbitrary and diffuse, that social life everywhere rests on the imperfect ability to reduce ambiguity and concentrate power. (11)

Culture, in this view, is less a matter of consensus than a matter of argument, "a confrontation of signs and practices along the fault lines of power" (18), that contains polyvalent, potentially contestable messages, images, and behaviors. It is important that in the turn toward understanding law culturally—as code, communication, resources with which to construct and contest meaning—we do not lose sight of the political stakes at issue, the material domains of signification, or the distributional effects consequent upon having one's meanings *mean something*. The role of law in institutions itself must be addressed—not simply as an overarching regulatory regime, or a body of institutions to which disputes are referred, but as a nexus of meaningful practices, discursive resources, and legitimating rhetoric—constitutive features of locally specific social relations of power. However imperfect, the law is a fundamental means for reducing ambiguity and concentrating power—stabilizing relations of difference and meaning.

Indeed, anthropologist Edmund Leach once provocatively defined law as the instrument of coercion that enables those with power to make certain interpretations or meanings dominate, and to make others live with those interpretations.[66] Recognizing that social boundaries were conventional and identities socially constructed, he suggested that "the maintenance of pure categories" was law's provenance: "The law, by which I here mean the customary rules of society, however they happen to be formulated, then pretends that it is normal for everything to be tidy and straightforward . . . The law seeks to eliminate ambiguity" (19). Whether or not one accepts so broad a definition for law (or believes that "societies" have customary rules), the role of law in limiting or denying ambiguity—consolidating power by stabilizing meaning—is central to its cultural study. To write "against culture" when engaged in sociolegal inquiry necessarily involves a healthy suspicion of legal definitions and juridical resolutions of meaning combined with an engaged commitment to exposing the exclusions and marginalizations, anxieties and aporias that pure categories always betray.

---

66. Edmund Leach, *Custom, Law and Terrorist Violence* (Edinburgh: Edinburgh University Press, 1977), 19.

Writing against 'Culture'

If a critical cultural legal studies might derive resources from anthropological misgivings about culture and the political necessity to write against it, another tradition also deserves our attention. Writing against Culture has also been the preoccupation of a group of scholars whose work is generally designated as cultural studies. Cultural studies is not "a tightly coherent, unified movement with a fixed agenda, but a loosely coherent group of tendencies, issues, and questions."[67] Summary overviews of cultural studies abound; metatheories of the field's coverage and import are now almost as ubiquitous as examples of the genre.[68] Aware that no state-of-the-art summary would be complete, or completely satisfy those who identify with the practice, I think the following, admittedly partial, trajectory is likely to find wide assent. Emerging from a widespread dissatisfaction with the Eurocentric elitism characteristic of those fields of humanities that traditionally took Culture as their object of inquiry, those practicing cultural studies rejected the modernist insistence upon the integrity and autonomy of the literary or artistic work and the value of studying cultural artifacts as self-sufficient wholes. They connected texts to the specific histories of their production, consumption, reception, and circulation within socially differentiated fields. In connecting the social life of textuality with everyday experience and attending to the social centralizations and marginalizations realized through rhetorical deployments, this approach shares many of the inclinations that shape contramodern anthropology. As Appaduari suggests,

> The subject matter of cultural studies could roughly be taken as the relationship between the word and the world. I understand these two terms in their widest sense, so that *word* can encompass all forms of textualized expression, and *world* can mean anything from the "means of production" and the organization of life-worlds to the globalized relations of cultural reproduction . . .[69]

---

67. Patrick Brantlinger, *Crusoe's Footprints: Cultural Studies in Britain and America* (New York: Routledge, 1990), ix.

68. Toby Miller provides an irreverent overview of the overviews and a copious bibliography in "Introducing *Screening Cultural Studies*," *Continuum* 7, no. 2 (1994): 11–44.

69. Appadurai, "Global Ethnoscapes," 196.

Cultural studies is anticanonical, attentive not to a nominated chain of great works by Great Men (Culture in Mathew Arnold's sense), but to larger social fields of inscription. Showing that "literature" is not a discrete form of discourse that can be clearly distinguished or elevated (although the rhetoric used to establish this belief as self-evident *is* a continuing area of scrutiny), literature is treated as sharing properties and relationships with discourses as various as travel writing, advertising, current affairs TV, medical texts, product labels, radio talk shows, political tracts, and legal treatises. The strategy is one that connects texts with larger cultural contexts recognizing the uneven "distribution of power and subjectivity across geopolitical space."[70]

> These passages beyond the text [in the formalist sense] or even beyond literature by supposedly literary critics are clear challenges to traditional ways of understanding the humanities disciplines. They are all also movements in the direction of a cultural politics that aims to overcome the disabling fragmentation of knowledge within the discursive structure of the university, and in some cases, to overcome the fragmentation and alienation in the larger society that that structure mirrors. In these ways most versions of literary theory point in the direction of a unified, inter- or anti-disciplinary theory and practice.[71]

To connect texts to contexts is not, however, to point to holistic systems of meaning—culture in the romantic or modern anthropological sense. Cultural studies eschews social organicism, or ideas that the life of a nation may be found embodied in its works of cultural expression. Assuming instead that lines of social difference underlie and animate all forms of representation, cultural studies is attuned to themes of gender, race, and class as they manifest themselves in cultural forms. Indeed, the drive to expand the field of "cultural" studies involves an acknowledgement that culture has been a contested term since its historical origination, marked with traces of the struggles in which it has been deployed:

---

70. Miller, "Introduction to *Screening Cultural Studies*," 17.
71. Brantlinger, *Crusoe's Footprints*, 16.

> From the late-eighteenth century forward, culture has been a term of ideological contention and "polysemy," in whose various conflicting uses [Raymond] Williams traced, as if in etymological miniature, the larger struggles of social groups and classes for power, freedom, and education—that is, for full social and cultural representation.[72]

In an influential overview of the field, Richard Johnson suggested that the term *culture* "remains useful not as a rigorous category, but as a kind of summation of a history. It references in particular the effort to heave the study of culture from its old inegalitarian anchorages in high-artistic connoisseurship and in discourses, of enormous condescension, on the not-culture of the masses."[73] Behind this history lies a struggle to reform leftist politics so as to include concerns with women, children, gays and lesbians, immigrants, and "minorities"—to acknowledge the cultural conditions of politics and the cultural characteristics of both domination and resistance. Johnson sees a Marxist influence on cultural studies to be indicated by the following shared premises:

> The first is that cultural processes are intimately connected with social relations, especially with class relations and class formations, with sexual divisions, with the racial structuring of social relations and with age oppressions as a form of dependency. The second is that culture involves power and helps to produce asymmetries in the abilities of individuals and social groups to define and realize their needs. And the third, which follows from the other two, is that culture is neither an autonomous nor an externally determined field, but a site of social differences and struggles.[74]

In accordance with Williams's dictum that "culture is ordinary," British cultural studies has focused upon "everyday life"—the structures and practices within and through which societies construct and circulate meanings and values.[75] Like contemporary ethnographers, practition-

---

72. Ibid., 41.
73. Richard Johnson, "What Is Cultural Studies Anyway?" *Social Text* 16 (1987): 38, 42.
74. Ibid., 39.
75. Brantlinger, *Crusoe's Footprints*, 37.

ers of cultural studies reject the modern insistence upon the integrity of authorial works. They study cultural forms not as timeless statements of value, but as "the real, the occasional speech of temporally and historically situated human beings."[76] Contingency and particularity, affect and ambivalence, iteration and enunciation are stressed rather than the eternal and the abstract in language and experience. Again, the movement is toward the cultural politics of quotidian practice. Rejecting modernity's boundaries between culture and everyday life as well as the related distinction between high culture and popular culture, cultural studies shifts attention to everyday cultural practices as the locus of both domination and transformation. Angela McRobbie stresses the scholarly "return to the terrain of lived experience":[77]

> How social relations are conducted within the field of culture, and how culture in turn symbolizes the experience of change, provide the points of reference for this body of work . . . much of the attention in cultural studies, and in this collection, is paid to the important but often unnoticed dynamics of everyday life: the sounds in the kitchen, the noises in the home, and the signs and styles on the street. (41)

Feminist concerns have been influential in shifting attention to the popular, the entertaining, and the personal as central to the reproduction of power and the transformation of meaning in contemporary societies.

Anthropologist Terence Turner (in response to the discontents within his own discipline about the propriety of "others" taking over the culture concept) quotes from a 1991 proposal for a specialization in cultural studies at Cornell University:

> "Cultural studies" is an interdisciplinary genre of cultural analysis and criticism . . . comprehends work on what has been described as the "social circulation of symbolic forms" that is, the institutional and political relations and practices through which cultural production acquires and constructs social meanings . . . a recognition of the role of "culture" in the sense of "symbolic constructions," in a broad range of social practices and identities . . . Alongside more

---

76. Connor, *Postmodernist Culture*, 120.

77. Angela McRobbie, *Postmodernism and Popular Culture* (London: Routledge, 1994), 40.

traditional areas of literary and historical study, [cultural studies is concerned with] cultural forms such as movies, television, video, popular music, magazines, and newspapers, and the media industries and other institutions which produce and regulate them . . . [78]

As he suggests, *culture* is nowhere in this statement treated as a reified entity or a bounded, internally consistent domain abstracted from historical forces. Rather, the emphasis is consistently on the social contextualizations of specific cultural forms as mediators of social processes and resources for social transformation. Indeed, the movement from determining structures to indeterminate (but overdetermined) practices in cultural studies has been pronounced.

Studying cultural processes "in the concreteness of the ordinary" requires multiple and shifting perspectives that consider all moments of a cultural form's social being in the world. This would include an existence in daily lives, in the realm of public representations, the contexts and conditions of its readings, the influence (and contestation) of those readings in private lives and social lifeworlds, the authorization, legitimation, denial, or injunction of those interpretations in institutional forums, and the potential transformation of such readings in the production of new cultural forms. Such multidirectional circuits of textuality are all too rarely addressed; more often than not, scholars focus on one or two movements in this journey as if the other moments in some way followed. As Johnson reminds us, we cannot know how a text will be read simply from the conditions of its production, any more than we can know which readings of a text will become salient meanings within people's everyday lives. Scrutinizing texts in terms of their formal qualities tells us nothing about their conditions of production or consumption, the basis of their authority, or their likely interaction with existing ensembles of cultural meanings in the experiences of specifically situated subjects. These "reservoirs of discourses and meanings are in turn raw material for fresh cultural production. They are indeed among the specifically cultural *conditions* of production."[79]

Although the term *postmodern* is much misunderstood by those who deploy it (often, in sociolegal studies, as a term of denigration that attributes a less substantive rigor, if not sheer triviality, to the work at

---

78. Terence Turner, "Anthropology and Multiculturalism:" What is Anthropology That Multiculturalism Should be Mindful of It?" *Cultural Anthropology* 8: (1993): 411, 420.
79. Johnson, "What Is Cultural Studies," 47.

issue), debates about postmodernity do have significance in this context.

> Of postmodernity it will be suggested that this remains most useful, not as an anti-foundationalist philosophical concept whose basis lies in the disavowal of truth-seeking in intellectual inquiry, and which thus differentiates itself from the project of modernity, but as an analytical/descriptive category whose momentum derives from its cutting free from the long legacy of meanings associated with modernity. The term postmodernity indicates something of the size and the scale of the new global and local social relations and identities set up between individuals, groups, and populations as they interact with and are formed by the multiplicity of texts and representations which are a constitutive part of contemporary reality and experience.[80]

Regimes of law are constitutive of the cultural conditions of production and reproduction of representations, providing both incentives to produce and to disseminate texts, regulating their modes of circulation, and enabling some while prohibiting other forms of reception and interpretation. Laws of copyright and contract, torts and telecommunications, investment and trade, publicity and privacy shape the direction and tempo of cultural flows. In global contexts these relationships become increasingly complex.

Issues of global cultural relations proliferate and press upon us, but the means and methods we have for addressing such issues are arguably inadequate, as Toby Miller points out.[81] In cultural studies, Miller suggests, the field is dominated by cultural and economic reductionism. Either the life of the text is wholly autonomous from its contexts of production and dissemination or the "truth of the text resides in its carriage" and "practices of making sense are entirely subordinated to the political economy of transmission" (29). A revitalized global cultural studies, however, would combine theories and methods across sites "in a liminal state that borrows from the interpretive strengths of textual analysis and the distributional strengths of cultural economics" (31). Adopting perspectives that combine the critical skepticism of

---

80. McRobbie, *Postmodernism and Popular Culture*, 26.
81. Miller, "Introducing *Screening Cultural Studies*," 29.

political economy with the antifoundationalism of poststructuralist philosophies, he suggests that we trace "actor networks, technologies of textual exchange, circuits of communication, and textual effectivity, traditions of exegesis, commentary and critical practice" (33). Whether we are concerned with the legal regulation and direction of cultural flows or with the flow of legal texts and juridical meanings, such an interdisciplinary, multisite, multilevel analysis recommends itself to a critical cultural legal studies. Such studies, I would suggest, must be capable of drawing relationships between forms of epistemology and types of power, between modes of interpellation, characteristic forms of agency, and specific activities of interpretation. Only such intersections permit consideration of the role of cultural flows in constitutions of subjectivities and identities—an increasingly significant domain of sociolegal studies and an important domain for the consideration of contemporary politics.

Legalities and Identities

Recent developments in both anthropology and cultural studies put renewed emphasis upon the centrality of subjectivity and the construction of identity in contemporary historical conditions. Recognizing the simultaneously contingent and compelling character of identity claims in political arenas, theoretical tools have been developed to deal sensitively with the nuances of such assertions. The intellectual history behind this agenda is complex; it involves a working through of issues of consciousness, ideology, interpellation, subject formation, hegemony, and psychoanalysis engaging the theoretical work of Marx, Althusser, Gramsci, Foucault, Bourdieu, and Lacan. Individual and collective identities are actively created by human beings through the social forms through which they become conscious and sustain themselves as subjects.

Although interpellation has not been a popular concept in sociolegal study, because it is too often reduced to a simplistic determinism and an implicit denial of agency,[82] some promising work has been done

---

82. See Rosemary Coombe, "Room for Manoeuver: Towards a Theory of Practice in Critical Legal Studies," *Law and Social Inquiry* 14 (1989): 69 and sources cited therein for a discussion of theoretical means for holding on to some of the strengths of the concept of interpellation without fully succumbing to its structuralist tendencies.

along these lines.[83] Concerns with identity, community, and subjectivity, however, are shared by many contemporary critical scholars of law and society who might be seen to share a cultural orientation with anthropologists and cultural studies scholars. The emphasis upon subjectively inhabited *forms* is not especially elaborated in critical sociolegal studies, although the resurgence of interest in narrative forms is a step in this direction.[84] One wonders what an empirically grounded study of metaphor or allegory in legal thought and consciousness might yield.

Many scholars of law and society explore the fashions in which identities are forged in relation to law, in accommodation and in resistance to it, acknowledging that law interacts with other forms of discourse and sources of cultural meaning to construct and to contest identities, communities, and authorities. Such approaches have been deemed by Elizabeth Mertz "a new social constructionism" in sociolegal studies.[85] She delineates this "innovative development" as a vision that embodies the following aspects:

> (1) a view of law as "underdeterminate" (but not entirely indeterminate); (2) an understanding that legal representations of social identities as fixed or coherent are often fictional, serving other than their apparent purposes; (3) a critical view of the constitution of the "local" in legal discourse, with careful attention to the ways in which local units and identities are actually created (at least in part) from the "top down" in interaction with national and international legal discourses; (4) a similarly critical understanding of the way in which concepts such as "customary law," "authentic indigenous voices," and "rationality" themselves reflect very particular social constructions that are far from neutral reflections of reality; and (5) a sophisticated analysis of the power of legal language to create epistemological frames. (1245)

---

83. See Anne Barron, "Citizenship and the Colonization of the Self in the Modern State," in *Postmodernism and Law: Enlightenment, Revolution and the Death of Man*, ed. Anthony Carty (Edinburgh: University of Edinburgh Press, 1991), 107–26.

84. See Patricia Ewick and Susan Silbey, "Subversive Stories and Hegemonic Tales: Toward a Sociology of Narrative," *Law and Society Review* 29 (1995): 197 and sources cited therein; Judith Greenberg and Robert V. Ward, "Teaching Race and the Law through Narrative," *Wake Forest Law Review* 34 (1995): 323.

85. Mertz, "Social Constructionism," 1243.

The "social constructionist" vision devotes particular attention to the provisional, fluid, strategic, and contested identities constructed in contexts mediated by law. In so doing, its proponents question the tendencies of legal doctrine and statutory dictates, which understand identities in static and fixed terms, embodying a unity and coherence that can be ascertained:

> [C]ommunities and identities are produced in the interstices of law and society, social and contextual creations, not the static or prefigured identities that populate legal fictions, and, too often, take on a life of their own, creating formative effects in social life . . . as people struggle to meet these definitions or to voice alternative visions. (1248)

Although the term *social constructionism* is somewhat inadequate a nomination for the tendencies of this range of scholarship (it harks back to an early sociological phenomenology that was less than attentive to inequalities in power and access to discursive resources),[86] such work portends the dawning of a cultural materialist study of law.

Carol Greenhouse suggests that the idea of cultural construction ties the poetics of identity to the materialities of power.[87] As examples she discusses two ethnographic studies of law in local constructions of identity.[88] Both Wendy Espeland and Susan Gooding "track the circulation of the law's signs and practices, emphasizing the perspectives of Indian litigants and their supporters. The law's transformative power in relation to Yavapev or Colville people's cultural identity inheres in the practical uses to which they put the law's idioms, limits, and opportunities as *their own* cultural expressions."[89] To appreciate the law's role in the cultural construction of identities, we must interrelate "the cul-

---

86. I speculate that the term is used to make such work appear less threatening to social science empiricists who would at least recognize this scholarship as stemming from a recognizable lineage.

87. Carol Greenhouse,"Constructive Approaches to Law, Culture, and Identity," *Law and Society Review* 28 (1994): 1231.

88. Susan S. Gooding, "Place, Race, and Names: Layered Identities in *United States v. Oregon*, Confederated Tribes of the Colville Reservation, Plaintiff-Intervenor," *Law and Society Review* 28 (1994): 1181; and Wendy Espeland, "Legally Mediated Identity: The National Environmental Policy Act and the Bureaucratic Construction of Interests," *Law and Society Review* 28 (1994): 1149.

89. Greenhouse, "Constructive Approaches," 1239.

tural, social, and legal technologies that fuse issues of representation indelibly to issues of practice and power."[90] Moreover, as implied earlier, the meaning of the cultural here does not point to culture in its modern (Romantic or racialist) senses, but upon shared meanings of experience generated in social practices. As Greenhouse puts it, "the analytical relevance of identity emerges as *social action*—as experience, not as a representational space, or, even less, a category, or type."[91] Law-and-society scholarship has been less than attentive to issues of social textuality—for example, the impact of legal inscriptions upon the availability and desirability of those cultural resources with which identities are iterated and enunciated.

More sophisticated variants of cultural studies are antipositivist in the sense that they do not presuppose that the social can be explored simply in terms of its Logos, positivities, or presences; it must be seen, as well, in terms of "counterfactuals,"[92] the missing, the hidden, the repressed, the silenced, the misrecognized, and in the traces of those persons and forces that are underrepresented or unacknowledged in any social formation.[93] For studies of law this might suggest that the law's real impact may be felt where it is least evident and where those affected may have few resources to pursue their rights in institutional channels, and that the law's workings may well be found in traces of struggles over signification—not only when law is institutionally encountered, but when it is consciously and unconsciously apprehended. It is at work when threats of legal action are made as well as when they are actually acted upon. People's imagination of what "the law says" may shape the expressive activities through which cultural meanings are created.

Moreover, the law's *failure* to acknowledge identities and meanings may play a constitutive role in shaping significations in the public sphere. For scholars concerned with gay and lesbian empowerment, for

90. Ibid., 1238.

91. Ibid., 1240. A culturally materialist approach to law in society must approach the concept of "experience," however, with some caution, avoiding any privileging of the phenomenological as more authentic or real than social meanings. For critical discussions of experience, see Diane Fuss, *Essentially Speaking* (New York: Routledge, 1993) and Joan Scott, "On Experience," in *Feminists Theorize the Political*, ed. Joan Scott and Judith Butler (New York: Routledge, 1992).

92. Brantlinger, *Crusoe's Footprints*, 64.

93. For a longer discussion of this problem in the field of legal history, see Rosemary Coombe, "Contesting the Self: Negotiating Subjectivities in Nineteenth-Century Ontario Defamation Trials," *Studies in Law, Politics and Society* 11 (1991): 3.

example, preoccupations with the presence or absence of identity and relations between the law's recognition and identity's cultural construction have taken on new urgency as the limitations of an identity-based legal strategy have become evident. Lisa Bower, reviewing the field of queer legal theory, suggests that the failure of American law to provide equality under the trope of identity led gay and lesbian activists to question a politics based upon identity and to engage instead in a cultural politics of categorical destabilization.[94] The resort to doctrinal categories and resolutions by queer legal theorists may then be misguided, for it presupposes the continued primacy of a politics addressed to the state in appeals for official recognition. Rather, she suggests, the relation between law and politics has been transformed in gay and lesbian activism, with the politics of official recognition as evidenced in rights claims taking a back seat to a more public and performative politics that aims to change popular consciousness and disrupt existing sex-gender categories and to transform people's identities and identifications. Such a politics takes dominant signifiers in public realms and invests them with new (and superficially perverse) meanings. Ironically, the limitations of the law's ability to recognize an identity has compelled a redefinition of community and a rearticulation of the politics of asserting difference. Indeed, a politics of identification based upon nonidentity might be seen to have been legally engendered.

The current proliferation of sociolegal studies dealing with identity is congruent with the contemporary anthropological uneasiness with the idea of culture as a noun—the conviction that we need to understand culture as a description of particular practices of meaningful articulation. Turner goes so far as to redefine culture *as* the act of identity construction:

> Cultures are the way specific social groups, acting under specific historical and material conditions, have "made themselves." The theoretical contribution of the anthropological approach to culture, in sum, has been the focus on the capacity for culture as a collective power emergent in human social interaction . . . Two features of the anthropological concept of the capacity for culture are particularly

---

94. Lisa Bower, "Queer Acts and the Politics of Direct Address: Rethinking Law, Culture, and Community," *Law and Society Review* 28 (1995): 1009.

relevant in this context; its inherently social character and its virtually infinite plasticity. The capacity for culture does not inhere in
individuals as such but arises as an aspect of collective social life
. . . Its almost infinite malleability, however, means that there are
virtually no limits to the kinds of social groups, networks, or relations that can generate a cultural identity of their own.[95]

Many varieties of cultural studies are motivated by a conviction that
"the empowerment of the basic human capacity for self-creation (i.e.,
for culture, in the active sense of collective self-production) for all members and groups of society"[96] is a political accomplishment. All social
practices have cultural meaning and potentially do subjective work.
There is no reason to limit the field to particular practices, nor to discrete genres of discourse, types of signs, or active pursuits. Ben Forest,
for example, shows how in the campaign to incorporate West Hollywood as a city, a gay male identity was consolidated from a specific
sense of place that became something of a new form of political subjectivity—"citizenship," if you will.[97] The supermarket, the corporate
prospectus, the football game, a particular car—these are all cultural
forms that may be engaged in social constructions of identity. Real life
is a textualized frame of experiential reference. It is important, however, to acknowledge that capacities for such creativity are not equally
distributed, nor are the cultural resources to construct and contest identities equally accessible or available.

Some of the most influential of early cultural studies monographs
addressed legal themes, looking at the ways in which legal discourse
constrained and empowered those outside its official circuits. From the
early "histories from below"[98] to the collective work on media representations in *Policing the Crisis*,[99] law was seen as central to consciousness and social structuration. Miller reminds us of Richard Hoggart:

---

95. Turner, "Anthropology and Multiculturalism," 426.

96. Ibid., 427.

97. Ben Forest, "West Hollywood as Symbol: The Significance of Place in the Construction of a Gay Identity," *Environment and Planning D: Society and Space* 13 (1995): 133.

98. See, for example, E. P. Thompson, *Whigs and Hunters: The Origin of the Black Acts*
(London: Basil Blackwell, 1978); E. P. Thompson, "The Moral Economy of the English
Crowd in the 18th Century," *Past and Present* 10 (1971): 75–109; Douglas Hay, *Albion's Fatal
Tree: Crime and Society in 18th Century England* (London: Allen Lare, 1977).

99. Stuart Hall et al., *Policing the Crisis: Mugging, the State, and Law and Order* (New
York: Holmes and Meier, 1978).

[T]he oldest of the three men conventionally catalogued as the founding parents of cultural studies, and the first director of the Birmingham Centre, he is oft-listed alongside Raymond Williams and Stuart Hall, but rarely made the subject of equivalent exegetical projections. It is worth remarking that, in Hoggart's phrase, cultural studies always had a significant engagement with the bureaucratic public sphere (also known as the law). Hoggart it was who gave the crucial testimony at the Lady Chatterley trial. Penguin Books it was that subsequently made the endowment-in-gratitude which was used to establish the Centre. And Hoggart it was that served on the United Kingdom's Pilkington Committee on Broadcasting. (Of course there are cultural studies exponents who argue that the British contingent has always been involved with questions of policy and broad politics, far from the security of the maddening text).[100]

This interest in law, however, seems largely to have dissipated (with the significant exception of work on intellectual property as a force in cultural production, circulation, reception, and reproduction).[101] There has been a tendency in cultural studies either to metaphorize law (as in the psychoanalytic Law of the Father)[102] or to fetishize it, according to it a

100. Toby Miller, "Culture with Power: The Present Moment in Cultural Policy Studies," *Southeast Asian Journal of Social Science* 22 (1994): 264, 270.

101. See Jane Gaines, *Contested Culture: The Image, the Voice and the Law* (Chapel Hill: University of North Carolina Press, 1991); Celia Lury, *Cultural Rights: Technology, Legality, and Personality* (London: Routledge, 1993); and Thomas Streeter, *Selling the Air: A Critique of the Policy of Commercial Broadcasting in the United States* (Chicago: University of Chicago Press, 1996). Intellectual property laws, which create private property rights in cultural forms (literature, advertising, music, brand names, corporate logos, indicia of government, and celebrity images, for example) afford especially fertile ground for a consideration of relationships between and among law, cultural forms, cultural meanings, subcultural formations, and hegemonic struggles. Historical studies of intellectual property provide further examples of the genre. See Mark Rose, *Authors and Owners: The Invention of Authorship* (Cambridge: Harvard University Press, 1993) and Martha Woodmansee, *The Author, Art and the Market* (New York: Columbia University Press, 1994), as well as the collected essays in Martha Woodmansee and Peter Jaszi, eds., *The Construction of Authorship* (Durham, NC: Duke University Press, 1994). A more comprehensive compilation of the historical literature may be found in Rosemary Coombe, "Contested Paternity: Histories of Copyright," *Yale Journal of Law and the Humanities* 6 (1994): 397. See also Pheng Cheah, David Fraser, Judith Grbich, eds., *Thinking Through the Body of the Law* (New York: New York University Press, 1996) for an interesting departure from the tendency to avoid addressing legal questions.

102. Gillian Rose, *The Dialectic of Nihilism: Post-Structuralism and Law* (London: Basil Blackwell, 1984); Alain Pottage, "The Paternity of Law," in *Politics, Postmodernity and Critical Legal Studies: The Legality of the Contingent,* ed. Costas Douzinas, Peter Goodrich, and Yifat Hachamovitch (London: Routledge, 1994), 147.

unity and canonical existence that would be rejected were it applied to other textual forms.[103] It is precisely the formalist emphasis upon texts as isolated works that a critical cultural studies of law would avoid, stressing not isolated decisions, statutes, or treatises, but the social life of law's textuality and the legal life of cultural forms in the specific practices of socially situated subjects.

One could argue, as Miller does, that "culture has always been about policy"[104] and that it is only recently that the appeal to legal policies as shaping cultural milieus has been heard as polemic. The introduction to Stuart Cunningham's book *Framing Culture* is one example:

> The Prices Surveillance Authority's 1989 report on book publishing in Australia didn't make it to your local bookstore or to the review section of your weekend paper, yet it may have more impact than a dozen bestselling novels. . . . the Australian Broadcasting Corporation's (ABC) television arts magazine, didn't feature what happened in recent years in the latest round of international negotiations in the General Agreement on Tariffs and Trade (the GATT), yet cultural goods and services are high on the list of tradeable commodities, and powerful nations view these markets as strategic sites for deregulation. Cultural commentators well versed in the intricacies of film style or art history may evince little interest in the commercial businesses, labour organisations, statutory authorities, or government departments without whose activities the world of culture as we know it would be unrecognisable.[105]

Miller remarks that the need to couch these observations in such combative form is the unfortunate consequence of an untenable distinction—albeit one that threatens to become entrenched—between semiotic and textual approaches and reformist and sociological ones. In short, it is a consequence of "the failure to breach the space between the humanities and the social sciences."[106] If cultural policy has become characterized by an "abstracted empiricism . . . in the service of the

---

103. See, for example, Gaines, *Contested Culture*.

104. Miller, "Culture with Power," 264.

105. Stuart Cunningham, *Framing Culture: Criticism and Policy in Australia* (Sidney: Allen and Unwin, 1992), 16.

106. Miller, "Culture with Power," 269.

state" (280), cultural theory has become a form of grand moralism in the service of critique: "A rapprochement between the two, where policy studies is not valorized over critique and vice versa, is the polite return to a network of interlaced concerns which has always been part of culture and should always have been part of cultural studies" (280). This artificial division in concerns may simply mirror an older and more entrenched split between "the requirement of the social sciences to concentrate on power" and the requirement of the humanities "to concentrate on systems of meaning" (280). The whole point of engaging in cultural studies was to overcome this disabling division. This must certainly be the aspiration of a critical cultural study of law. The heuristic value of exploring law *culturally*, I suggest, is a more focused and politicized emphasis upon meaning in domains traditionally preoccupied with questions of power. Similarly, the dividends realized from studying culture *legally* is the greater specificity and materiality afforded to understandings of power in fields largely focused upon meaning. The social force of signification and the material weight of meaning are simultaneously brought to the fore in such endeavors.

One way of studying the (multi)cultural life of law in late capitalist conditions would be to "take surfaces seriously" in the global cities from which transnational flows are managed and in which migrants with culturally diverse frames of reference cross paths.[107] Such scholarly work would involve the production of ethnographies of "place," recognizing that what is specific to place is the local experience of the intersection of forces generated elsewhere. The intersections of legal sensibilities evident in cross-cultural encounters in urban spaces provide promising venues for studying law culturally and culture legally to reveal evolving relationships between power and meaning. My own ethnographic work with anthropologist Paul Stoller in Harlem among African street vendors, for instance, suggests that legal regulations and their interpretation provide the very stuff out of which cultural identities are constructed and social distinctions established and maintained. We discovered that the commercial texts that litter city streets are more than mere "noise" that detract from deeper cultural harmonies or "fluff" that can be brushed away to find the true fabric of social life. The trademarks on people's clothes, logos on the goods sold by street vendors, the videos and cassettes playing, the celebrity names and images that adorn T–shirts and baseball caps (including their counterfeit and bootleg versions), and the billboards that loom over city streets are not

---

107. Coombe, "Cultural Life of Things."

simply facades for something "deeper" or "thicker" that the omniscient scholar should ideally discern, but legally regulated texts that condense conflicted meanings in various social imaginaries that may be provisionally evoked. These are the lingua franca through which meanings of race, ethnicity, class, and gender are negotiated, the means through which the African and the American and their intersection in the African–American are being articulated.[108] These are contested cultural forms that express conflictual meanings about culture, race, and identity. Intellectual property laws are obviously imbricated within such commercial landscapes, but other nexuses of transnational migrations and flows in other research sites will certainly reveal the centrality of other fields of law in orienting practices and consciousness, shaping and transforming contemporary frames of reference. A cultural legal studies or a legally informed cultural studies would trace the interconnections of diverse regimes of power and knowledge and their local meanings in specific sites of transnational intersection.

Contingencies of Law and Culture

In her 1993 presidential address to the American Anthropological Association, Annette Weiner asserted that

> culture is no longer a place or a group to be studied. Culture, as it is being used by many others, is about political rights and nation-building. It is also about attempts by third-world groups to fight off the domination of transnational economic policies that destroy these emergent rights as they establish their own nation-states . . . culture has now become the contested focus of complex economic and political transformations. These shifts irrevocably alter the culture concept as anthropologists have used it in the past, and in less complex contexts.[109]

Culture, then, has become a favored idiom for political mobilization against the transnational centralization of political-economic power in defense of local interests.[110] But why and in what contexts are claims

---

108. Rosemary Coombe and Paul Stoller, "X Marks the Spot: The Ambiguities of African Trading in the Commerce of the Black Public Sphere," in *The Black Public Sphere,* ed. Black Public Sphere Collective (Chicago: University of Chicago Press, 1995).
109. Annette Weiner, "Presidential Address," *American Anthropologist* 95 (1995): 14.
110. Turner, "Anthropology and Multiculturalism."

made in the idiom of culture and when are similar assertions made as claims to sovereignty or rights to development? "Ethnic" culturalisms, moreover, have emerged simultaneously with culturally focused identity politics and subcultures among nonethnic groups in overdeveloped capitalist societies. In battles over multiculturalism, for example, we see distinctions between conservative and critical positions emerging. Conservative forms of multiculturalism reproduce the reifications of modern anthropology, fetishizing difference, and romanticizing essentialist forms of otherness.[111] By tearing issues of identity out of political and economic contexts, identity is abstracted from the conditions of its production, and consequentially historically specific cultural subjects are disempowered.[112] For critical multiculturalists, however, culture is not an end but a means to political ends that entail struggles for recognition of historically shaped differences and for social equalizations of the power to shape the meanings of basic political concepts and principles. Film theorists Ella Shohat and Robert Stamm suggest that the egalitarian vision of representation proposed by a critical multiculturalism does not imply an uncritical pluralism of diverse cultures but instead involves a dismantling of dominant concepts of culture:

> Multiculturalism and the critique of Eurocentrism are inseparable concepts . . . Multiculturalism without anti-Eurocentrism runs the risk of being merely accretive . . . Critical multiculturalism refuses a ghettoizing discourse that would consider groups [i.e., cultures] in isolation. It is precisely this emphasis on relationality that differentiates it from liberal pluralism . . . and substitutes for [the latter's] discourse of tolerance one which sees all [difference] in relation to the deforming effects of social power . . .[113]

It remains to be seen, however, whether such distinctions will be juridically recognized and legally legitimated in the courts and legislatures of those jurisdictions with policy commitments to multiculturalism or whether respect for cultural difference will simply entrench existing

111. See Eva Mackey, "Postmodernism and Cultural Politics in a Multicultural Nation: Contests over Truth in the *Into the Heart of Africa* Controversy," *Public Culture* 7 (1995): 403; Koglia Moodley, "Canadian Multiculturalism as Ideology," *Ethnic and Racial Studies* 6 (1983): 320; and Turner, "Anthropology and Multiculturalism" for discussions.

112. Turner, "Anthropology and Multiculturalism."

113. Ella Shohat and Robert Stamm, *Multiculturalism and Ideology: Unpacking Eurocentrism* (New York: Routledge, 1995).

hierarchies. Kristin Koptiuch, for example, has shown how the "culture" predominantly asserted in criminal cases evoking the "cultural defense" is one that ratifies (and naturalizes by culturalizing) male-on-female violence by Asian men, eerily amplifying nineteenth-century orientalist stereotypes.[114] This is one area of law where the resurgence of culture serves to reinscribe Romanticist imaginaries rather than enable postcolonial emancipations.

To explore the diverse contexts in which "culture" itself is legally evoked and to consider the current stakes of its deployment would be a fruitful area for critical cultural legal study. Certainly "culture" is the banner under which many battles are being fought, rights asserted, defenses propounded, and properties claimed. No longer a disciplinary preserve, "culture" is a lively rhetorical vehicle in new social movements that challenge Enlightenment universalities. From battles over multiculturalism and speech codes, the so-called cultural defense, "workplace cultures" in sexual harassment suits, the protection of "eco-cultures," the assertion of distinctive corporate cultures for "managing" diversity, and the exemption of "cultural industries" from free-trade obligations, to efforts to repatriate cultural properties, "culture" is cropping up in legal domains of adjudication administration, negotiation, arbitration, and regulation. As the historical genealogies of the term suggest, *culture* is a symbol whose fields of connotation have always been complex and conflicted. Culture currently appears to be undergoing yet another historical transformation. The law will play a powerful role in defining its new meanings. Particular visions of culture are routinely validated in juridical domains while other versions are delegitimated. A culturally materialist inquiry might track the resonances of the culture concept as it assumes new valences in political struggles and legal forums.

To conclude, we should avoid insisting on any singular paradigm for the study of law and culture. Paradigmatic understandings are especially misguided given the inherent instabilities that have historically provided opportunities for the disruption of the positivity of the terms and their mutual interdependence in colonial histories. Rather than privilege any particular mode of linking them, we might attend to

---

114. "'Cultural Defense' and Criminological Displacements: Gender, Race, and (Trans)Nation in the Legal Surveillance of US Diaspora Asians," in *Displacement, Diaspora and Geographies of Identity,* ed. Smadar Lavie and Ted Swedenburg (Durham, NC: Duke University Press, 1996).

the various ways in which the terms have been historically articulated, while recognizing the political stakes of their current destabilizations and restabilizations in struggles enacted in multiple forums. Rather than definitively and authoritatively elaborate the appropriate form of their intersection, we might become more critically cognizant of the historical forces always already at work in the world articulating this relationship. We might position ourselves to address how relationships between law and culture have been established and maintained in the world, effecting new distributions of wealth and new inequalities of power, legitimating some identities and delegitimating others, recognizing some communities of self-fashioning while prohibiting others, provoking new identifications and disrupting others. To do so, however, requires a perspective situated within and upon the everyday practices of signification and their institutional acknowledgement, where material relations between meaning and power are forged.

This endeavor will demand more than an abstract or linguistically modeled "constitutivism." It requires a focus upon concrete fields of struggle and their legal containment, the legal constitution and recognition of symbolic struggle. We need to attend to law's capacity to fix meaning while denying it as an operation of power, its tendencies to recognize culture in some social spaces and deny its significance in others, and its sporadic and arbitrary acknowledgments of the social production of meaning. To do so would be to recognize culture as signification, but also to address its materiality: to recognize both the signifying power of law and law's power over signification as evidenced in concrete struggles over meaning and their political consequence. Processes of globalization have multiplied these struggles, as significations travel with new speed and in new media, and multiple contexts of reception overlap or are brought into juxtaposition, creating new meanings and motivating new redeployments. New understandings of the boundaries between law and culture will undoubtedly be wrought by such transformations.

The Cultural Work of Copyright: Legislating Authorship in Britain, 1837–1842

Martha Woodmansee

A bill is pending in the United States Congress to extend copyright protection from the present term of an author's life plus fifty years to life plus seventy years postmortem.[1] The Senate committee handling the bill, the Judiciary Committee, is chaired by Orrin Hatch, and one of the expert witnesses he invited to testify several months ago on September 20, 1995, was Alan Menken. Menken is the house composer for the current generation of Disney animations—*The Little Mermaid* (1989), *Beauty and the Beast* (1991), *Aladdin* (1992), and *Pocahontas* (1995)—and he testified on behalf of authors. Menken spoke ardently in favor of term extension. Reading from a prepared statement, he explained to the Committee that he "literally grew up with music," got a college degree in it (after switching from "pre med"), and then went out to seek his fortune:

The research for this paper, begun at the invitation of Austin Sarat, was carried out at the Newberry Library with generous support from the National Endowment for the Humanities. It profited from conversations there with Paul Gehl and James Turner, as well as with my collaborator Peter Jaszi, who participated in its composition in all but the narrow Romantic sense that the paper seeks to place in critical relief. The footnotes that follow use shortened references; full source citations appear in the list of Works Cited at the end of the chapter.

1. "Copyright Term Extension Act of 1995" (H.R. 989, S. 483). Since this writing, the 104th Congress has ended without acting on the bill, but term extension is certain to be back on the legislative agenda for the 105th Congress in 1997.

The world of American music was at my doorstep, and with the optimism of youth, I set out to claim its legacy. As anyone who sets out in the music business knows, the path is neither smooth nor direct. My early years were spent, not in concert halls but in ballet classes and cabaret studios where I earned my money as an accompanist while struggling for recognition as a song writer. I often wondered if I would ever realize my dream of writing music that would be sung and loved by people the world over. But I never doubted, if I did realize this dream, that as an American I would be supported by a system of laws in copyrights that would secure my creations not only for me but for my children and their children after that.[2]

Copyright is an "exclusive right" to exploit an intellectual property economically—a right that, because it prevents others from making any kind of economic use of the property, has traditionally been granted for only very "limited times" as an incentive to induce creative individuals to make valuable new ideas public by guaranteeing them a portion of the profits of their industry.[3] So the Judiciary Committee was eager to ascertain the incentive value of tying intellectual property up for an additional twenty years. How, committee members wished to know, might an exclusive right of life plus seventy years be expected to spur "authors" like Menken on to *more* new creative ventures than did the present term of life plus fifty years postmortem?

Menken, however, addressed the committee's concerns in a language of entitlement rather than of incentive. "It's ironic," he observed, "that this great country which has spawned cultural treasures unsurpassed in the world should deny the creators of those treasures protections commensurate with those guaranteed by 'creators' rights' in Europe." The European Union has recently adopted the German term of life plus seventy years. That the United States should hesitate to follow suit Menken found "unjustifiable to all Americans, particularly at a time when we are positioning ourselves as the world leader on the global information superhighway. And this is unjustifiable to song

---

2. *Hearing of the Senate Judiciary Committee*, 18.

3. United States copyright law has its source in the U.S. Constitution, art. 1, sec. 8, clause 8 of which grants Congress the power "to Promote the Progress of Science and useful Arts, by securing for limited Times to Authors and Inventors the exclusive Right to their respective Writings and Discoveries."

writers such as myself and to our children and grandchildren, who will be deprived of their legacy unless we extend our term of copyright."[4]

The vision of authorial entitlement to which Menken thus gave expression has become pervasive in copyright in recent times, to the great detriment of the "public domain," or intellectual "commons," on which all of us must continuously draw in the production of new works, for this vision has operated to justify longer and longer terms of protection, against more and more kinds of unauthorized uses, to more and more different kinds of creative works. In this chapter I explore the genesis of this vision of authorial entitlement in the history of copyright. I then return to the present to examine recent developments like the push for term extension somewhat more fully. The moment in copyright history that I examine was one of intense dialogue between the legal and literary cultures, but such dialogue has since ceased almost completely. An overarching aim of the chapter is thus to suggest why dialogue urgently needs to be reopened.[5]

The authorial ethos to which Menken gave expression is commonly believed to have its source in the 1710 Act of Anne, the first British copyright statute, and the subsequent history of copyright is thought to be one of progressive recognition of authors' rights in legal culture.[6] I want to take issue with this narrative. "Authorship" entered the domain of law with Anne, to be sure, but only as the stalking-horse of a book trade concerned to shore up its historic monopoly in the face of competition from domestic and foreign "pirates."[7] The book trade remained the key player in the subsequent development of British copyright law down through the eighteenth century. The decisions of the courts—the eighteenth century saw no further important legislation—contain only scattered and relatively indistinct traces of this vision. It was not until the nineteenth century that authorship acquired the powerful charge that so transfixes lawmakers today. Specifically, I

---

4. *Hearing of the Senate Judiciary Committee*, 19.

5. A first step in reopening dialogue may be found in the collaborative interdisciplinary work of the Society for Critical Exchange (see Woodmansee and Jaszi, eds., *Construction of Authorship*; and Woodmansee and Jaszi, "The Law of Texts").

6. This is the thrust of recent studies like Mark Rose's *Authors and Owners* (1993) and John Feather's *Publishing, Piracy and Politics* (1994) as well as of the classics of Drone (1879) and Birrell (1899).

7. See Woodmansee, "The Genius and the Copyright," 437–38; and Woodmansee and Jaszi, *Construction of Authorship*, 6–7.

want to suggest that it acquired this charge in the extended parliamentary debate that culminated in the Copyright Act of 1842.

This legislation, only the second major revision of British copyright since the Act of Anne, is extraordinary in having been largely the work of authors. It was sponsored by an accomplished author-judge who was the MP for Reading, Sergeant Thomas Noon Talfourd, acting on the inspiration as well as intermittent advice and encouragement of the soon to be poet laureate, William Wordsworth, its object was to secure "just" remuneration for *authorial* service to the nation, and it consisted largely of the telling and retelling of the *lives* of authors, living and dead.

When Talfourd introduced the bill in May 1837, books were protected from unauthorized reprinting for twenty-eight years from publication, extendable automatically for the life of the author. This was the term established in the Copyright Act of 1814, the first major reform of the Statute of Anne.[8] Now, in a second reform, Talfourd proposed to extend this term to the author's life plus sixty years postmortem. This proposal represented a very substantial extension, especially since the bill provided for living authors to recover copyrights they had sold to publishers at the expiration of the twenty-eight-year term, and then to enjoy the very same protection they could expect on new books—the life of the author plus sixty years. The bill met substantial opposition both inside and outside Parliament. Action on it dragged on for more than five years, and when the bill finally passed into law in July 1842, it had been whittled down to a term of forty-two years or the author's life plus seven years postmortem, and the "reversion" clause had been dropped. The new law nevertheless represented a substantial victory for proponents, for one of its chief objectives was to confer dignity on the profession of authorship, and five years of parliamentary attention accomplished that and more.

Talfourd's bill, as it came to be known, also generated a substantial body of writing—petitions from well-known authors and from representatives of the book trade, pamphlets and articles in newspapers and

---

8. How the copyright term came to be extended in this way remains a mystery, for the legislation was apparently introduced to clarify the mechanisms of legal deposit—the requirement imposed on printers and booksellers by the Act of Anne to supply nine libraries in England and Scotland with a free copy of all new publications—and deposit seems to have been the focus of the debate that led up to the bill's passage. See Feather, *Publishing, Piracy and Politics,* 97–121.

periodicals, and transcripts of parliamentary debates and committee reports, not to mention private correspondences about the bill. In locating documents, we are fortunate to be able to draw on John Feather's fine bibliographical work[9] in addition to the standard histories of copyright all the way back to John J. Lowndes's contemporaneous *Historical Sketch of the Law of Copyright; with Remarks on Serjeant Talfourd's Bill* (1840; 2d ed. 1842).[10] In this chapter, part of a longer study in progress, I intend to focus on parliamentary debate of the bill.[11]

The Case for Extension

Talfourd argues in three major addresses to the House of Commons (May 18, 1837; April 25, 1838; and February 28, 1839) that the existing copyright law prevents writers from making a fair profit on the fruits of their labor. Demand for most literary offerings may flag before protection lapses—indeed, in the vast majority of cases, it will be satisfied within months or even days of publication—but some literature may still be, or may just be becoming, profitable. This is what is occurring, according to Talfourd, to much of the nation's best literature. It begins to become profitable only after the author's death, with the result that even as the public is benefiting most from his work, his descendants go penniless. For as the law currently stands, Talfourd points out, when an author dies, his writings enter the public domain. Thus it is with the descendants of Milton and Coleridge, Burns, Scott, and Defoe, to name but a few. Talfourd relates the *life* of each to drive home his point—that in stipulating that their writings enter the public domain when they die, existing law has prevented the nation's most revered authors from providing for their families in the style they deserve.

This patrimonial argument for extending the term of copyright— the notion that authors have earned the right, accordingly, are entitled

---

9. "Publishers and Politicians, Part II"; also reprinted in Feather, *Publishing, Piracy and Politics*, 122–48.

10. See Drone, *A Treatise on the Law of Property in Intellectual Productions*, 144–64. See also Barnes, *Authors, Publishers, and Politicians*, 116–37. For some further contemporaneous discussions, see John Lockhart's essay review, "The Copyright Question," Archibald Alison's "The Copyright Question," Thomas Tegg's *Remarks on the Speech of Sergeant Talfourd,* and the anonymous works *A Few Words on the Copyright Question, Observations on the Law of Copyright,* "The Copy-right Law," and "The New Copyright Bill."

11. The official records of the debate are collected in *Parliamentary Debates.* References will be given in the text.

to establish families on a secure financial footing, to create estates—is reiterated frequently by supporters of the bill, suggesting not only that authorship was on the way to becoming a respectable bourgeois profession, but that as a group authors had come to represent an important enough national resource to warrant nurturing by the state.[12] Talfourd goes so far as to compare them in this regard to Britain's military heroes, asking fellow members of Parliament whether they would treat them as shabbily as they treat authors.

> Did we tell our Marlboroughs, our Nelsons, our Wellingtons, that glory was their reward, that they fought for posterity, and that posterity would pay them? We leave them to no such cold and uncertain requital; we do not even leave them merely to enjoy the spoils of their victories, which we deny to the author—we concentrate a nation's honest feeling of gratitude and pride into the form of an endowment, and teach other ages what we thought, and what they ought to think, of their deeds by the substantial memorials of our praise. Were our Shakspeare and Milton less the ornaments of their country, less the benefactors of mankind? (May 18, 1837, vol. 38, col. 874)

If authors' service to the nation compares with that of its great military heroes, Talfourd asks, does it not at least owe them "the spoils of their peaceful victories"—opportunity to enjoy the profits produced by their writings? Rather than remunerate authors thus minimally, however, Talfourd contends, Britain expropriates them: seizes the patrimony of their children by turning their writings over to the public upon their demise.

Once in the public domain, according to Talfourd, their works are at the whim of ignorant and/or unscrupulous entrepreneurs who, in the interest of turning a profit, reprint, excerpt, anthologize, and abridge them without the least regard for authors' intentions. Thus, whereas their descendants might be expected to protect the integrity of their work—so as to ensure their revered ancestor's reputation—current law allows their work to be "garbled," "mangled," "disfigured."

---

12. For overviews of the history of the profession of authorship during this period in Britain, see Collins, *The Profession of Letters*; Bonham-Carter, *Authors by Profession*, 33–90; and Cross, *The Common Writer*.

Authors not only lose out financially, but their pride of workmanship, their reputation, is also assaulted.

This situation has global consequences, according to Talfourd, for colonial expansion has vastly extended the audience of British authors:

> The great minds of our time have now an audience to impress far vaster than it entered into the minds of their predecessors to hope for: an audience increasing as population thickens in the cities of America, and spreads itself out through its diminishing wilds, who speak our language, and who look on our old poets as their own immortal ancestry. And if this our literature shall be theirs; if its diffusion shall follow the efforts of the stout heart and sturdy arm in their triumph over the obstacles of nature; if the woods stretching beyond their confines shall be haunted with visions of beauty which our poets have created, let those who thus are softening the ruggedness of young society have some present interest about which affection may gather, and at least let them be protected from those who would exhibit them mangled or corrupted to their transatlantic disciples. (April 18, 1837, vol. 38, cols. 878–79)

In this imperialist vision—a rich commingling of political, theological, and hermeneutical as well as patrimonial registers—Britain's authors have replaced its admirals, and British dominance is postulated to depend upon direct, or pure, dissemination of the Authorial Word—dissemination unadulterated by colonial admixture. Such transmission depends in turn on a substantially extended copyright term being vested postmortem in the only individuals who may be counted on to ensure it—authors' descendants.

At the center of Talfourd's case is a *life* of a living author that warrants the copyright reform he proposes:

> Let us suppose an author, of true original genius, disgusted with the inane phraseology which had usurped the place of poetry, and devoting himself from youth to its service; disdaining the gauds which attract the careless, and unskilled in the moving accidents of fortune—not seeking to triumph in the tempest of the passions, but in the serenity which lies above them—whose works shall be scoffed at—whose name made a by-word—and yet, who shall persevere in his high and holy course, gradually impressing thought-

ful minds with the sense of truth made visible in the severest forms of beauty, until he shall create the taste by which he shall be appreciated—influence[,] one after another, the master-spirits of his age—be felt pervading every part of the national literature, softening, raising and enriching it; and when at last he shall find his confidence in his own aspirations justified, and the name which once was the scorn admitted to be the glory of his age—he shall look forward to the close of his earthly career, as the event that shall consecrate his fame and deprive his children of the opening harvest he is beginning to reap. As soon as his copyright becomes valuable, it is gone. (May 18, 1837, vol. 38, col. 877)

"This is no imaginary case," Talfourd concludes, "I refer to . . ."—and then, having left them hanging a little longer, he pronounces the name of William Wordsworth. Many House members would already have guessed his identity, for Wordsworth's (in)famous prefaces are the source of Talfourd's key ideas here and even of several of his formulations.[13] We will return briefly to the poet's intensive involvement in— his virtual orchestration of—the legislation subsequently. Of interest in the present context is what his *life* tells us about Talfourd's bill, and that is—in the words of an opponent—that it is an "author's bill" in the high romantic sense, for what he here sketches is the making of a kind of secular prophet—a writer, to be sure, but a writer who disdains to place his genius in the service of the expressed human needs that we associate with the everyday business—and pleasures—of life in favor of a "high and holy course" that involves making the truth "visible." The object of Talfourd's bill is to reward, and in this way encourage, authorship in this exclusive—indeed, grandiose—sense.

Talfourd freely admits this intent. Responding a year later to petitions filed against the bill by members of the book trade, he admits that ensuring "to authors of the highest and most enduring merit a larger

---

13. In his famous "Preface" of 1800, Wordsworth sought to promote *Lyrical Ballads* by distinguishing them from the popular "magazine" poetry of the day, which he asserts to be vitiated by "gaudiness and inane phraseology" (*The Prose Works of William Wordsworth*, vol. 1, 123). His efforts failed to gain him a wide readership, however, and in the "Essay, Supplementary to the Preface" of 1815, he relates a self-serving history of English poetry in which he tells his readers that *all* of the great poets from Spenser to Percy met with similar fates during their lifetimes while lesser talents flourished. The lesson of his history, Wordsworth writes, is that "every Author, as far as he is great and at the same time *original*, has had the task of *creating* the taste by which he is to be enjoyed" (*Prose Works*, vol. 3, 80).

share in the fruits of their own industry and genius" is the bill's "main and direct object." "[W]hatever fate may attend the endeavour," he adds,

> I feel with satisfaction that it is the first which has been made substantially for the benefit of authors, and sustained by no interest except that which the appeal on their behalf to the gratitude of those whose minds they have enriched, and whose lives they have gladdened, has enkindled. The statutes of Anne and of George 3rd, especially the last, were measures suggested and maintained by publishers; and it must be consoling to the silent toilers after fame, who in this country have no ascertained rank, no civil distinction[,] in their hours of weariness and anxiety to feel that their claim to consideration has been cheerfully recognised by Parliament, and that their cause, however feebly presented, has been regarded with respect and with sympathy. (April 25, 1838, vol. 42, col. 556)

The Case against the Bill

> It is painful to me . . . to oppose my hon. and learned Friend on a question which he has taken up from the purest motives, and which he regards with a parental interest. These feelings have hitherto kept me silent when the law of copyright has been under discussion. But as I am, on full consideration, satisfied that the measure before us will, if adopted, inflict grievous injury on the public, without conferring any compensating advantage on men of letters, I think it my duty to avow that opinion and to defend it. (February 5, 1841, vol. 56, col. 344)

Thus did Thomas Babington Macaulay deliver the death blow to Talfourd's bill in February 1841. The bill had been debated in every session of Parliament since its introduction, and while a majority of the House of Commons probably favored it, it was opposed by a well-organized and determined minority—an alliance of radicals, utilitarians, and free traders that the then shaky Whig government could not afford to alienate. This minority could not defeat the bill, but through skillful manipulation of parliamentary procedure it had managed to obstruct the bill's progress for over three years.[14] Now Macaulay, who had yet to

---

14. Feather, "Publishers and Politicians, Part II," 56–57, 59.

contribute a word to the debate, threw his measured periods into the cause.

Although a necessary incentive to writers, copyright is a kind of monopoly, he argues, and "the effect of monopoly generally is to make articles scarce, to make them dear, and to make them bad" (col. 348). Unless books are an exception, therefore, the task is to keep the term of protection as short as possible without canceling the incentive it provides. Macaulay thinks sixty years postmortem is much too long: "[A]n advantage that is to be enjoyed more than half a century after we are dead, by somebody, we know not whom, perhaps by somebody unborn, by somebody utterly unconnected with us, is really no motive at all to action" (col. 349). Macaulay obviously does not share Talfourd's patrimonial sentiments—his dynastic urge.

To illustrate his point, Macaulay offers a *life* of Samuel Johnson:

> Dr. Johnson died fifty-six years ago. If the law were what my hon. and learned Friend wishes to make it, somebody would now have the monopoly of Dr. Johnson's works. Who that somebody would be it is impossible to say, but we may venture to guess. I guess, then, that it would have been some bookseller, who was the assign of another bookseller, who was the grandson of a third bookseller, who had bought the copyright from Black Frank, the Doctor's servant [and residuary legatee], in 1785 or 1786. Now, would the knowledge, that this copyright would exist in 1841, have been a source of gratification to Johnson? Would it have stimulated his exertions? Would it have once drawn him out of his bed before noon? Would it have once cheered him under a fit of the spleen? Would it have induced him to give us one more allegory, one more life of a poet, one more imitation of Juvenal? I firmly believe not. I firmly believe that a hundred years ago, when he was writing our debates for the Gentleman's Magazine, he would very much rather have had twopence to buy a plate of shin of beef at a cook's shop underground. Considered as a reward to him, the difference between a twenty years' term and a sixty years' term of posthumous copyright would have been nothing or next to nothing. But is the difference nothing to us? I can buy Rasselas for sixpence; I might have had to give five shillings for it. I can buy the Dictionary—the entire genuine Dictionary—for two guineas, perhaps for

less; I might have had to give five or six guineas for it. (February 5, 1841, vol. 56, cols. 349–50)

Macaulay's Johnson casts doubt on the utility to writers of the extension proposed in Talfourd's bill while simultaneously suggesting that the bill will do disservice to the reading public by raising the price of books. That is because, finding themselves in need of money, authors like Johnson will sell their copyrights outright, handing over to publishers the full advantage of the extended term. As evidence Macaulay relates another *life,* that of Milton's granddaughter, chosen because her fate had been adduced by Talfourd to demonstrate the need for posthumous copyright. In Macaulay's hands the woman's poverty demonstrates just the opposite: it is the result rather of the perpetual copyright in force at the time. Milton's copyrights belonged to his publisher, Tonson, to whom he had sold them outright. Accordingly, Macaulay points out,

> everybody, who wants them, must buy them at Tonson's shop, and at Tonson's price. Whoever attempts to undersell Tonson is harassed with legal proceedings. Thousands who would gladly possess a copy of Paradise Lost, must forego that great enjoyment. And what, in the meantime[,] is the situation of the only person for whom we can suppose that the author, protected at such a cost to the public, was at all interested? She is reduced to utter destitution. Milton's works are under a monopoly. Milton's grand-daughter is starving. The reader is pillaged; but the writer's family is not enriched. Society is taxed doubly. It has to give an exorbitant price for the poems; and it has at the same time to give alms to the only surviving descendant of the poet. (February 5, 1841, vol. 56, cols. 352–53)

Macaulay also takes issue with Talfourd's claim that an author's works are best entrusted to his heirs. There is a greater danger that "valuable works will be either totally suppressed or grievously mutilated" when their copyrights remain in the hands of the family than when they are transferred to booksellers (col. 353). Macaulay is thinking of the censorship undertaken by families out of disagreement—moral, political, religious, and so forth—with an author's views. He offers as illustration Richardson's novels and Boswell's *Life of Johnson.* In both cases, he argues, there is reason to doubt that the prudish heirs would have allowed their ancestors' works to be reprinted had they held the copyrights. But another kind of "mutilation" was already common and was becoming more so at this time: the kind of cannibalizing of a work for parts to be used in new works that advertising has exploited to such effect in our own times. That Talfourd was not able to imagine a family perpetrating such "acts of disrespect" against an ancestor is in keeping with the traditional, patriarchal politics that inform his position generally.

Macaulay's broadside was no doubt in part effective because he was a famous author. But he also summed up with customary economy and urbanity key points that more radical critics of the bill had been raising from the start. Literacy had continued to increase throughout the century, and several innovations in printing and papermaking had reduced the price of books.[15] Many MPs feared that the resulting "diffusion of knowledge"—to use the radical Joseph Hume's term (February 27, 1839, vol. 45, col. 934)—would be slowed, even disrupted, by the legislation. For it would retain in, or return to, copyright books in or about to enter the public domain and become available for reprinting in inexpensive editions. Their fears are neatly summed up by Hume:

> Of all means of public instruction and education, cheap publications were the most important and the most effectual, and the main cause of the diffusion of information in them for the last ten years, had been the cheap publications which had been produced . . . . The present object appeared to be, to drive the country back to those barbarous times, when information was conferred to but a small section of the community. (February 19, 1840, vol. 52, col. 421)

Radical opponents of the bill take the side of the user, casting their objections in a rhetoric of divergent class interests. They even charge

---

15. The invention of the Fourdrinier papermaking machine and development of stereotyping in the first decade of the century were followed by the invention and development of the power press, revolutionizing printing and publishing. Distribution was also facilitated by the growth of the railroad. See Feather, *A History of British Publishing,* 129 ff. For the evolution at this time of our modern "mass" reading public, see Altick, *The English Common Reader.*

the House with authorial collusion—with taking the part of authors in complete disregard for the welfare of the public. Are not many MPs themselves authors, opponents of the bill ask (with good reason). "It was a genteel thing to be an author," Warburton is recorded as observing, "and for that reason they found protection in that House" (February 19, 1840, vol. 52, col. 404). Wakley had earlier made the same point with more wit when he quoted before-and-after prices of books by members that had passed into the hands of the bookseller Thomas Tegg for remaindering: Bulwer-Lytton's two-volume *England and the English*, originally priced at 1£ 11s 6d, was being remaindered by Tegg for 1s a volume; and Benjamin Disraeli's *Vivian Grey*, also published at 1£ 11s 6d, had been bought by Tegg for 8d a volume (May 9, 1838, vol. 42, col. 1060–61). Tegg, who specialized not only in remainders but also in abridgments and inexpensive reprints of books in the public domain, had been a vocal opponent of the bill from the beginning.[16] In the course of the long debate, he came to symbolize the processes of distribution that the bill addressed and thus appears as the hero or scourge of the trade, depending on the viewpoint of a given speaker.

Compromise

Talfourd barely responded to Macaulay's eleventh-hour intervention. Audibly stunned by the way in which the latter "had thrown the weight of his authority, the grace of his eloquence, and the fascination of his style into the scale, in opposition to th[e] measure," Talfourd spoke only briefly, concluding his rather random remarks with the hope that "the voices of Wordsworth, Southey, of Moore and Rogers, of Coleridge, speaking, as it were, from the grave, and of the son of Sir Walter Scott—would weigh against all the powers and genius of his right hon. Friend's address" (February 5, 1841, vol. 56, col. 360). But they did not, and in the question that followed, the second reading of the bill was deferred for six months by a vote of 45 to 38. This was the last that was seen of his bill, for the Whig government fell in June 1841, and in the subsequent election Talfourd was not returned to Parliament.

A Tory victory in the election created conditions that were more conducive to the legislation, for its strongest supporters now sat on the

---

16. See Tegg's *Remarks on the Speech of Sergeant Talfourd.*

government side. Moreover, its sponsors—in addition to Viscount Mahon (Philip Henry Stanhope), who initiated the bill, William Gladstone, who was to join the cabinet the next year, and the reactionary Tory Robert Inglis—were better politicians than Talfourd. Compromise is everywhere audible when Mahon takes the floor to introduce the bill, but most notably in the methodical way in which he takes up, one by one, the questions Macaulay had raised over a year earlier. In the process several *lives* get retold—those of Boswell's delicate son and Richardson's prudish grandson, and, for the nth time, the life of Dr. Johnson. Macaulay's Johnson, it will be recalled, demonstrated the complete uselessness of term extension to authors: he would have preferred "a plate of shin of beef" to the knowledge that the heirs of his footman, "Black Frank," would derive benefit from his works long after he died. Now, in Mahon's hands, Johnson's life proves just the opposite. I again quote liberally to convey the extraordinary fascination that authors held for these politicians at the dawn of Victoria's reign.

> It will be recollected, that he had married very early, that he had lost his wife ere he had passed the prime of manhood, and that he had toiled through the remainder of his life mainly in mournful seclusion, amidst the gloom of constitutional melancholy. . . . Why was he doomed to that gloom and that seclusion? Why, but from the effect of that very law which denied him adequate property in his own productions, or sufficient rewards for his labours, and forbid him to surround himself once more with the charities of home. Why might he not have hoped, under another law, to have some one dearer and nearer than "Black Frank" to soothe his dying moments, or receive his parting breath? How unfair to urge the desolate state of Dr. Johnson—the very evil produced under the present law, as an argument against a change of that law! How painful would have been the feelings of that great and good man, had he foreseen that the circumstances of his distress would be distorted into an argument for prolonging the distresses of others! (April 6, 1842, vol. 61, col. 1355)

Mahon constructs for Johnson a *life* of morbid isolation for which the inadequacy of copyright was the prime cause. Had he just had the kind of postmortem protection now under parliamentary consideration, Johnson would have been on a financial footing to remarry after the death of his wife, to start a family, and in this way, Mahon implies, to turn his life around. With a healthy investment in the future, Johnson would not have suffered the melancholy for which he is remembered. Authors need a patrimony.

Mahon's defense of the bill culminates in the imperial considerations of Talfourd's very first speech. Having, in the interest of compromise, proposed a much reduced term of twenty-five years *post mortem auctoris,* Mahon says that he considers it his duty to inform the House that more dramatic progress may be occurring elsewhere in the world: "From Russia down to Spain—from the states most attached to ancient customs, down to those chiefly rent asunder by civil strife—attempts have been successfully made to increase the encouragements to men of letters" (April 6, 1842, vol. 61, col. 1360). In France, Mahon notes, action is under way to extend the term of protection from the current ten (twenty if an author leaves kindred) to fifty years postmortem. The rationale for the extension will be of interest to the House, he thinks, for it appears to lie in the crucial role that France assigns authors in its global agenda. Mahon reads aloud from a report that the "great poet and upright statesman" Lamartine had laid before the Chamber of Deputies the previous year:

> The whole of Europe is at this moment inspired by one common thought and care for the protection of literature. It is the part of France to take the lead of Europe. Her high station in the civilised world has been won for her by the hand of her artists, and by the pen of her poets and historians, even more than by the sword of her soldiers. After so many other victories, could France leave to neglect or to spoliation those powers of thought that have achieved a mighty and pervading empire over all time and all space? Let it be the part of France to take the lead of Europe. (April 6, 1842, vol. 61, col. 1360)

Lamartine asserts French preeminence in terms certain to stir rivalry in the British Parliament: for all its military defeats, France still holds worldwide cultural preeminence. To remain competitive, Mahon suggests, Britain will need to adopt a copyright bill that does greater justice to its eminent authors. Winding down, he notes that these authors' prominence in former debates makes it unnecessary to name them again here. "[T]hey will perhaps most be felt" if each member of Parliament "recall[s] them in silence to his own recollection. Like the statues of the ancient heroes withheld from a solemn procession, 'Praefulge-bant eo ipso quod effigies eorum non visebantur' [They were distinguished by the very fact that their images were not seen]" (April 6, 1842, vol. 61, col. 1361).

Lest this means of contributing to Britain's global aspirations seem nebulous, Mahon concludes his case for the new bill by celebrating a simpler, more direct contribution: that of a book like Southey's *Life of Nelson* to the superiority of Britain's navy.

> [P]erusal of the *Life of Nelson* has kindled, has cherished, and has kept alive the feelings of professional pride and honourable emu-lation. . . . Depend upon it, many a young heart has, in the hour of danger, beat high with the recollection which that book inspired . . . . But, further still, may not many a young man who would oth-erwise have preferred a life of safe and quiet application, and cer-tain profit at home in trade or commerce, have been impelled to the service of the country by these glowing pages? (April 6, 1842, vol. 61, col. 1362)

In this final flourish, *The Life of Nelson* displaces Admiral Nelson, sym-bolically wresting cultural superiority away from France.

It must have come as a surprise to many in the House of Commons when Macaulay thereupon rose in support of the bill. In the fourteen months since his dramatic intervention against Talfourd's bill, Macaulay had evidently devoted some attention to copyright because he was now armed with a proposal of his own and with a barrage of facts and figures to demonstrate its advantages. Instead of the twenty-five years postmortem that Mahon proposed adding to the twenty-eight-year term authors already enjoyed, Macaulay proposes that the latter term of twenty-eight years just be extended another fourteen years: an author should enjoy "copyright for life, or for forty-two years, whichsoever shall be the longer" (April 6, 1842, vol. 61, col. 1364). He therewith launches into a dizzying comparison of the way in which the two proposals dispose of the literature not only of England but of ancient Greece and Rome, of France, Spain, and Germany. The ostensi-ble object of the performance, which runs to over four printed pages, is to show how much greater justice his own proposal does. Following an elaborate comparison of the fortunes of "Madame D'Arblay and Miss

Austen"—the only mention of women writers in the entire debate, even though by this time at least one-third of all "polite" literature (i.e, novels, poems, plays, and literary essays) was being written by women[17]— Macaulay concludes that in contrast with Mahon's plan, his own plan tends to reward "the best books":

> Take Shakespeare. My noble friend gives a longer protection than I should give to Love's Labour's Lost, and Pericles, Prince of Tyre; but he gives a shorter protection than I should give to Othello and Macbeth.
>
> Take Milton. Milton died in 1674. The copyrights of Milton's great works would, according to my noble friend's plan, expire in 1699. Comus appeared in 1634, the Paradise Lost in 1668. To Comus, then, my noble friend would give sixty-five years of copyright, and to the Paradise Lost only thirty-one years. Is that reasonable? Comus is a noble poem: but who would rank it with the Paradise Lost? My plan would give forty-two years both to the Paradise Lost and to Comus.
>
> Let us pass on from Milton to Dryden. . . . Of all Pope's works, that to which my noble friend would give the largest measure of protection is the volume of Pastorals, remarkable only as the production of a boy. Johnson's first work was a Translation of a Book of Travels in Abyssinia, published in 1735. It was so poorly executed that in his later years he did not like to hear it mentioned. . . . To this performance my noble friend would give protection during the enormous term of seventy-five years. To the Lives of the Poets he would give protection during about thirty years. Well; take Henry Fielding; it matters not whom I take, but take Fielding. His early works are read only by the curious, and would not be read even by the curious, but for the fame which he acquired in the later part of his life by works of a very different kind. What is the value of the Temple Beau, of the Intriguing Chambermaid . . . ? Yet to these worthless pieces my noble friend would give a term of copyright longer by more than twenty years than that which he would give to Tom Jones and Amelia.
>
> Go on to Burke. . . . (April 6, 1842, vol. 61, cols. 1365–68)[18]

---

17. See Cross, *Common Writer*, 166–67.

18. As Macaulay's speech is reported in the third person in Hansard's *Parliamentary Debates*, I quote here from Macaulay, *Prose and Poetry*, 747.

We need not follow Macaulay to the ancient world or even to contemporary Europe to grasp the point he is arguing—or to sense that this registry of authordom somehow exceeds the requirements of the task at hand. He concludes:

> To Lear, to Macbeth, to Othello, to the Fairy Queen, to the Paradise Lost, to Bacon's Novem Organum and De Augmentis, to Locke's Essay on the Human Understanding, to Clarendon's History, to Hume's History, to Gibbon's History, to Smith's Wealth of Nations, to Addison's Spectators, to almost all the great works of Burke, to Clarissa and Sir Charles Grandison, to Joseph Andrews, Tom Jones and Amelia, and, with the single exception of Waverley, to all the novels of Sir Walter Scott, I give a longer term of copyright than my noble friend gives. Can he match that list? Does not that list contain what England has produced greatest in many various ways, poetry, philosophy, history, eloquence, wit, skilful portraiture of life and manners? I confidently therefore call on the Committee to take my plan in preference to the plan of my noble friend. (April 6, 1842, vol. 61, col. 1371)[19]

So excessive a display surely could not have been necessary—or, indeed, sufficient—to demonstrate the preferability of his own proposal to Mahon's and would seem to be intended in part to convey Macaulay's conversion, if not to the bill's animating principle, then to the cause of authorship.[20]

This is how Mahon understood it, and after briefly restating his case for the term that he himself proposed, he invites some kind of compromise: "if [Macaulay] were prepared to adopt, with his term of forty-two years, a diminished term after life, he would willingly accede to such a proposal" (April 6, 1842, vol. 61, col. 1393). The required proposal is put forward by Peel, who had been returned to office as prime minister in the elections the previous year. Speaking for the first time in the long debate, Peel expresses hope that it will prove "possible to com-

---

19. Ibid., 750.

20. His nephew writes that Macaulay "enjoyed the satisfaction of having framed according to his mind the Statute which may fairly be described as the charter of his craft" (Trevelyan, *The Life and Letters of Lord Macaulay*, vol. 2, 38). In the statute's designation as an act "to afford greater Encouragement to the Production of Literary Works of lasting Benefit to the World," Macaulay's contribution would seem to find explicit acknowledgment.

bine the two propositions, and besides the forty-two years of the amendment to give an author's family a right for seven years after his death" (col. 1394). In the ensuing vote, this weighty voice of compromise prevails.

But not before a last salvo is fired by the opposition. Although he will support Macaulay's proposal "as the least of two evils," the radical Wakley explains, he cannot resist calling attention to its paucity of argument—Macaulay's failure to support his statements with facts that would show a need for the House to take any action at all. Wakley's intervention will have no impact on the outcome of the debate, which is palpably decided, but this final salvo nevertheless merits our attention because it helps place the debate as a whole in perspective. At the center of Wakley's remarks is a dramatic reading of several poems by Wordsworth, performed not to contribute to the celebration of authorship begun by Mahon and Macaulay, but to expose its pretensions. By placing before the House poems that "anyone might have written," he proposes to reduce authorship to somewhat more human proportions, raising the question why parliamentary measures should be warranted. "The extracts he was about to read to the House were from the works of a very distinguished poet, Mr. Wordsworth," Wakley is reported as saying.

> This course had been forced upon him. He had never done anything of the kind before; but surely, if hon. Gentlemen were anxious to give an extended protection to authors, they could not object to hear what were the kind of works which they proposed to protect. The first poem he would read was entitled *Louisa:*—

> I met Louisa in the shade,
> And, having seen that lovely maid,
>   Why should I fear to say
> That she is ruddy, fleet, and strong,
> And down the rocks can leap along,
>   Like rivulets in May?

> And she hath smiles, to earth unknown,
> Smiles that, with motion of their own,
>   Do spread, and sink, and rise,
> That come and go, with endless play,

And, ever, as they pass away,
  Are hidden in her eyes.

  She loves her sire, her cottage home,
Yet o'er the moorland will she roam
  In weather rough and bleak;
And when, against the wind, she strains,
O, might I kiss the mountain rains
  That sparkle on her cheek!

  Take all that's mine beneath the moon,
If I with her but half a noon
  May sit beneath the walls
Of some old cave, or mossy nook,
When up she winds along the brook
  To hunt the waterfalls.

This was a gem! He assured the House he did not read these
extracts with any invidious purpose. No man entertained a higher
respect for Mr. Wordsworth than he did; but if the House was prepared to give protection to works containing matter of that
description, he did contend that men of science, who had conferred the highest blessings on the human race, had a strong claim
on the Legislature [as well], and some [more] protection ought certainly to be bestowed upon them. The next poem he would read
was addressed *To a Butterfly:* —

  I've watched you now a full half-hour,
Self-poised upon that yellow flower,
  And, little butterfly! indeed
I know not if you sleep or feed.
  How motionless!—Not frozen seas
More motionless! and then
What joy awaits you, when the breeze
Hath found you out among the trees,
  And calls you forth again!

  This plot of orchard ground is ours;
My trees they are; my sister's flowers;

Here rest your wings when they are weary;
Here lodge, as in a sanctuary!
Come often to us, fear no wrong,
   Sit near us on the bough!
We'll talk of sunshine and of song,
And summer days when we were young,
Sweet childish days, that were as long
   As twenty days are now.

If they gave a poet an evening sky, dew, daises, roses, and a rivulet, he might make a very respectable poem. Why, anybody might do it. [Another member interjects "try it."] Try it! he had tried it. . . . He thought, however, a member of society might employ his talents to much better advantage than in the composition of such productions as he had quoted. Who could not string such lines together by the bushel? He could write them by the mile. (April 6, 1842, vol. 61, cols. 1380–82)

After reading one further poem, *The Stock-Dove*, Wakley asks whether his fellow MPs believe that "any act of Parliament they could frame would ever give to such authors a pecuniary advantage."

Wakley speaks as if these poems had only recently been published, but in fact they had appeared in 1807 in *Poems, in Two Volumes*—as had disparaging comments very like Wakley's, in the reviews that appeared at that time. The reviews had savaged the work: it consisted by and large of "common-place ideas" clothed "in language not simple, but puerile . . . namby pamby" (to quote Byron).[21] But thirty-five years of accomplishments had made such remarks sound unseemly—or so we may gather from the care taken by subsequent speakers to dissociate themselves from them. Yet Wakley's remarks call attention to a feature of the poems that is being effaced by the legislation—as also by its animating spirit Wordsworth. And that is their collective, corporate, even collaborative roots.

It is not simply that, as Wakley complains, Wordsworth has reworked "common-places"—inherited ideas and forms that have been worked and reworked by poets before him. The poems are the result of a process that was collaborative in a narrower sense. As has more

---

21. Quoted in Gill, *William Wordsworth*, 266.

recently come to light with the publication of the journals of Wordsworth's sister Dorothy, the entire family participated in the preparation of *Poems, in Two Volumes*. A more famous poem from the collection, "Daffodils," illustrates the collaborative procedure dramatically.[22] Recording the sights and sounds of an after-dinner walk with William in her journal, Dorothy notes:

> When we were in the woods beyond Gowbarrow Park we saw a few daffodils close to the water-side. We fancied that the lake had floated the seeds ashore, and that the little colony had so sprung up. But as we went along there were more and yet more; and at last, under the boughs of the trees, we saw that there was a long belt of them along the shore, about the breadth of a country turnpike road. I never saw daffodils so beautiful. They grew among the mossy stones about and about them; some rested their heads upon these stones as on a pillow for weariness; and the rest tossed and reeled and danced, and seemed as if they verily laughed with the wind, that blew upon them over the lake; they looked so gay, ever glancing, ever changing. This wind blew directly over the lake to them. There was here and there a little knot, and a few stragglers a few yards higher up; but they were so few as not to disturb the simplicity, unity, and life of that one busy highway.[23]

A good deal of both the letter and the spirit of this entry is assimilated into William Wordsworth's later poem, but without any reference to its author. Dorothy's substantial contribution—indeed, her very participation—has been completely effaced—her five "we's" assiduously replaced by "I's," transforming the couple's collective experience into a solitary one. The resulting poem relates the poet's moving experience of a phenomenon of nature that produces renewed pleasure whenever it is relived in memory:

> I wandered lonely as a cloud
> That floats on high o'er vales and hills,

---

22. While I draw different conclusions, I learned about this collaboration from David Gewanter's paper, "'Daffodils' and Authority: Wordsworth's Collaborative Lyric," presented in April 1991 at a conference that the Society for Critical Exchange organized on "Intellectual Property and the Construction of Authorship." A selection of the conference papers is contained in Woodmansee and Jaszi, *Construction of Authorship*.

23. Dorothy Wordsworth, *The Grasmere Journals*, 84–85.

When all at once I saw a crowd,
A host, of golden daffodils;
Beside the lake, beneath the trees,
Fluttering and dancing in the breeze.

Continuous as the stars that shine
And twinkle on the milky way,
They stretched in never-ending line
Along the margin of a bay:
Ten thousand saw I at a glance,
Tossing their heads in sprightly dance.

The waves beside them danced; but they
Out-did the sparkling waves in glee:
A poet could not but be gay,
In such a jocund company;
I gazed—and gazed—but little thought
What wealth the show to me had brought:

For oft, when on my couch I lie
In vacant or in pensive mood,
They flash upon that inward eye
Which is the bliss of solitude;
And then my heart with pleasure fills,
And dances with the daffodils.[24]

In the final stanza, the poet's pleasurable recollection of his experience of the daffodils becomes a metaphor for the poetic process per se, constructing it as an operation not of several minds in collaboration but of a single individual mind in interaction with the natural world. Ironically, the very lines in which this vision is set forth were supplied—as William elsewhere confirms—by his wife, Mary Hutchinson: "They flash upon that inward eye / Which is the bliss of solitude."[25]

"Daffodils" exposes the element of truth in Wakely's irreverent protest against term extension. A corporate, collaborative work, the poem calls our attention to the element of collaboration at the heart of

---

24. William Wordsworth, *Poems, in Two Volumes*, 207–8.
25. Wordsworth ascribed these lines to Hutchinson in a note dictated to Isabella Fenwick (*Poems, in Two Volumes*, 418).

creative production generally even as it dramatizes the process by which such collaboration gets denied. We inevitably draw upon the work of others in our creative activities—if not contemporaries working in the close proximity of the Wordsworths, then those working at some temporal remove whom we may or may not acknowledge as "influences." Copyright encourages us to deny others' contributions to our creative production by awarding the exclusive right to exploit it economically to "authors"—to essentially *solitary* originators. Although a profoundly collaborative work, "Daffodils" was confirmed as William's property upon publication, and nobody, not even Dorothy or Mary, could have reproduced it in whole or in part without his permission. Today Dorothy would even run the risk of being charged (albeit erroneously) with infringement of William's copyright for publishing her (prior) prose description of the daffodils, so dramatically has the scope of the "work" to which an author may claim legal protection expanded in the century and a half since passage of the 1842 bill.

Copyright owes this rapacious ethos in significant measure to Wordsworth himself, and his hand may be discerned throughout the parliamentary debates. Wordsworth had long been interested in copyright. At the time of the 1814 reform, he had felt that the extension being contemplated was much too short, and in anticipation of its debate in Parliament, he had complained in a letter to Richard Sharp that

> it requires much more than [twenty-eight years] to establish the reputation of original productions, both in Philosophy and Poetry, and to bring them consequently into such circulation that the authors, in the Persons of their Heirs or posterity, can in any degree be benefited, I mean in a pecuniary point of view, for the trouble they must have taken to produce the works.[26]

To benefit writers the "originality" of whose work forces them to look to posterity for recognition, copyright would need to extend well beyond the term being contemplated, Wordsworth believes. Only "useful drudges," he complains to Sharp, may expect to realize a profit from their investment within twenty-eight years—

---

26. Letter to Richard Sharp, September 27, 1808 (William Wordsworth, *Letters: Middle Years*, 266).

flimsy and shallow writers, whose works are upon a level with the taste and knowledge of the age; while men of real power, who go before their age, are deprived of all hope of their families being benefited by their exertions.[27]

It would be many years before Wordsworth got involved in copyright reform, but when he did, it was to implement the ideas sketched in this letter of 1808.

There is no subsequent record of intervention until three decades later, when Wordsworth succeeded in interesting Talfourd in the cause.[28] Talfourd, who entered Parliament in 1831, had been an admirer of Wordsworth since 1813 and a friend since 1815, when they were introduced by Charles Lamb. That year Talfourd, who was then a law student of twenty, wrote a fifty-eight-page "Estimate [of] the Poetical Talent of the Present Age" for *The Pamphleteer* that diverged sharply from contemporary opinion to pronounce Wordsworth "the greatest genius of the age."[29] Several more substantial appreciations of the poet, including "On the Genius and Writing of Wordsworth" for the *New Monthly Magazine* in 1820, figured among Talfourd's very considerable literary and critical output.[30]

Wordsworth was sixty-seven when Talfourd introduced his bill, and his poetry was just beginning for the first time to produce substantial income. "[W]ithin the last three years or so my poetical writings have produced for me nearly 1500 pounds," he wrote Gladstone in 1838, but he then went on to complain that under existing copyright "much the greatest part of them either would be public property to-morrow, if I should die, or would become so in a very few years."[31] From letters like this, it appears that the prospect of copyrights lapsing just as they were becoming valuable is what finally goaded Wordsworth into action. When he became involved, he not only

---

27. Ibid., 266.

28. On Talfourd, see in addition to the substantial entry in the *Dictionary of National Biography*, vol. 19, 343–46: *A Memoir of Mr. Justice Talfourd. By a Member of the Oxford Circuit;* and Ward, "An Early Champion of Wordsworth."

29. Talfourd, "An Attempt to Estimate the Poetical Talent of the Present Age," 465.

30. The only readily available collection of Talfourd's writings is Talfourd, *Critical and Miscellaneous Writings.*

31. Letter to William Ewart Gladstone, March 23, 1838 (William Wordsworth, *Letters: Later Years, 1835–1839*, 536).

coached Talfourd, supplying material for his speeches, but personally wrote to dozens of members of Parliament and other influential acquaintances to drum up support for the bill, fired off several anonymous letters to newspapers, organized a campaign of petitions from well-known authors, and, reluctantly, even petitioned Parliament himself.[32] Talfourd quotes from the petition in his third major speech of February 28, 1839.

A more thorough examination of Wordsworth's hand in the Copyright Act of 1842 is beyond the scope of this chapter. In conclusion I want rather to return to the present to sketch some of the ways in which the vision of authorial entitlement that triumphed there is making itself felt today.[33]

The Legacy of 1842

A convenient point of entry is provided by the copyright initiative with which I began—the term extension bill that is currently pending in Congress (as well as in the British Parliament).[34] In place of the poet-lobbyist Wordsworth we now have Alan Menken urging nearly the same term extension to the Senate Judiciary Committee that was contained in Talfourd's proposal. Menken also deploys the same rhetoric of authorial entitlement, but—and this is one of two crucial differences in these two moments in the history of copyright—Menken is in the employ of Disney, Inc. It is Disney and other such large entertainment and information industries that are the moving force behind this legislative initiative. This is not to say that Menken does not stand to gain from another term extension, just that he will gain only if Disney does.

What does Disney anticipate? As a "corporate author," it may currently expect to garner royalties from its productions for seventy-five

---

32. Wordsworth's writings on copyright are collected in *Prose Works*, vol. 3, 309–27. See in addition Zall, "Wordsworth and the Copyright Act of 1842"; Noyes, "Wordsworth and the Copyright Act of 1842: Addendum"; Moorman, *William Wordsworth*, vol. 2, 550–55; Feather, "Publishers and Politicians, Part II"; Eilenberg, "Mortal Pages"; and Woodmansee, *The Author, Art, and the Market*, 145–47.

33. The groundbreaking investigation of the impact of Romantic theory on twentieth-century American copyright law is my collaborator Peter Jaszi's article "Toward a Theory of Copyright." Further treatments of the impact of Romantic theory may be found in Woodmansee and Jaszi, *Construction of Authorship*, and "Law of Texts"; and Jaszi and Woodmansee, "Ethical Reaches of Authorship."

34. See note 1. Since this writing, the British Parliament has enacted term extension. This occurred in December 1995.

years—insofar as they remain popular. If the term extension bill passes, there will be an additional twenty years, or ninety-five years of royalties. It is of course impossible to say whether *The Little Mermaid, Beauty and the Beast, Aladdin,* or *Pocahontas* will still be in circulation nearly a century from now, so it is not certain that Menken's heirs will profit from the animations. But it is certain that if the bill does not pass, Mickey Mouse will enter the public domain within just a few years, because *Steamboat Willy,* the cartoon that introduced Mickey, was created in 1928. It would be interesting to know the annual profit produced by this figure globally and the profit Disney anticipates from it over the next twenty years as it begins to be distributed throughout the world electronically—assuming, that is, that another piece of copyright legislation that has just come before the Congress, the National Information Infrastructure (NII) Copyright Protection Act of 1995, becomes law, subjecting the domestic electronic environment, and by almost inevitable extension the global one as well, to rigorous regulation. But at what cost to the public?

To sketch first the cost of term extension, if the present bill passes—and passage is likely—this legislation will return to copyright hundreds of thousands of letters, manuscripts, out-of-print books, forgotten films, and the like created in the 1920s and 1930s that were about to enter the public domain, bringing to a halt countless creative projects, prospective as well as in progress, that make use of copyrighted materials—for example, biographies, textbooks, and critical editions, to name only the most obvious scholarly and educational projects that will be affected. One shudders for scholars like Patrick Parrinder, who has been working for years on a revised team-edition of H. G. Wells.[35] Wells was due to enter the public domain in 1996 but now will remain in copyright until 2016. The big loser, however, will be the reading public, for it will now be another twenty years before new, corrected editions of Wells and other such modern classics become available. As readers of Lawrence, Woolf, Joyce, Hardy, and Yeats are painfully aware, good editions generally coincide with the lapse of copyright, for there is little incentive for publishers to improve their editions as long as they are protected from competition. Although term extension stands to cost the public dearly, it has met little opposition in Congress. This is the second important difference between the present legislative

---

35. As reported by Sutherland in "The Great Copyright Disaster." See also Parrinder, "Who Killed Clause 29?"

moment and the deliberations that culminated in the Copyright Act of
1842. In a disturbing departure from the British precedent, there has
emerged no Wakley, Hume, or Warbuton—least of all a Macaulay—to
speak out against the Copyright Term Extension Act of 1995. The public has no advocate in the U.S. Congress.[36]

And what is likely to be the cost of the NII legislation that will subject the digital networks to the discipline of copyright?[37] Many of us
have begun to view our professional lives as intimately bound up with
the progress of electronic data technology—and particularly the technology of digital networks, whether the Internet or the promised electronic data superhighway of the future. As anyone knows who has
used a network to send or receive E-mail, to access distant libraries, to
tap into data bases, or to participate in electronic bulletin boards, the
network environment of today is polyvocal, polymorphous, and even
chaotic, characterized by the exchange of tremendous amounts of miscellaneous information with little apparent concern for claims of proprietorship. The network is like a gigantic hypertext, an ever changing
work of collaborative authorship.

From our standpoint, the liberating potential of this development
would seem to lie precisely in the networks' freedom from the sorts of
controls—legal and otherwise—to which older information technologies such as print are subject. But to traditional proprietors of information such as Time-Warner and Disney, this vision is a profoundly threatening one. The very ease with which material can be copied and
distributed digitally has made these copyright owners want to submit
the Internet and the networks of the future to more rigorous copyright
discipline.[38]

In short, the battle lines have been drawn over the future of the
Internet and its successors. On one side are those who see its potential

---

36. The bill's single detractor in the hearing of the Senate Judiciary Committee from
which I quote was my collaborator, the law professor, Peter Jaszi (see "Statement of Professor Peter Jaszi"). House testimony against the bill appears to have been equally "academic" (see Karjala). For more general reservations against term extension, see Ricketson,
"The Copyright Term." See also Litman, "The Public Domain."

37. Like the term extension bill, the NII legislative initiative also bogged down in
the 104th Congress, in this case due to opposition by a broad coalition including both
information consumers (especially librarians and educators) and companies engaged in
building the infrastructure of the NII; however, digital copyright too may be expected to
be taken up again in the 105th Congress.

38. See Samuelson, "The Copyright Grab" and "Digital Media and the Changing
Face of Intellectual Property Law."

as a threat to traditional notions of individual proprietorship in information and who perceive vigorous extension of traditional copyright principles to the new information environment as the solution. On the other side are those who believe that the network environment could become a new cultural "commons" if its development is not stifled by premature or excessive legal controls. Given the stakes, it is impossible that a network "commons" will be preserved as a pristine "proprietor-free zone." Some measure of regulation is inevitable, and it may even be essential if information proprietors are to participate fully in the networks. But users have a stake in assuring that the form of that regulation meets their needs as well as those of information proprietors. We need to insist that discussion of the legal future of the networks is informed by a considered balancing of competing interests rather than by the charged Romantic rhetoric of "authorship."

Works Cited

[Alison, Archibald.] "The Copyright Question." *Blackwood's Magazine* 51 (1842): 107–21.

Altick, Richard D. *The English Common Reader: A Social History of the Mass Reading Public, 1800–1900.* Chicago: University of Chicago Press, 1957.

Barnes, James J. *Authors, Publishers and Politicians: The Quest for an Anglo-American Copyright Agreement 1815–1854.* London: Routledge and Kegan Paul, 1974.

Birrell, Augustine. *Seven Lectures on the Law and History of Copyright in Books.* London: Cassell, 1899.

Bonham-Carter, Victor. *Authors by Profession.* Vol. 1. Los Altos, CA: William Kaufmann, 1978.

Collins, A. S. *The Profession of Letters: A Study of the Relation of Author to Patron, Publisher and Public 1780–1832.* London: Routledge and Kegan Paul, 1928.

"The Copy-right Law." *The Monthly Review* 145 n.s. (1838): 52–63.

Cross, Nigel. *The Common Writer: Life in Nineteenth-Century Grub Street.* Cambridge: Cambridge University Press, 1985.

Dictionary of National Biography. Vol. 19. Oxford: Oxford University Press, 1921–22.

Drone, Eaton S. *A Treatise on the Law of Property in Intellectual Productions in Great Britain and the United States.* Boston: Little, Brown, and Co., 1879.

Eilenberg, Susan. "Mortal Pages: Wordsworth and the Reform of Copyright." *English Literary History* 56 (1989): 351–74.

Feather, John. *A History of British Publishing.* London: Routledge, 1988.

———. "Publishers and Politicians: The Remaking of the Law of Copyright in

Britain 1775–1842. Part I: Legal Deposit and the Battle of the Library Tax." *Publishing History* 24 (1988): 49–76.

———. "Publishers and Politicians: The Remaking of the Law of Copyright in Britain 1775–1842. Part II: The Rights of Authors." *Publishing History* 25 (1989): 45–72.

———. *Publishing, Piracy and Politics: An Historical Study of Copyright in Britain.* London: Mansell, 1994.

A Few Words on the Copyright Question, Shewing It to Be One of Public Interest: With Some Objections to Mr. Sergeant Talfourd's Bill to Change the Present Law of Copyright. London: Scott, Webster, and Geary, n.d.

Gewanter, David. "'Daffodils' and Authority: Wordsworth's Collaborative Lyric." Paper presented at a conference arranged by the Society for Critical Exchange, "Intellectual Property and the Construction of Authorship." Cleveland, April 1991.

Gill, Stephen. *William Wordsworth: A Life.* Oxford: Clarendon, 1989.

Hearing of the Senate Judiciary Committee. Subject: Copyright Protections. Washington, DC, September 20, 1995. Unofficial transcript of U.S. Senate Judiciary Committee. Washington, DC: Federal News Service, 1995.

Jaszi, Peter, and Martha Woodmansee. "The Ethical Reaches of Authorship." *South Atlantic Quarterly* 95 (1996): 947–77.

Jaszi, Peter. *Statement of Professor Peter Jaszi. On S. 483, The Copyright Term Extension Act of 1995. Before the Senate Judiciary Committee,* September 20, 1995.

———. "Toward a Theory of Copyright: The Metamorphoses of 'Authorship.'" *Duke Law Journal* (1991): 455–502.

Karjala, Dennis S. *Written Testimony of Dennis S. Karjala. Representing United States Copyright and Intellectual Property Law Professors. House of Representatives Subcommittee on Courts and Intellectual Property. Hearings on H.R. 989,* July 13, 1995.

Litman, Jessica. "The Public Domain." *Emory Law Journal* 39 (1990): 995–1023.

[Lockhart, John G.] "The Copyright Question." *Quarterly Review* 69 (1842): 186–227.

Lowndes, John J. *Historical Sketch of the Law of Copyright; with Remarks on Serjeant Talfourd's Bill: and an Appendix of the Copyright Laws of Foreign Countries.* 2d ed. London: Saunders and Benning, 1842.

Macaulay, Thomas B. *Prose and Poetry.* Edited by G. M. Young. Cambridge: Harvard University Press, 1970.

A Memoir of Mr. Justice Talfourd. By a Member of the Oxford Circuit. London: Butterworths, 1854.

Moorman, Mary. *William Wordsworth: A Biography.* 2 vols. Oxford: Clarendon, 1957–65.

"The New Copyright Bill." *The Eclectic Review* 3 n.s. (1838): 693–704.

Noyes, Russell. "Wordsworth and the Copyright Act of 1842: Addendum." *Publications of the Modern Language Association* 76 (1961): 380–83.

Observations on the Law of Copyright in Reference to the Bill Introduced into the House of Commons by Mr. Sergeant Talfourd. London: Scott, Webster, and Geary, 1838.

Parliamentary Debates. 3d Series. Vols. 38–62. London: Thomas Curson Hansard, 1838–42.

Parrinder, Patrick. "Who Killed Clause 29?" *Times Literary Supplement* 4845 (9 February 1996): 16.

Ricketson, Sam. "The Copyright Term." *International Review of Industrial Property and Copyright Law* 23, no. 6 (1992): 753–85.

Rose, Mark. *Authors and Owners: The Invention of Copyright.* Cambridge: Harvard University Press, 1993.

Samuelson, Pamela. "The Copyright Grab." *Wired* (January 1996): 135–38, 188–91.

———. "Digital Media and the Changing Face of Intellectual Property Law." *Rutgers Computer and Technology Law Journal* 16 (1990): 323–40.

Sutherland, John. "The Great Copyright Disaster." *London Review of Books,* 12 January 1995, 3.

Talfourd, Thomas Noon. "An Attempt to Estimate the Poetical Talent of the Present Age, Including a Sketch of the History of Poetry, and Characters of Southey, Crabbe, Scott, Moore, Lord Byron, Campbell, Lamb, Coleridge, and Wordsworth." *Pamphleteer* 5 (1815): 413–71.

———. *Critical and Miscellaneous Writings of T. Noon Talfourd, Author of "Ion."* 2d American ed. Philadelphia: A. Hart, 1852.

———. "On the Genius and Writing of Wordsworth." *New Monthly Magazine* 14 (1820): 498–506, 648–55.

Tegg, Thomas. *Remarks on the Speech of Sergeant Talfourd.* London: Bradbury and Evans, 1837.

Trevelyan, George Otto. *The Life and Letters of Lord Macaulay.* 2 vols. London: Longmans, Green, and Co., 1878.

Ward, William S. "An Early Champion of Wordsworth: Thomas Noon Talfourd." *Publications of the Modern Language Association* 68 (1953): 992–1000.

Woodmansee, Martha. *The Author, Art, and the Market: Rereading the History of Aesthetics.* New York: Columbia University Press, 1994.

———. "The Genius and the Copyright: Economic and Legal Conditions of the Emergence of the 'Author.'" *Eighteenth-Century Studies* 17 (1984): 425–48.

Woodmansee, Martha, and Peter Jaszi. "The Law of Texts: Copyright in the Academy." *College English* 57 (1995): 769–87.

———, eds. *The Construction of Authorship: Textual Appropriation in Law and Literature.* Durham, NC: Duke University Press, 1994.

Wordsworth, Dorothy. *The Grasmere Journals.* Edited by Pamela Woof. Oxford: Clarendon, 1991.

Wordsworth, William. *The Letters of William and Dorothy Wordsworth: The Later Years, 1835–1839.* 2d ed. Vol. 6, Pt. 3. Edited by Ernest de Selincourt and Alan G. Hill. Oxford: Clarendon, 1982.

———. *The Letters of William and Dorothy Wordsworth: The Later Years, 1840–1853.* 2d ed. Vol. 7, Pt. 4. Edited by Ernest de Selincourt and Mary Moorman. Oxford: Clarendon, 1988.

———. *The Letters of William and Dorothy Wordsworth: The Middle Years, I:*

1806–1811. Edited by Ernest de Selincourt and Mary Moorman. Oxford: Clarendon, 1969.

———. *Poems, in Two Volumes, and Other Poems, 1800–1807*. Edited by Jared Curtis. Ithaca, NY: Cornell University Press, 1983.

———. *The Prose Works of William Wordsworth*. 3 vols. Edited by W. J. B. Owen. Oxford: Clarendon, 1974.

Working Group on Intellectual Property Rights of the Information Infrastructure Task Force. *Intellectual Property and the National Information Infrastructure*. Washington, DC: Information Infrastructure Task Force, 1995.

Zall, Paul M. "Wordsworth and the Copyright Act of 1842." *Publications of the Modern Language Association* 70 (1955): 132–44.

Law and the Order of
Popular Culture

Carol J. Clover

Explanations for the appeal of trials tend to focus on the crime or the punishment and run along psychosexual lines. In crime scenarios, the argument goes, we can indulge all manner of perverse fantasies, but safely, under the cloak of law and order. Following Foucault, who saw in the fascination with trials a displaced fascination with torture, we speak of our engagement with the punishment and the processes of discipline that subtend it.[1] Such explanations have a lot of force, and the last two decades have seen a something of a scholarly industry along these lines. But they don't explain everything, including the obvious fact that some cultures are more, some vastly more, trial interested than others. In the West, there is a world of difference between English-speaking countries and the Continent on just this point. Especially Americans are said to be trial obsessed, and it is also the case that the courtroom drama of film and television is an overwhelmingly Anglo-American phenomenon. Robin Lakoff tells how students in a class she taught at the University of Barcelona were hard pressed to explain how a Spanish trial worked but could describe an American one in detail.[2] A Stockholm newspaper recently began a review of a new television series by noting, "The average Swedish tv-viewer knows more about

---

1. "We are far removed indeed from those accounts of the life and misdeeds of the criminal in which he admitted his crimes, and which recounted in detail the tortures of his execution: we have moved from the exposition of the facts or the confession to the slow process of discovery; from the execution to the investigation; from the physical confrontation to the intellectual struggle between criminal and investigator." Michel Foucault, *Discipline and Punish: The Birth of the Prison*, trans. Alan Sheridan (New York: Vintage, 1979), 69.

2. Robin Tolmach Lakoff, *Talking Power* (New York: Basic Books, 1990), chap. 5.

the American justice system than the Swedish one. . . . We even know more about the British system than our own."[3] Although these stories and others like them say a lot about the hegemonic status of American media and of English-language culture more generally, they also point to a real difference. After all, Swedes and Spaniards also commit murder and mayhem and are also punished. But Swedes and Spaniards don't "trial-watch" the way Americans do, and they don't turn trials into entertainment nearly to the extent the Anglo-American world does. How to explain this cultural divide? Either the Anglo-American world has a greater investment in the deep pleasures of crime and punishment, in which case we have to wonder why, or such explanations do not tell the whole story.

The part of the story not told, the part that is culture specific, is the terrain of this chapter. The reader will notice that the line I have drawn between courtroom-drama-producing culture and if not non-, then less-, courtroom-drama-producing culture coincides with the line between the two major legal systems of the West, that of the Continent and that of the Anglo-American world. It is something of a truism that the basis of the Anglo-American form in an adversary system and in oral presentation before a jury makes our trials fundamentally more dramatic than the inquisitorial and professionally judged trials of the Continent. To the extent that the Anglo-American fondness for courtroom dramas has been discussed at all—remarkably little, given the scope of the phenomenon—it has been related in a vague way to that truism. But on the whole, it is striking is how little the truism has actually been investigated and how underappreciated are its implications for and in the study of popular culture. Film scholarship has not taken up the courtroom drama; no history of it has been written, and the form has no standing in the pantheon of genres.[4] There has been more interest on the law side in the so-called law-and-film movement, but even here, the focus has been not on generic issues, but on individual works that are felt to rise above the pack by virtue of their legal intelligence,

---

3. *Dagens Nyheter,* 21 January 1995, 14 (my translation).

4. The only full-length study to date is Thomas Harris's *Courtroom Drama's Finest Hour* (Metuchen, NJ: Scarecrow, 1987), a set of appreciative readings, with little categorical attention, of *Twelve Angry Men, Witness for the Prosecution, I Want to Live!, Compulsion, Anatomy of a Murder, Inherit the Wind, Judgment at Nuremberg,* and *The Verdict.* For a speculation on the official nonstatus of a popularly recognized form, see my "'God Bless Juries!'" in *Refiguring American Film Genres: History and Theory,* ed. Nick Browne (Berkeley and Los Angeles: University of California Press, 1997).

ethical interest, engagement with worthy issues, and quality of cinema—*Twelve Angry Men, Boomerang, Witness for the Prosecution, The Fury, To Kill a Mockingbird,* and the like.[5]

But surely the question to be asked about the trial movie (by which term I refer to both television and film courtroom dramas) has less to do with the value of particular instances than it does with the fantastic generativity of the form in Anglo-American popular narrative. And surely that generativity devolves not on crime or punishment, at least not primarily, nor other points of content, nor law in the large sense or justice, but—as the truism would have it—something about Anglo-American procedure. I am aware that this proposition runs athwart the opinion of some academic lawyers that the differences between Anglo-American and Continental law have been overstated and indeed to a considerable extent discursively constructed, but I would argue, at the risk of circularity, that popular culture itself—above all, film and television narrative—makes a strong prima facie case for the difference of the Anglo-American system, and further that popular culture isolates, as the source of that difference, exactly those features of the procedural structure that attend the adversarial system and the jury.

Thus the proposition of this chapter: that real-life trials become movies (by which I mean both film and television dramas) as easily as they do in the Anglo-American world both because trials are already movielike to begin with and movies are already trial-like to begin with. The first half of that proposition is hardly news, although the reception-oriented account that follows differs from the usual dramaturgically derived model in some crucial respects. It is the second half that concerns me here. When I say that Anglo-American movies are already trial-like to begin with, I mean to make a three-part, essentially historical claim: that the plot structures and narrative procedures (even certain visual procedures, in film and television) of a broad stripe of Amer-

---

5. See especially Norman Rosenberg, "Hollywood on Trials: Courts and Films, 1930–1960," *Law and History Review* 12 (1994): 341–67. In note 8, Rosenberg suggests that by comparison with the law-and-literature enterprise, the law-and-film venture is canonless. To the extent that this is so (and I would argue that it is only somewhat so), it is surely a function of the time lag. Other recent studies of note include Richard K. Sherwin, "Law Frames: Historical Truth and Narrative Necessity in a Criminal Case," *Stanford Law Review* 47 (1994) and *Movies as Legal Texts,* ed. John Denvir (Urbana and Chicago: University of Illinois Press, 1996). Not about film, but pertinent to the relation of law and narrative, is Paul Gewirtz and Peter Brooks, eds. *Law's Stories: Narrative and Rhetoric in the Law* (New Haven and London: Yale University Press, 1996).

ican popular culture are derived from the structure and procedures of the Anglo-American trial; that this structure and these procedures are so deeply embedded in our narrative tradition that they shape even plots that never step into a courtroom; and that such trial-derived forms constitute the most distinctive share of Anglo-American entertainment. I emphasize that I am using the term *narrative* here to mean the textual process of plot making, not as it is being used in legal circles to refer to particular stories or plots or tale types. My interest is neither in courtroom "storytelling" nor in movie "stories" of trials. It is not in "stories" at all. It is in the extent to which the narrative substructure of so much of our cinema rhymes with the narrative substructure of our trial and in what kind of cultural conclusions can be drawn from the commonality. Needless to say, these are larger arguments than I can make here, but I hope that the case study that follows will at least suggest the direction of the larger project of which this chapter is a part.[6]

At issue in the Anglo-American trial are its two grossest features: the adversarial structure and the jury. The roots of the adversarial structure are in the illiterate, tribal, and stateless world of Germanic Europe—a world in which, in the absence of central authority, the two parties were responsible for collecting evidence, bringing suit, pleading cases, and enforcing judgments.[7] England alone retained the "adversarial" or "accusatorial" or "party-presentational" outlines of Germanic procedure, even after the emergence of a state, and to this day the "Anglo" trial retains the form of a two-sided contest, a duel, with the judge as something of a referee. The origins of the jury are disputed and depend on how one defines it. Although the trial jury proper is dated to the years following 1215, protojuries of one sort or another go much further

---

6. Carol J. Clover, *Our Trial: Movies and the Adversarial Imagination* (provisional title), to be published by Princeton University Press.

7. My account here is drawn from the usual sources (Pollock and Maitland, Plucknett, Millar), Thomas Green's *Verdict According to Conscience: Perspectives on the English Criminal Trial Jury, 1200–1800* (Chicago : University of Chicago Press, 1985), and my own research into the Anglo-Saxon and Old Norse primary texts. There is, in my view, some truth to the suspicion that the distinction as it has been articulated for the last century between the Anglo-American and Continental legal systems is discursively constructed, but that is not to say that there *is* no distinction. I came to this project as a medievalist with a long-standing interest in Germanic legal systems, and I am convinced that the distinction *as far as procedure is concerned* is, if anything, more deepgoing than the standard accounts allow and that—as this chapter should suggest—it has had profound consequences on popular narrative from the early Middle Ages on.

back, and, looking at the earliest records, one has the sense that the primitive adversarial trial presupposed by nature some third body, agreed upon by the parties (or by a process agreed upon by the parties), charged with arriving at, if not a final verdict in the modern sense, then some significant decision that terminated the hearing. The fact that the use of juries has been curtailed in Britain (90 percent of the world's jury trials are now American) and that even in the United States many trials are bench-tried should not detract from the stubbornly central position of the jury in the rhetorical architecture of the Anglo-American trial. In either case, the jury and the adversarial structure were early welded together, and from the combination proceed many other characteristics of the form, notably the degree of procedural formalism and the emergence, in later centuries, of the elaborate rules of evidence.

No one appreciated more than Tocqueville what it might mean to live in a nation of once and future jurors. It is first and foremost to the institution of the jury that he ascribed the peculiar and widespread interest of Americans in lawsuits and legal logic. "The jury," he declared, "extends this habit [of legal thought] to all classes. The language of the law thus becomes, in some measure, a vulgar tongue; the spirit of the law, which is produced in the schools and courts of justice, gradually penetrates beyond their walls into the bosom of society, where it descends to the lowest class, so that at last the whole people contract the habits and tastes of the judicial magistrate." By bringing common people to the law, the jury brings the law to common people, and hence the legal habit of mind "extends over the whole community and penetrates into all the classes which compose it; it acts upon the country imperceptibly, but finally fashions it to suit its own purposes."[8] More particularly, the legal system provides a rhetorical and logical template that gives shape to all manner of social forms above and beyond the court of law. So it is, Tocqueville wrote, that "scarcely any political question arises in the United States that is not resolved, sooner or later, into a judicial question," that "all parties are obliged to borrow, in their daily controversies, the ideas, and even the language, peculiar to judicial proceedings," and that "the jury is introduced into the games of schoolboys."[9] Just what Tocqueville meant by "games of schoolboys"

---

8. Alexis de Tocqueville, *Democracy in America*, vol. 1 (New York: Vintage, 1990), 280. Although Tocqueville was mainly interested in civil trials, his remarks apply in the main to criminal ones as well.

9. Ibid., 280, 318.

we don't know, but the gist is clear: so fundamental is the adversarial jury trial in the American imaginary that, as a ghost matrix with a life of its own above and beyond its source, it turns up in and structures even the sheerest forms of play. No one even vaguely acquainted with American culture can help being struck by the prescience of that observation. Not only in film and television drama, but in board games, interactive software, Internet tribunals, television game shows, and radio talk shows, we enact and reenact trials, in the process positioning ourselves, as Tocqueville also appreciated, first, last, and always as triers of fact.

The relentless juror orientation (even when the ostensible point of view is that of a lawyer, judge, or police detective[10]) of Anglo-American trial-derived popular culture obliges us to ask an obvious question: what trial is it that the jury sees? Again at the risk of circularity, I want to suggest that the juror's trial differs somewhat from the official trial of lawyers, judges, and textbooks, whose accounts indeed seem so often designed to correct the lay impression; that if the juror's trial gets lots of things wrong, it gets some things, including the underlying epistemology, exactly right; and that it is these things, the things the juror's trial gets right, that have been so crucial in the production of popular culture.

By way of getting at what are for popular culture the salient features of the adversarial trial as a form, let us imagine a generic instance as it might be experienced, as a strictly formal operation, by a generic jury. Make it that favorite of popular fantasy, a murder trial in which the two sides are roughly balanced.[11] By "trial," we mean the main

---

10. The positioning of the film audience as jury is one of the most fundamental and consistent rules of the courtroom drama. It is surely for that reason that the jury is largely unseen in trial movies (typically glimpsed in a couple of camera pans). An exception of sorts is the subclass of thrillers in which a juror becomes involved with a lawyer (or the defendant, or whatever), but most of these films have only marginally to do with a trial or indeed with the jury experience. The real exception to the unseen-jury rule is, of course, *Twelve Angry Men*. In considering that film's anomalous status, it is worth remembering that it is based on a French original (the 1950 French film *Justice est faite*—though what the French were doing making a movie about a jury is another question); that it was a failure at the box office and owes its present status to a belated resuscitation on the part of art-film and law-interested viewers; that despite its jury-room framing, it enacts the phases and processes of the trial (prosecution arguments, defense arguments, evidence, cross-examination, etc.) and reaches offscreen, out to us, for a verdict; and that after a couple of pale imitations, it produced no progeny. For a fuller account of *Twelve Angry Men*'s reception history, see Clover, "'God Bless Juries!'"

11. From the privileged status of murder in trial and detective or mystery narratives, it is reasonable to conclude that an interest in criminal violence is what drives the forms. That must be largely true, but it is worth remembering that a fair share of fictional

hearing. That stretch is neatly tripartite, consisting of a long examination bookended by opening statements and closing arguments, with the verdict as a kind of coda.[12] It matches, as many have pointed out, the architecture of classic drama. It also matches the architecture of the standard screenplay.[13]

The opening statements (like the closing arguments) present us with the two positions in narrative form. Even at this early point, the story of guilt is likely to have the upper hand: it is more coherent, seems more explanatory of the rudimentary facts, and is braced by our prima facie assumption that the state must have a powerful case in order to bring it to court. At the end of the opening statements, there is an abrupt shift of gears, almost a change of tense, as we enter the examination phase. The highly bound, reasoned, syntactic, storytelling mode of the opening statements comes to a halt and the "text" collapses into a jumble of physical items and arrested moments: weapons, carpet fibers, testimony about drug reactions, behavior at the funeral, and so on. As if in freeze-frame close-up, these fragments now become the object of our investigation, but disarticulated and disordered, as though unrelated to one another or to any larger story. The examination is a limit case of narrative parataxis—a stretch of textual bits and pieces, without coordinating conjunctions, as causally unbound as possible. It is also, or can be, a limit case of narrative agglutination, testing our ability to register and process not just contested data, but lots of them.

Governing this extraordinary discourse are two formal systems: what has been called the "engine" of cross-examination (that is, the scheduled alternation between direct and cross), and the rules of evidence, the underlying assumption of which is that an event (the stabbing murder of a 7-Eleven clerk, let's say) can be broken down into particles of fact that preexist narrative and that, scrutinized singly and initially outside of story, these fact particles will, in the mind of the beholder, assemble toward their own best explanation. The mind of the

---

trials are about other things (slander, negligence, adoption or custody, drugs, etc.). The sine qua non of the American-style detective narrative (the basis of thrillers, including courtroom thrillers) is not murder, but some sort of paranoid risk to the investigator figure, which murder nicely but not exclusively supplies.

12. For different accounts of the Anglo-American trial-as-drama, see especially John E. Simonett, "The Trial as One of the Performing Arts," *American Bar Association Journal* 62 (1966): 1145–47 and Milner S. Ball, "The Play's the Thing: An Unscientific Reflection on Courts under the Rubric of Theater," *Stanford Law Review* 28 (1975–76): 81–115.

13. Syd Field, *Screenplay: The Foundations of Screenwriting* (New York: Dell, 1984).

beholder posited by the "text" of the examination is thus exceptionally attentive, itself a party in the meaning-making process. "The premium on close attention is large," as Scott Turow has noted. It wants "a certain intricacy of mind."[14]

Not just one, but two, backstories (to borrow a film term) present themselves piecemeal for assembly. The first is the declared one, the story of the crime that we are asked to reconstruct a bit at a time. Every datum of the examination is or claims to be a piece of the puzzle, but we are also made aware—through objections, witness slips, and the like—that there are more data out there that are being kept from us, and we can't help puzzling over what they are and what might account for their status as outtakes.[15] The other backstory is the unintended one of the trial as a performance, evoked by sidebar conferences, objections, excessive or otherwise unexpected behavior on the part of court apparatus that might prompt speculation (Does the judge favor the prosecution? Does the defense attorney really believe her client, or is she just doing her job? Are the lead attorneys on the two sides really lovers, as one juror speculates who saw them eating lunch together? Who are all those thuggish-looking people in the gallery—is the defendant mob connected and as his jurors are we in danger?[16]). The rules of evidence and protocol that are designed at the point of production to maximize fairness are, at the point of reception, a veritable machine for the production of paranoid speculation far beyond the trial's official parameters.

Paranoid speculations (there are hidden stories that we can unlock if we remain hyperalert to the clues) are also prompted by one of the most remarkably primitive features of the adversarial trial, one that has

---

14. Scott Turow, *Presumed Innocent* (Farrar, Straus, and Giroux, 1987), 258. Needless to say, the sort of narrative I am describing here conforms closely to Roland Barthes's "hermeneutic code" in *S/Z* (New York: Hill and Wang, 1974); see also Peter Brooks, *Reading for the Plot: Design and Intention in Narrative* (Cambridge: Harvard University Press, 1992).

15. Film metaphors permeate descriptions of trials. To judge from Court TV's live coverage, the opening statement is now characterized by the first attorney as "a preview of coming attractions" as frequently as it is the conventional "road map" or "blueprint." As for outtakes, consider Alan Dershowitz's account of a trial: "A legal case is somewhat like a long, unedited film containing thousands of frames, only a small portion of which ultimately appear on the screen as part of the finished product. The role of the legal system—police, prosecutor, defense lawyer, judge—is to edit the film for trial (*Reversal of Fortune: Inside the von Bülow Case* [New York: Simon and Schuster, 1986], xxii–xxiii).

16. Exactly these speculations were rampant among the jurors with whom I served in a five-week criminal trial in 1990.

its roots in Germanic antiquity: the separate collection and presentation of evidence. Where evidence is separately collected, it can be separately suppressed, destroyed, tainted, fabricated, delayed, planted, altered, and so on, and although official accounts of the legal system remind us that evidence meddling is illegal, the fact is that it *does* happen, and it does happen to some extent because it *can* happen. No wonder we indulge fantasies (in trials both real and imaginary) of evidence cheating. At some level we understand that the separate-collection structure provides the opportunity for it, the competitive structure of the trial provides the motive for it, the raft of rules against it admits the possibility of it, and, as in the O. J. Simpson trial, real lawyers level accusations of it. So too the separate presentation of evidence, which rests on the no less antique assumption that, as Macaulay put it, the fairest decision will be reached when "two men argue as unfairly as possible on both sides" insofar as such a procedure guarantees that "no more important consideration will altogether escape notice."[17] What this means in practice is that the prosecution and defense create respectively the worst and the best possible versions of the incontrovertible facts. The system pays lip service to truth and justice, but the adversarial structure contemplates an odd, even cynical, notion of truth, one we might count as postmodern were it not so manifestly archaic: not the "real" or "whole" or "philosophical" truth of Platonic argument (and indeed of the Continental trial), but a truth of exhausted possibilities, what is left standing after every possible explanatory story has been tried out against it. And what kind of truth can it be that falls not to a wise professional or a trained panel, but to us?

But what unsettles us particularly about the system of arguing "as unfairly as possible" is that the two sides are not arguing *equally* unfairly. We may or may not be able to articulate the principle of different burdens (the prosecution's to prove its case beyond a reasonable doubt, the defense's merely to raise enough doubt), but we see its discursive consequences in a structure that pits a prosecution X not against a defense Y, but against a defense not-X, X being a relatively fixed and coherent story with some commitment to a single account of "what really happened" and not-X being a site of proliferating scenarios, including mutually exclusive ones, of what *might* have happened. What this boils down to in practice, for the jury, is different truth statuses for

---

17. Thomas Babington Macaulay, *The History of England*, vol. 4 (Leipzig: Bernhard Tauchnitz, 1855), 84–85.

X and not-X, the sense that while the prosecution is bound by the explanation it believes to be true, the defense is free to make up whatever explanations it wants. It is against the law, we are told, to suborn perjury. But we are also aware that between absolute truth and plain perjury there is a large playing field, and that much of the defense lawyer's art is avoiding the end zones. Even if we did not see this idea repeatedly thematized in movies ("don't tie my hands by telling me what happened"), we would deduce it from real trials—for example, the so-called Reginald Denny beating trial, in which defense counsel for the accused argued (1) you have the wrong man, and (2) the crowd made him do it. The inventive nature of the not-X position is neatly spelled out in Racehorse Haynes's oft-quoted defense against the charge that his dog bit someone last night: my dog doesn't bite, my dog was tied up last night, I don't believe you got bit, and I don't have a dog. Although none of these defenses is itself a story, singly and together they imply a tale of false accusation (for reasons left to the paranoid imagination).[18] What jurors know, in other words, is that the adversarial trial is also a machine for the production of not just "versions," or "stories," or "theories of the case" (as lawyers call them), but something that looks to us an awful lot like lies.

And where there are lies, there are liars. It is no wonder, given the adversarial structure's drive toward invention and the plain fact that at least some of the people who take the oath to tell the truth will lie, that we are such hyperalert readers of demeanor, watching witnesses for the smallest twitch, shift of glance, tightening of the mouth. It is by the same token no wonder that we should be so drawn to the idea of scientific lie detection. There is something deeply unsettling about our trial's relation to truth, and in venues ranging from law school to television talk shows and fiction, we endlessly explain our legal system to each other and ourselves, as if we don't really quite get it—as if one more formulation might finally unboggle our minds and put into focus how it is that unfairness gets us fairness, a widening gyre works to narrow things down, lying produces truth, and truth is nothing more or less

18. Cf. Alan Dershowitz, "Life is Not a Dramatic Narrative," in *Law's Stories: Narrative and Rhetoric in the Law*, ed. Peter Brooks and Paul Gewirtz (New Haven and London: Yale University Press, 1996), 99–109. To propose, as Dershowitz does, that the explanatory plots that circulate in court are imported from secular narrative culture—film, television, fiction, drama—is to deny the narrative-generating nature of the adversarial structure and indeed the extent to which the "stories" of secular narrative culture originate in the courtroom.

than the best story so far. A culture with such a system might well want a truth machine, and so it is that the polygraph has been embraced in the United States as in no other country ("as American as apple pie") and that, despite its liminal status as evidence, it hovers over the discourse of the trial ("I'll prove I'm telling the truth: give me a polygraph!") and is a commonplace in film and television forms relating to trials.[19]

All of this is played out on a strict schedule of turn taking—yet another peculiarity of the Anglo-American trial. In the early phases of the hearing, we are (for reasons suggested earlier) likely to be on the prosecution side, though apprehensively, thanks to points scored by the defense in cross-examination. But midway through the examination, when the sides have switched places in the presentation of their cases and we face defense testimony, we arrive at a crossroads, a time when we must choose between sturdy and familiar X and the alluring plausibility of a not-X. Textually viewed, it is the most charged moment of the proceedings, one that, once negotiated, delivers us into the most characteristic experience of the adversarial trial: of being pulled rhythmically back and forth, in the almost machinelike alternation of direct examination with cross-examination, between the two positions. We are told to form no conclusions along the way, an instruction that seems to presume a "pure" process of data gathering that resists interim explanations. What cognitive science would say about such a model I don't know, but it is emphatically at odds with the procedure of trial movies and detective fiction, which invite us to an initial conclusion, then unsettle that conclusion with new evidence, then invite us to a new conclusion, and so on, in a succession of tentative hypotheses, one replacing another in a long line. Indeed, it is that process—particularly the moments of textual vacuum, when a fresh piece of evidence undoes our working story without quite providing us with a replacement—that are so central to our experience of this brand of hermeneutic narrative. I strongly suspect that on this point too, popular culture has it right, and that for the jurors, the process of the examination is an exercise in more-or-less anxious plot making and unmaking. It is in any

---

19. "Many Europeans have never heard of the lie detector but there lurks some vague familiarity with the concept in the mind of nearly every American who can read and wears shoes. . . . Instrumental lie detection—polygraphic interrogation—is a 20th century phenomenon and as American as apple pie." David Thoreson Lykken, *Tremor in the Blood: Uses and Abuses of the Lie Detector* (New York: McGraw Hill, 1981), 9, 27.

event a process that calls not only for "close attention" and a "certain intricacy of mind," but a powerful memory and an active paranoid imagination.

With the closing arguments, the text reverts to syntactic narrative with a vengeance as each side tries to gather all the evidence into a master bundle. But all the narrative in the world can't fully still all the prospects opened in the examination. In practice, many trials fall short of full closure (hung juries, appeals, public dissatisfaction with the verdict, lingering doubts, etc.), and even when there is a verdict and it sticks, at least the jurors may feel slightly unnerved; it is, after all, the job of the adversarial system to come up with equally plausible scenarios, and it's not easy to dump the possibilities you've come to know so well. Commonplace has it that art improves on life in this respect, that imaginary trials provide the strong ending (in the form of a Perry Mason–style confession, for example) that real trials often lack.[20] This is true of most trial movies, but by no means all of them. A surprisingly large minority conclude on a tone of uncertainty or flatly with a question mark, and lest we imagine this to be a postmodern development, consider the 1916 film *By Whose Hand?*, a courtroom whodunit in which, after teasing us with two candidates between whom it has been alternating throughout, a final intertitle declares "By Whose Hand? You Are the Jury—You Decide!"[21] Different though they are, these two con-

20. For example, "The trial structures disorder and thus makes it less disturbing and even enjoyable. It is the sustained process of imposing legal order on criminal violence that reaffirms that life's disorder can be controlled. One of the cultural appeals of a television series like Perry Mason, a series that all but defined law for a generation of Americans, was the patterned closure of each program. The truth was always outed, the true criminal revealed; and the vindicated innocence of Perry Mason's client stood for the vindicated order that the legal process predictably imposed. The appeal of the classic detective story is similar, given its reiterated form: a puzzle of violence presented and ultimately solved (and solved through orderly reasoning). Real-life trials obviously do not have the neatness represented on *Perry Mason*, but they have some of its patterned quality—and, above all, they usually reach closure" (Paul Gewirtz, "Victims and Voyeurs: Two Narrative Problems at the Criminal Trial," in *Law's Stories: Narrative and Rhetoric in the Law*, 135).

21. Needless to say, this is not a plot that just happens not to close. It is conceived as open-ended, and it clearly means for that open-endedness to be part of its appeal. Other examples of more-or-less unclosed trial movies are *Reversal of Fortune, Anatomy of a Murder, Criminal Justice, A Question of Guilt, They Won't Believe Me!, A Woman's Face,* and *Twelve Angry Men.* Many trial movies based on actual cases have as their aim exactly to "unclose" the real-life trial: the various Lindbergh movies, for example, or *Brother's Keeper* or *The People v. Jean Harris* or *I Want to Live!* On *By Whose Hand?* (also known as *Who Killed Simon Baird?*), see the review in *Variety,* 14 April 1916, 26. Although I too have the impres-

clusions—firmly closed and more or less open—can be seen as responses to the same problem, that problem being a textual structure designed to produce not a full stop, but a dash or series of dots. Right down to the ending, popular culture grasps the essence of the adversarial trial.

In an often-cited 1966 article on "The Trial as One of the Performing Arts," John E. Simonett declared that trials unvarnished would never make it on television. The American experience since the reversal of the ban on cameras in the courtroom has proved him not just wrong, but absolutely so. In fact, the features of the modern trial Simonett thought killed it as performance—the "advent of modern discovery procedures," the "final rehearsal of pretrial, with counsel knowing in advance who the witnesses will be and what they will say," and the law's "delay, recesses, and conferences away from the bench"—seem to bother Court TV junkies not one whit.[22] And even before trials were televised, courtroom galleries all over the country were peopled with regular visitors known as court watchers; they too seemed, and seem, little bothered by the modern constraints and indeed grade judges and attorneys on their performances.[23] In the United States, at least, where trials are, audiences are.

---

sion that there has been an increase in unclosedness in movies of the last two decades, the fact that there have been unclosed trial movies in every decade of the century (including the first) indicates that the possibility inheres in the form. The adversarial structure is always already postmodern, in a manner of speaking.

22. The phrase "If Court TV were any more addictive, it would be illegal" is said to have originated as a graffito during the Menendez trial. Court TV included it in a promotional sequence that ran throughout most of 1994.

23. In an article on the particularly active Chicago court watchers, Karen Dillon writes, "Courtwatching, which has been a tradition in Chicago for decades, is a serious business for the buffs, as they are affectionately called by lawyers and judges in the federal building. A self-dubbed shadow jury, they offer suggestions to lawyers during a trial, rate lawyers, judges and witnesses for their performances in court, and predict verdicts and sentencings with surprising accuracy" ("Friends of the Court," *American Lawyer,* April 1989, 130). About six regular court watchers were present every day of the five-week trial on whose jury I sat in Alameda County in 1990. Various reports (including the *American Lawyer* one just quoted) suggest that although the numbers have declined since the advent of trial television, a hard core remains committed to the live event. The *Court-watchers Newsletter* bears out the claim of Judy Spreckels, who has been attending Los Angeles–area trials off and on for forty-six years, that it is "procedure, not personalities," that keeps her coming back: "I like the courtroom atmosphere, the discipline, the points of law, the brilliance of people coming up with a better lie and telling it often enough to be believed" (Amy Wallace, "Courthouse is Clubhouse for the Menendez Watchers," *Los Angeles Times*, 15 June 1994, A33).

And—to turn finally to movies—where audiences are, producers and directors are. If Tocqueville were among us today, he would surely not be surprised at the ways our entertainment system seizes on real trials (Menendez, O. J. Simpson); how it makes up trials that should have happened but didn't (the Oswald trial movies[24]); how it "retries" real cases, perhaps affecting their course (*The Thin Blue Line*, which led to a verdict reversal); how it turns real trials into mainstream dramas (the Scopes trial in *Inherit the Wind*); how it re-creates trials using the transcript as script (*The Trial of Jean Harris*, for example, which never leaves the transcript *or* the courtroom); how it produces fictional trial stories (the classic courtroom drama); and, finally, how it generates fictional stories that follow the trial recipe even though they never set foot in the courtroom.

The last claim is the extreme one. But because, paradoxically, the trialness of a narrative can be most clearly seen for what it is when there is no diegetic trial involved, and also because the courtroomless courtroom drama or the trial-less trial movie is especially popular at the moment, the category is doubly interesting for our purposes, and it is to it that I want to devote the remainder of this chapter.

Let me take as my example *Basic Instinct*. Written by Joe Esterhazs and directed by Paul Verhoeven, *Basic Instinct* (1992) was marketed as a thriller or suspense drama. More generally, it fits in the detective genre, with some connections to film noir insofar as it concerns a depressed detective drawn irresistibly to a woman richer, smarter, and stronger than he is and likely fatal as well. Such generic labels (thriller, film noir, suspense drama, etc.) are based on character, setting, and manifest plot; any of them will do. What I want to propose is that the narrative machine underneath the manifest plot, whatever its label, is the trial. There may be no trial *in* the movie, but there is a trial underneath and behind it; the movie itself mimics the phases, the logic, and the narrative texture of the trial.

The video box cover tells the plot up to a point:

Michael Douglas stars as Nick Curran, a tough but vulnerable detective. Sharon Stone costars as Catherine Tramell, a cold, calcu-

---

24. Notably *On Trial: Lee Harvey Oswald* (directed by David Greene, Charles Fries Productions, 1977) and *The Trial of Lee Harvey Oswald* (directed by Ian Hamilton, produced by Showtime, 1986). The latter film features Vincent Bugliosi as the prosecutor, Gerry Spence as the defense attorney, a real federal judge, real witnesses, and a jury of real Dallas citizens.

lating, and beautiful novelist with an insatiable sexual appetite. Catherine becomes a prime suspect when her boyfriend [a former rock star] is brutally murdered [with an ice pick]—a crime she had described in her latest novel. But would she be so obvious as to write about a crime she was going to commit? Or is she being set up by a jealous rival? Obsessed with cracking the case, Nick descends into San Francisco's forbidden underground where suspicions mount, bodies fall, and he finds within himself an instinct more basic than survival.

After Nick has become enmeshed with Catherine, she abruptly dismisses him, saying that she has no use for him any more now that she's finished the novel she was writing about him and has killed off his character. Nick's cop friend Gus is then stabbed to death with an ice pick (by whom, we don't know, but it might be Catherine, and she might have thought Gus was Nick). Nick goes home from this unsettling incident to find Catherine waiting for him, and instead of running for his life, he goes to bed with her (thus the basic instinct of the title).

The first thing we see in *Basic Instinct* is a naked couple having wild sex, the woman on top. They pause briefly while she ties his hands to the bed (from his reaction it looks to be part of their routine). More wild sex, and when it reaches fever pitch, the woman reaches for an ice pick and then, with tremendous force, stabs him to death. At which point the scene cuts—to the next day with the cops there (in the same place) investigating the scene. Now begins the movie proper.

Standard film practice avoids putting crucial plot information in the first few moments, as though acknowledging that audiences take a while to sink into the terms. But some kinds of film, notably thrillers, routinely break the convention, opening the way *Basic Instinct* does, with an abrupt entry sequence showing a crime as it is being committed, without introduction or explanation, and often before the credits. This kind of opening jolts us into the movie, but more than that, it works as a test or a tease: we know we're supposed to be paying close attention and we do as well as we can, but we don't quite get it—partly because we're not yet in in full concentration (the theater lights may still be dimming) and partly because the scene doesn't show us everything, including, of course, the very thing that will matter most in the story to come. That thing in this case (a case of identity) is the woman's face. We see her blond hair and her body but not the one thing that will distinguish her from the other two blond, thin, like-breasted women in the movie: Roxie (Catherine's girlfriend) and Beth (Nick's ex-girl-friend), both of whom will soon become suspects as well. In other words, it's not that the gradual-entry convention just happens to be broken here; it's that it's being precisely exploited, to catch us off guard and leave us insecure in our perception of exactly what we most need to know.

We will be reminded of our faulty apperception every time the scene is referred to throughout the film, right up to the last minute. We'll be asked to recollect it each time we see Catherine naked, espe-cially when she's having sex with Nick: is this the same body we saw at the beginning? Are the breasts the same? Is the hair the same? Is she moving the same way and doing the same things? We'll flash back again during certain sequences with Beth (again, this is Nick's former girlfriend), because although she has dark hair, the evidence keeps building up against her, and sure enough, it emerges at some point that she is given to wearing blond wigs and impersonating Catherine. But the moment at which we most urgently recall the first scene is during the last, when Nick and Catherine go to bed together, a scene that mim-ics the opening sequence down to fine details. Again wild sex, woman on top. But the question this time is not who the woman is; we know it's Catherine. It is whether Catherine is the same woman we saw in the opening sequence. So again we work the comparison: is the body the same? the breasts? the hair? the movements? and so on. It's when she reaches for the ice pick at the side of the bed that the question seems answered: yes, this woman and that woman are one and the same. Until, in the final seconds of the film, she withdraws her hand from the ice pick, letting it lie—throwing the whole thing open again.[25]

The first thing to notice here is that the overall structure of *Basic Instinct*, with its homologous first and last scenes, rhymes with the overall structure of the trial. That is, the opening scene of the movie is

---

25. That is, her putting the ice pick down indicates that Catherine elects not to kill Nick, at least not now. Does she halt because she's basically not a killer (she didn't kill her boyfriend and although she *does* want to kill Nick, she doesn't have it in her)? Or does she halt because she *is* a killer, or at least used to be, but can't kill Nick because she has devel-oped feelings for him? Even if this is not a halt but a hesitation, soon to be overcome, it needs explaining. My own informal survey suggests that although most viewers (maybe two-thirds) believe Catherine did it, a sizable and articulate minority vote for Beth. A sec-ond viewing brings out more clearly the elaborate system of clues implicating Beth, the larger point being that *Basic Instinct* "jurifies" its audience as surely as do the movies about Alger Hiss or Barbara Graham.

the functional equivalent of the opening statements (in which the crime is stated and the problem of the trial announced—in this case, identity), and the closing scene of the movie is the functional equivalent of the closing arguments, a recapitulation of the opening statement, but expanded and more knowing, and with a full context. And between these matching bookends lies a long middle, the movie proper, in which the text duplicates with remarkable intensity and fidelity the paratactic operations of the examination phase of the trial.

That phase begins, in the movie as in a trial, with an abrupt shift of gears: a dramatic cut from the dreamlike murder sequence, which seems somehow to be in the past tense even while it's happening, to the police investigation of the crime scene the day after, the movie's present tense. At this point, linear narrative shuts down and the text collapses into a concatenation of physical objects, bodily gestures, slips of tongue, random snatches of information—initially disordered and disarticulated bits and pieces whose relation to one another we will figure out only slowly and piecemeal, a process that is the sine qua non of the form and the source of much of our spectatorial pleasure.[26] In the second scene (the police investigation), we are shown in choppy sequence a number of objects close-up with a significant pause on each: a Picasso on the wall; a bloody ice pick; lines of cocaine on a mirror; semen stains the sheets (which we see in fluorescent relief through special glasses Nick puts on), and so on. In the following two scenes, when we encounter first Roxie and then Catherine, the camera will treat their faces the same way it treated the objects in the earlier scene, only closer up and with even longer pauses. The camera does more than report here; it probes, almost as if it were a lie detector.[27] So the "examination" phase of the movie goes, bouncing paratactically from the close-up of an ice pick to a long shot of a speeding car to a snatch of a telephone

---

26. Like many other trial movies, *Basic Instinct* is a whodunit. This is the most popular formula, but it is by no means the only one. In other trial movies, both overt and covert, the question is not who, but why or how. The fact that so many overt trial movies are based on real cases whose outcome is known makes it clear that the real art and interest of these narratives is less in the answer than in the process of discovery.

27. Early motion picture technology was seized upon by the justice system as having lie-detection potential, the idea being that because lies reveal themselves in movement over time, moving pictures (which can be replayed and run slow motion) can capture them in a way that still photography cannot. As early as 1903, motion film was being used by courts as a means of determining whether insurance claimants were lying or telling the truth.

conversation to a deliberate super-close-up of Catherine's face as she says, "No, I didn't kill him." We are in a discourse so familiar to us as late-century American filmgoers that we don't even see how odd it is as narrative—and as cinema, how constructed.

That the killer is a woman we already know: we saw her ourselves. The question is what woman. Remember that Catherine's latest novel was exactly about a woman who kills a former rock star with an ice pick. But does that fact point to Catherine's guilt? As the box cover put it (in the dueling-stories mode), "would she be so obvious as to write about a crime she was going to commit? Or is she being set up by a jealous rival?" The alternatives are spelled out in dramatic detail in sixth scene of the film, when the police consult a psychologist, Dr. Lamont.

> *Dr. Lamont:* "I see two possibilities. One: the person who wrote this book is your murderer and acted out the killing described in ritualistic literal detail. Two: someone who wants to harm the writer read the book and enacted the killing described in the book to incriminate the author."
>
> *Nick:* "What if the writer did it. Then what are we dealing with?"
>
> *Dr. Lamont:* "You're dealing with a devious, diabolical mind. You see, this book had to have been written at least six months, maybe even years, before it was published, which means that the writer had to have at least planned the crime in the subconscious, back then. Now, the fact that she carried it out indicates psychopathic obsessive behavior in terms not only of the killing itself, but also in terms of the applied advance defense mechanism."
>
> One of the cops asks what that might mean, and *Beth* (who in addition to being Nick's ex-girlfriend is a court psychiatrist), translates: "He means that Catherine intended the book to be her alibi. She's going to say, 'do you think I'd be dumb enough to kill anyone in the exact way I described in my book? I wouldn't do that, because then I'd know I'd be the suspect'."
>
> *Nick:* "Ok, so what if it's not the writer. What if it's someone who's *read* the book?
>
> *Dr. Lamont:* "You're dealing then with someone so obsessed that he, or she, is willing to kill an irrelevant and innocent victim in order to place blame on the person who wrote that book. I'm

talking about a deepseated, obsessional hatred, and an utter lack of respect for human life."

Gus (Nick's cop buddy): "So however you cut it, we're dealing with someone very dangerous. And very ill."

The "trialness" of *Basic Instinct* is right on the surface in this scene. We have the testimony of the expert witness (even though it's just a conversation in the police station). We have the two-story structure spelled out, and in a way that reflects the differing burdens of the adversarial system: on one hand, the known quantity of the prosecution (*the* writer: Catherine) and, on the other, the ambient alternative of the defense (*a* reader: not Catherine), an alternative that is the site of proliferating possibilities.[28]

At first the finger of suspicion points to Catherine. So systematically does the film spell out her motive (she's a man-hating lesbian of almost Nietzschean dimensions), her means (she owns ice picks and likes using them), and her opportunity (she can seduce men at will) that her guilt seems self-evident during the first third or so of the movie— the portion corresponding to the prosecution's case in the trial. But in the same way that even during the prosecution's case the defense may, in cross-examination, insinuate other possibilities, so *Basic Instinct* lodges early on the Roxie possibility and then the Beth one. Around the middle of the film, when Beth becomes a real contender in our ongoing reconstruction of the past, we have effectively moved into the trial's defense case.

It is from this point that *Basic Instinct* and films like it come into their own as the engine of the examination kicks into high gear. The bits of evidence now come thick and fast; every conversation is loaded with them. One will incriminate Roxie, the next Catherine, and then Beth, and so on. Likewise all the historical data floating about the text: one bit will adhere to Catherine, the next to Roxie, the next to Nick, and so forth. The backstories we have been struggling to piece together now

---

28. Actually, *Basic Instinct* is relatively simple in this respect. It really gives us only two suspects, Roxie and Beth, although there's a gesture toward a third in the figure of Hazel Dobkins (the older woman who is discovered to have once murdered her husband and children). In addition, the film hints throughout at a secret and ominous society of women, lesbian and otherwise, which men (and the movie spectator) will glimpse but never know.

begin to take shape. Practically every character has one in this film, but the main ones are Catherine's and Beth's, which at first seem separate but then, in one of the film's crucial revelations, turn out to be ominously linked: they were lovers in college and somehow, from the obsessive psychic bond that developed between them, murders happened (of their psychology teacher, of Catherine's parents and husband, of Beth's husband). During the last third of the film, the text becomes so saturated with possibilities that it is all but unfollowable (certainly unsummarizable) and so laden with information about the past that it seems in danger of being swamped by the particulars of its backstory. There are films in this tradition that *are* so swamped—*The Big Sleep* being the famous case in point. We have to wonder about the kinds of audience pleasure presumed by such a text. At the very least, we can say the exercise involves "a certain intricacy of mind," which in turn involves a certain paranoia—a paranoia that is played out both *in* the text (in the character of Nick) and *by* the text (engaging us in the anxious reading of clues and imagining of plots to explain them). If the particulars are new, the basic narrative recipe is deeply familiar, probably the most potent American culture has ever produced.

Finally, there is the cinematography of *Basic Instinct*, which becomes increasingly polygraphic in its close-up probe of faces, particularly the faces of Catherine and Beth, searching them for signs of lies and truth. Their performances lean heavily on their ability to appear as though they *could* be lying—not as though they *are* lying, but as though they might be lying but then again they might not be. Clearly that skill is a prerequisite for movies of this kind, playing as they do in the terrain of aesthetic paranoia and the Freudian fetish: I know Catherine's tears *look* real, but even so . . . I suggested earlier that this is the heart of the jury experience—believing and disbelieving simultaneously, trying to hang on to a story that you're also trying to let go of, working to avoid narrative aporia. If that is so, then Nick is not only our surrogate inside the movie; he's also the consummate juror. That particular brand of indecision—I know Catherine did it, but even so—is the condition of his character and the condition of our spectatorship: it's what draws him into bed and us into the plot. He may be a cop in the fiction of the story, but functionally speaking he's no better off than we are. When *Basic Instinct* ends by showing us Catherine, in bed with Nick, reaching for an ice pick only to put it back again, it joins a very long tradition of trial movies that not only play themselves out in the shadow of reasonable doubt, but never leave that shadow, never quite reveal the paranoid truth, never fully resolve the fetishistic quandary. By whose hand? You are the jury; you decide.

Let me end my discussion of *Basic Instinct* with some notes on its genealogy. Esterhasz, who wrote it, also wrote *Jagged Edge*. And indeed what is *Basic Instinct* but *Jagged Edge* with the sexes reversed? The investigator figure in *Jagged Edge* (the Nick figure) is a woman (played by Glenn Close) and the rich and scary prime suspect (the Catherine figure) is a man (played by Jeff Bridges), with whom the investigator falls in love. The plots—the proportions and the plot moves—are otherwise very much the same. It's also the case that the opening and closing scenes of *Jagged Edge* are virtually identical to the opening and closing scenes of *Basic Instinct* insofar as a sexual murder is the first thing we see and an echo murder is the last.[29] But unlike *Basic Instinct*, *Jagged Edge* is an explicit trial story: the investigator is not a cop, but a lawyer; the prime suspect is not just any rich person, but a rich client; and the site of official transactions is not a police station, but a courtroom. *Jagged Edge* is what we might call a third-act courtroom thriller (with most of its courtroom action in the third act). But the genealogy does not end there. *Jagged Edge* is also explicitly based on another movie, Hitchcock's 1947 film *The Paradine Case*, with Gregory Peck as the barrister who falls in love with his beautiful client, the prime suspect in the murder of her very rich husband. In that film, however, the trial begins early on and effectively frames the diegetic action of the film as a whole. *The Paradine Case* is a classic courtroom drama, in other words, complete with robes and wigs and courtroom grandstanding in the English manner—"the wordiest script since the death of Edmund Burke," James Agee called it. We have, then, in reverse order, a full-fledged courtroom drama as the explicit model for a third-act courtroom thriller, which is in its turn the explicit prototype of a detective thriller that never goes near a court or a lawyer. (*Basic Instinct* would seem to have offspring of its own in a film like *Body of Evidence*, in which, interestingly, the courtroom has been restored.) Scratch the surface of variation, though, and you find the same basic structure and plot moves. The courtroom is optional, the sexes reversible, the investigator's profession variable; but all three films follow the same narrative blueprint, and they all play the same textual game.

---

29. *Jagged Edge* closes more completely. In the echo crime at the end, the Jeff Bridges figure does attack the Glenn Close figure, and she does shoot him.

My point should be clear. If *Basic Instinct* is a shadow form of the Anglo-American trial, so must be lots of other films normally classified as thrillers—by no means all of them, but a significant subset.[30] (I am convinced that the detective novel in general is back-formed from the Anglo-American trial, a proposition that has the virtue of explaining why it should be that the form originated in the United States and England and for all its Continental adaptations, remains conspicuously Anglo-American to this day.) And of course there are all the bona fide courtroom dramas—films like *Witness for the Prosecution, Anatomy of a Murder, Paths of Glory, Cry in the Dark, Philadelphia, A Few Good Men* (my list runs to the many hundreds)—plus all those films that are counted in other genres but take the manifest form of trials: comedies like *My Cousin Vinny*, noir films like *They Won't Believe Me!*, Westerns like *Sergeant Rutledge*, gangster movies like *Billy Bathgate*, romantic comedies like *Defending Your Life*, documentaries like *Brother's Keeper*, melodramas like *Peyton Place*, horror movies like *Audrey Rose*, musicals like *Les Girls*, baseball movies like *Eight Men Out*, historical romances like *Somersby*, and porn films like *In Defense of Savannah*. Add all this up and we are looking at a healthy share of Anglo-American film production.

It is also its most culturally marked share. The kind of movie narrative at issue here—fragmented, evidence-examining, forensically visualized, backstory-driven, X-not-X-structured, polygraphically photographed, intricately plotted, doubt-cultivating, and jury-directed—is, if not culturally specific, then culturally characteristic. In his 1957 classic *The Rise of the Novel*, Ian Watt proposed that certain qualities in English prose fiction—notably its formal realism and its "circumstantial view of life"—were conditioned by the English court of law.[31] The rise of Continental critical theory, in the years to follow, effectively shut down considerations of the local, like Watt's, in favor of the general. What I am suggesting here is that although much has been gained in,

30. *Basic Instinct* and *Jagged Edge* are more neatly symmetrical than most thrillers, which, instead of an echo crime at the end, have some other form of "closing argument." On the other hand, other trial-derived thrillers use the flashback (a cinematic device employed from more or less the moment of its invention by the trial form) far more than *Basic Instinct* and *Jagged Edge*, which eschew it. All in all, *Basic Instinct* is no more trial-like than most other thrillers and can be regarded as fairly typical as far as its plotting goes.

31. Ian Watt, *The Rise of the Novel : Studies in Defoe, Richardson and Fielding* (Berkeley and Los Angeles: University of California Press, 1957), esp. 31–34 and passim. Watt's way of thinking about law and literature has been followed up with respect to the case (as exemplary precedent) by Gary E. Strankman in his "Law and the Rise of the English Novel" (manuscript provided by the author).

say, the large project of Foucault (to return to my starting point), some-thing has also been lost, at least in areas in which the difference of Anglo-American law might matter. Watt's move toward cultural speci-ficity via the legal system seems to me powerfully suggestive and is the context for my proposal, in this chapter, that a broad and distinctive streak of Anglo-American popular entertainment derives from the peculiar epistemology of the adversarial jury trial.[32]

---

32. Although they are not the subject of this paper, I might note that Continental trial movies are fewer and farther between and have a rather different shape, tending toward scenarios in which the hapless individual is borne down upon by the over-whelming apparatus of state or church authority (the Joan of Arc or Joseph K. model), hence calling upon a fundamentally different kind and level of engagement on the part of the spectator.

Cinema Scopes: Evolution, Media, and the Law

Marjorie Garber

Hear no evil, see no evil, speak no evil.
—Legend of the "Three Wise Monkeys," carved over the door of
the Sacred Stable in Nikko, Japan

The "world's most famous court trial" attracted media attention and headlines from around the globe. Radio and print journalists, photographers, and movie camera crews swelled the crowd and provided economic benefits to the community, since they needed hotel rooms, food services, and sundries. Potential jurors vied with one another for a coveted place on the panel and hence in the spotlight. Many testified that despite all the publicity they knew nothing about the affair that could prejudice them.[1] Movie cameras cranked, and electronic hookups flashed the news from the courtroom. "My gavel," the judge announced with pride, "will be heard around the world."[2] This was a trial that would be tried in the media, as many noted, with some witnesses and testimony denied to the jury yet heard and read by national audiences seemingly insatiable in their appetite for trial-related news.[3] The year was 1925, and the place was Dayton, Tennessee.

1. "In the examination of the jury panel, one venireman after another testified that he had never heard any discussion of evolution until after Scopes was indicted and that, while there had been a 'right smart' of it since that time, he himself had not paid much attention to it. Eleven of the 19 veniremen had stated this general fact. Ten of the 11 were taken onto the jury." Ray Ginger, *Six Days or Forever? Tennessee vs. John Thomas Scopes* (London: Oxford University Press, 1958; reprint, 1981), 99.

2. Ibid., 99, 103.

3. "Although Judge Raulston prevented the defense from presenting its case to the jury in Dayton, he did not prevent them from submitting it to the American people: the statements by the expert witnesses were presented verbatim by newspapers in all parts of the United States, including the South." Ibid., 164.

The Scopes trial—or the "Bible-evolution" trial—or the "monkey trial"—was one of a number of high-profile twentieth-century courtroom events that have each in turn been dubbed the trial of the century: others include the Leopold and Loeb trial, the Lindbergh kidnapping trial, the Nuremberg war-crimes tribunal, the Patty Hearst trial, and the trial of O. J. Simpson. What made the trial of John Thomas Scopes the "world's most famous court trial" (to quote the title of the published trial transcript[4]) was in part the publicity and media attention that surrounded it: like Daniel Boorstin's famously tautologous definition of a celebrity, a person well known for being well known, the Scopes trial gained its visibility from the very intensity of media coverage and, quite specifically, from the convergence of radio, movie camera, still photography, print reporting, and commercial advertising that directed international attention upon a small town in Tennessee.

In the 1990s there have been striking signs of renewed interest both in the trial and in the issues. A revival of *Inherit the Wind* starring George C. Scott and Charles Durning was mounted on Broadway by Tony Randall's National Actors Theater. A symposium at Tennessee's Vanderbilt University explored "Religion and Public Life Seventy Years after the Scopes Trial."[5] Politician Pat Buchanan magnanimously informed reporter Sam Donaldson, "Sam, you may believe you're descended from monkeys . . . I think you're a creature of God."[6] And the legislature of the state of Tennessee in 1996 considered a bill allowing school boards to dismiss teachers who present evolution as a fact rather than a theory. Creationism was now known, alternatively, by the name of "intelligent design." The bill, perhaps unsurprisingly, became known as the "Monkey Bill."[7]

What is the scope of "Scopes" in our time? In considering the ways in which this peculiar confluence of religion, science, public education, and law seems to recur in twentieth-century American

---

4. *The World's Most Famous Court Trial* (Cincinnati: National Book Company, 1925; reprint, Birmingham, AL: Legal Classics Library, 1984).

5. November 2–3, 1995. The Robert Penn Warren Center for the Humanities at Vanderbilt University, Nashville, TN.

6. Maureen Dowd, "Media Martyr," *New York Times*, 3 March 1996, 15.

7. Peter Applebome, "Creationism Fight Returns to Nation's Classrooms," *New York Times*, 10 March 1996, 1, 22.

public life, I want to look at three moments in the trial's reception, three ways in which the "monkey trial" might be regarded
as a primal scene: 1925, the date of the actual court case, *Tennessee
v. Scopes;* 1960, the date of the Stanley Kramer film *Inherit the
Wind,* which was based on the hit 1955 Broadway play of the
same title; and the mid-1990s, when, for a variety of reasons, the
Scopes trial, Darwinism, and evolution returned to public attention and concern.

The observations that follow will be divided into three parts:
"Hear No Evil," "See No Evil," and "Speak No Evil." In this motto of
the "Three Wise Monkeys," meaning seems to fluctuate between antithetical poles: an injunction to avoid *evil,* or an injunction to avoid
knowledge. But as the ensuing cultural narrative will suggest (and,
indeed, as readings of the first book of Genesis by Milton and others
have repeatedly shown), it is not always possible, feasible, or even
desirable to tell the two apart.

Hear No Evil: The Media Trial, Radio, and Translation

People, this is no circus. There are no monkeys up here. Let us have
order.
    —Officer Kelso Rice, bailiff of the court in *Tennessee v. Scopes*[8]

If an army of monkeys were strumming on typewriters they *might*
write all the books in the British Museum.
    —Sir Arthur Stanley Eddington, *The Nature of the Physical World*
                                                              (1928)

It was "the first great media trial in American history" and "the first
trial broadcast nationwide by the new medium of radio" so that "every
word could be hung upon by all those Americans blest with a crystal
set, static permitting."[9] "We are told," preened William Jennings Bryan
in his last court speech, "that more words have been sent across the
ocean by cable to Europe and Australia about this trial than has ever

---

8. *World's Most Famous Court Trial,* 282.
    9. Thomas G. Barnes, introduction to *The World's Most Famous Court Trial* (Birming-
ham, AL: Legal Classics Library, 1984), 18.

been sent by cable in regard to anything else happening in the United States."[10]

The paradox of publicity for the Scopes trial was that the message of "modernism" was so desperately and determinedly not to be heard. The more Bryan boomed and boasted, the more radio transmitters were set up in the courtroom, the more eager was Tennessee not to send forth a new message about the modern theory of evolution. "You're not supposed to say God on the radio." "You're not supposed to say Hell, either," admonish characters in Inherit the Wind.

In this trial, as in some others we could name, notoriety produces "greatness": the World's Greatest Court Trial. While it had in fact an enduring impact upon the law, it had if possible an even greater immediate effect in the cultural imaginary, because the trial was itself the production site of its own publicity, the occasion for media display. As much as the nascent film industry was represented, the key media innovations for this trial were the radio and the overseas cable. Hearing, rather than seeing, was principally at issue, which was perfectly appropriate, since the question being asked was whether there were some ideas too dangerous for Tennessee's (and America's) children to hear.

The trial had begun as a "test case," brought by the American Civil Liberties Union, the ACLU, to test "gag laws" that enjoined a certain orthodoxy on teachers. Tennessee's 1925 "Butler Act" was a prime example. "BE IT ENACTED BY THE GENERAL ASSEMBLY OF THE STATE OF TENNESSEE [it declared], That it shall be unlawful for any teacher in any of the Universities, Normals and all other public schools of the State which are supported in whole or in part by the public school funds of the State, to teach any theory that denies the story of the Divine Creation of man as taught in the Bible, and to teach instead that man has descended from a lower order of animals."[11] Scopes—the "Bert Cates" of Inherit the Wind—had volunteered to test the statute, at the urging of a neighbor, George Rappelyea (a New York engineer, married to a local woman and living in the community) who was hostile to fundamentalist Christianity. Scopes was not, that is, an innocent, a martyr, a revolutionary, or a patsy. He was twenty-four years old and didn't know much

---

10. World's Most Famous Court Trial, 316.

11. House Bill 185, Public Acts of Tennessee for 1925. Cited in Sprague de Camp, The Great Monkey Trial (Garden City: Doubleday, 1968), 2.

biology. He was hired principally as an athletic coach, responsible for the football, basketball, and baseball teams. Reporter H. L. Mencken, in town to cover the trial, observed that "even in his shirtsleeves" Scopes "would fit into any college campus in America save Harvard alone."[12]

As it turned out, in an ironic twist revealed after the conclusion of the trial, Scopes had in fact skipped the lesson on evolution he was supposed to teach that day, giving the time over instead to working out some vital team plays. Guiltily he confessed as much to a news service reporter, swearing him to silence until after the Tennessee Supreme Court got the case on appeal. His biggest fear had been that his students, who (coached by defense lawyers) testified eloquently about the teaching of evolution in the classroom, would remember that it had never happened. "You know I pleaded 'not guilty,'" Scopes told the reporter.[13] This was another way in which, ironically, the students, and the nation, would "hear no evil." The "evil" doctrine had never in fact been taught in the targeted classroom. And Scopes was determined that that absence of hearing, that failure of evolution in fact to get a hearing, would never itself be heard.

Nonetheless, Scopes was found guilty and fined $100 by the judge. The fact that the judge himself (rather than the jury) set the fine became grounds for appeal. The defense had sought to quash the indictment, and, failing that, sought to present the constitutional issue to the jury, proposing to present expert testimony on evolution from a group of distinguished scholars in various academic specialities, from paleography to comparative anatomy. Judge Raulston ruled that such testimony from "foreigners" (hailing from towns like New York and universities like Harvard) was inadmissible. This ruling precluded any trying of the case on the merits of evolution and the rights of fundamentalists (who paid the local taxes and hired the local teachers) to decide what should be taught in school. These issues perforce, would have to be debated in the court of appeals. Defense lawyer Clarence Darrow therefore cleverly chose to forgo a closing argument, thus depriving the eager Bryan of the last word and the national soapbox he craved, and the case went on to a higher court.

The celebrity status of the lawyers had guaranteed the crowd: for the defense, the legendary Clarence Darrow; for the prosecution,

---

12. H. L. Mencken, *Baltimore Sun*, July 20, 1925, 1F.
13. de Camp, *Great Monkey Trial*, 432.

William Jennings Bryan, the famous Democratic orator and populist, known throughout the land for his "Cross of Gold" speech at the 1896 Democratic National Convention, and since then a perennial presidential candidate, Woodrow Wilson's former secretary of state, and now a sought-after speaker at Chautauqua gatherings, where he often delivered a speech called "The Menace of Darwinism."[14]

Darrow, the Chicago lawyer who appeared for the defense, had come direct from his victory as the defending attorney in the Leopold and Loeb case in New York—a case that, as we'll see, was mentioned pointedly within the Scopes trial as evidence that Darrow himself believed in the possibility of corruption through the teaching of dangerous ideas. Drawn together in the 1880s in their support of the downtrodden, Darrow and Bryan had split over evolution. Urged by his friend H. L. Mencken, Darrow volunteered for the defense. This classic confrontation thus pitted a criminal trial lawyer of tremendous reputation—Darrow had defended labor leaders, radicals, anarchists, communists, and socialists—against a public figure, Bryan—who hadn't tried a case in thirty-six years.

What were the issues under dispute? One was local option. Bryan had famously and repeatedly declared in his speeches and writings that "the hand that writes the paycheck rules the school."[15] Another issue, still relevant today, was that almost oxymoronic concept, "academic freedom." John Randolph Neal, Scopes's Tennessee lawyer, had put his understanding of the case clearly: "The question is not whether evolution is true or untrue, but involves the freedom of teaching, or what is more important, the freedom of learning."[16] But the defense strategy that was finally adopted, with Darrow in control, was to reverse the roles of plaintiff and defendant and to put fundamentalism itself on trial. "My object, and my only object," said Darrow, "was to focus the attention of the country on the programme of Mr. Bryan and the other fundamentalists in America."[17] This he did spectacularly by actually calling Bryan to the stand as a witness on the truth of the Bible.

But which Bible?

One thing that religious fundamentalism has in common with cer-

14. de Camp, *Great Monkey Trial*, 42.

15. William Jennings Bryan, *Commoner*, January 1923, 1–2.

16. Ginger, *Six Days or Forever?* 45.

17. Clarence Darrow, *The Story of My Life* (New York, Charles Scribner's sons, 1932), 249.

tain kinds of law, and indeed with certain kinds of literary criticism, is an emphasis upon the literal, upon what is sometimes called "the letter of the law." Here the opposite of fundamentalism is, in religious jargon, *modernism,* a term that connotes, in Christian churches, movements that attempt to define church teachings in the light of modern revolutions in science and philosophy.

How can Christian fundamentalists believe in the literal truth of a Bible they can read only in translation?

In the Scopes trial, which purported to test the competing "truths" of various ways of reading the Bible and human history, William Jennings Bryan was called as an expert witness and was deposed (devastatingly) by Darrow on the literal truth of Genesis. Did God really make the world in six days? Six days of twenty-four hours? Where did Cain get his wife, since no extra woman is mentioned in the Bible? Did Joshua really make the sun stand still? Bryan's answers put him into immediate disfavor with his supporters. Witness the following excerpt from the trial transcript.[18]

> *Darrow:* "You think those were not literal days?"
> *Bryan:* "I do not think they were twenty-four-hour days. . . . My impression is they were periods, but I would not attempt to argue as against anybody who wanted to believe in literal days."
> *Darrow:* "Now, if you call those periods, they may have been a very long time."
> *Bryan:* "They may have been."
> *Darrow:* "The creation may have been going on for a very long time?"
> *Bryan:* "It might have continued for millions of years."

Consternation in the court.

In 1924 Bryan had written, "Give the modernist three words, 'allegorical,' 'poetical,' and 'symbolical,' and he can suck the meaning out of every vital doctrine of the Christian Church and every passage in the Bible to which he objects."[19] But as disconcerting as these admissions of figure were (we are talking, it is well to remember, about reading practices, about allegory and interpretation), even more disconcerting was

---

18. *World's Most Famous Court Trial,* 302–3.

19. William Jennings Bryan, *Seven Questions in Dispute* (Philadelphia: Sunday School Times Co., c. 1924), 106.

what might be regarded as a more "fundamental" question. What was the Bible?

When the prosecution sought to enter "the Bible" into evidence, defense attorney Arthur Garfield Hays registered an objection: "What is the Bible?" he asked, rhetorically.

> Different sects of Christian disagree in their answers to this question. . . . The various Protestant sects of Christians use the King James version, published in London in 1611, while Catholics use the Douay version, of which the Old Testament was published by the English college at Douay, in France, in 1609 and the New Testament by the English college at Rheims in 1582, and these two versions are often called, respectively, the Protestant Bible and the Catholic Bible. The original manuscripts, containing the inspired word of God, written in Hebrew, in Aramaic and in Greek, have all been lost for many hundreds of years, and each of the Bibles mentioned is a translation, not of those manuscripts, but of translations thereof into the Greek and Latin. The earliest copy of the Old Testament in Hebrew now in existence was made as late as the eleventh century, though there are partial copies made in the ninth and tenth centuries. The oldest known Greek manuscripts of the Bible, except a few fragments, belong to the fourth and fifth centuries. Each party claims for its own version the most accurate presentation of the inspired word as delivered to mankind and contained in the original scriptures. Which version does the Tennessee statute call for? . . . Does it intend to distinguish between the different religious sects in passing this law?
>
> There is nothing in the statute that shows they should be controlled in their teaching by St. James [sic] version. The statute might have said that, but it did not. And yet, with an unaccountable confidence they have presented a book to your honor, and attempt to put that book in evidence with the confidence of a man not learned in religion, because any man learned in religion knows it is no more the version of the Bible than a dozen or half a dozen other books. Therefore, your honor, we object to the Bible going in evidence, or that book going in evidence, but insist that the prosecution prove what the Bible is before they put it in evidence.[20]

---

20. *World's Most Famous Court Trial*, 123.

John Washington Butler, the author of the Butler Law, was flabbergasted: what did they mean, more than one Bible? The idea was news to him, was (to use one of Judge Raulston's favorite words) "foreign" to him. The Bible was God's word. It never occurred to Butler that that "word" might be a translation, much less (or, therefore) an interpretation.[21] As Butler had said, in explaining why he wrote the statute, "The Bible is the foundation upon which our American government is built . . . The evolutionist who denies the Biblical story of creation, as well as other Biblical accounts, cannot be a Christian . . . It goes hand in hand with Modernism, makes Jesus Christ a fakir, robs the Christian of his hope and undermines the foundation of our Government. . . ."[22]

Judge Raulston asked whether Prosecutor Hays would raise the same objection if they attempted to file any other Bible, and then quickly overruled him: "Let your objection be overruled. Let it be introduced as the Bible."[23]

Here fundamentalism as a reading practice encounters what seem like insuperable difficulties: how can you believe in the literal truth of a document whose language you cannot read? And here the answer is, all too often, a version of Judge Raulston's: "Let your objection be overruled." Evidence on this point was further complicated by the expert testimony of a rabbi. Darrow had brought an entire gaggle of "foreigners" down to Tennessee to support his case: university scholars with expertise in anthropology, geology, paleontology, genetics, comparative anatomy, and religion. None of these experts was permitted to testify before the jury ("Hear No Evil"), but their views were read into the record. On the question of translation, Rabbi Herman Rosenwasser of San Francisco testified as follows:

> In the Bible there are four distinct terms for man: Adam, Enoch, Gever and Ish. Some of these are used as meaning animals. . . . In the first chapter of Genesis, the word 'Adam' is used. The word Adam means a living organism containing blood. If we are descended from Adam we are descended from a lower order—a living, purely [sic] organism containing blood. If that is a lower order of animal, then Genesis itself teaches the man is descended from a lower order of animals.[24]

---

21. Ginger, *Six Days or Forever?* 122; de Camp, 294.
22. Ginger, *Six Days or Forever?* 4.
23. *World's Most Famous Court Trial*, 123.
24. *World's Most Famous Court Trial*, 228.

Translation might thus reveal that the Bible supports, rather than contradicts, the theory of evolution. Yet we will soon see that the theory of evolution itself is subject to antithetical senses.

In a little paper on "The Antithetical Sense of Primal Words," first published in German in 1910, revised and translated into English in 1925, the same year as the Scopes trial, Sigmund Freud (having come upon a pamphlet published in 1884 that described the capacity of some words in "the Egyptian language" to mean both a thing and its opposite—"strong" and "weak," for example), notes that this phenomenon accords with his observations on the way dreams work, by bringing a category of thought to the surface without evaluating it. English-language examples exist in words such as *cleave* (meaning both "to cling to" and "to cut apart") and in the modern slang term *bad,* meaning "good," which in fact Freud and his philological expert both trace to the Old Saxon word *bat,* which means "good."

Could *evolution* itself be such a word?

Consider Raymond Williams's definition in his useful anatomy of culture, *Keywords: A Vocabulary of Culture and Society. Evolution* was singled out by Williams himself in his introduction as a "spectacular example" of a word that has undergone a profound change. It turns out that *evolution* has its roots in theology—deriving from a word meaning "to roll out." "It was soon applied, metaphorically, both to the divine creation and to the working out, the developing formation, of Ideas or Ideal Principles." According to Williams, it was only after the promulgation of the theory of the origin of species, from Charles Darwin and Herbert Spencer, that "evolution lost, in biology, its sense of inherent design, and became a process of natural historical development."[25] To make things both more complicated and more interesting, *evolution* began to be contrasted with *revolution,* slow change with fast, violent change. Even though some kinds of "evolutionary" change, like social Darwinism, could be ruthless or damaging, the evolution/revolution dyad protected the concept of "evolution." "Revolution," by contrast, was the bad twin, unnatural and radical. But the overlap and confusion between evolution as (1) inherent development, (2) unplanned natural history, and (3) slow and conditioned change became matter for constant scrutiny.

---

25. Raymond Williams, *Keywords: A Vocabulary of Culture and Society* (New York: Oxford University Press, 1985), 21.

The relationship between evolution and revolution, as it happens, was a crux for Adamists (as they called themselves) in post-Scopes Tennessee, where in December 1927 a high school teacher was asked by a student, "What was the difference between evolution and revolution?" J. H. Tate, a teacher at Farragut High School, replied by asking the student to look up *evolution* in the dictionary, where she found the definition, "A process of development." Tate, a good teacher, supplemented this answer with what he must have regarded as benign examples: the electric light and the breeding of animals. Another student disagreed, however, maintaining, "Evolution means to come from a monkey." Tate replied cautiously—he was himself a fundamentalist—that Darwin had written about such a theory, "but no man ever said the theory was true."[26] The next day, irate parents demanded (and got) his ouster for mentioning evolution in the school. As for the meaning of *evolution*, one parent told the principal he didn't know what it meant, and he didn't want his children to know, either.

See No Evil: The Evolution of Evolution

> I am a camera with its shutter open, quite passive, recording, not thinking. . . . Some day, all this will have to be developed, carefully printed, fixed.
> —Christopher Isherwood, *Goodbye to Berlin*

> There's a possibility that even an invisible man has a socially responsible role to play.
> —Ralph Ellison, *Invisible Man*

Films, like plays and novels, exist in multiple time: the time in which they are set, the time in which they are made, and the time in which they are seen or read. Thus, to take a very common example, Shakespeare's *Henry V* depicts the historical battle of Agincourt between the French and the English in 1415, in the middle of the Hundred Years' War; it was written by Shakespeare and performed by his company in 1599, celebrating the majesty of the English state and its queen, among the most powerful in Europe; when it was filmed by Laurence Olivier

---

26. Maynard Shipley, *The War on Modern Science: (A Short History of the Fundamentalist Attacks on Evolution and Modernism)* (New York: Knopf, 1927), 160; Norman F. Furniss, *The Fundamentalism Controversy (1918–1931)* (New Haven, CT: Yale University Press, 1954), 95–96.

in 1944, in the middle of World War II, it again celebrated English pluck and English ascendancy in the dark days of a war (Olivier's declamation of the Crispan Crispian speech on a Manchester patriotic radio program was a cause for national pride); and when once again an English actor and director filmed Henry V in 1989, the vivid sense of a post-Falklands, post-Vietnam anomie suffused the Kenneth Branagh production, making it quite a different play, quite a different story, despite the fact that it contained the same characters, the same plot, and the same language.

The Stanley Kramer film of *Inherit the Wind* occupies similarly multiple sites in time. When we watch it some seventy years after the Scopes trial, forty years after the stage play on which it was based, thirty-five years after Kramer's film (starring Spencer Tracy, Frederic March, and Gene Kelly) was first seen in American theaters, we see history as a palimpsest, or a set of nested boxes.

Which film do we see?

A friend of mine who was a trial lawyer for a number of years and now teaches literature commented on the rather smug tone of film—its air of self-congratulation, almost of self-righteousness. As a film of the late 1950s and earliest 1960s, coinciding with the election of John F. Kennedy, *Inherit the Wind* is apparently unreflectively liberal. Is it smug, or is it anxious? As we will see in a few moments (and as your own experience of human nature may already have taught you), it is not always so easy to distinguish between these two positions.

Inherit the Wind is a film set in the American South in 1925. It was adapted from a hit Broadway play of the same name, written by Jerome Lawrence and Robert E. Lee and starring Paul Muni—a play that was produced in 1955 and was thus presumably developed for the stage in the same year as the landmark school integration case, *Brown v. Board of Education* (1954). Kramer's film was released in 1960, in the early years of the civil rights movement. It features numerous scenes of picketing and marching, with virulent expressions of hatred on the part of some of the townspeople. Yet it contains not a single black character, not even an extra in the crowd scenes. Viewed from the race-conscious 1990s, the film seems astonishingly "white."

Why should that be? Is it that this particular film director was simply not interested in the question of race? Manifestly not. Stanley Kramer's films are frequently, indeed insistently, concerned with racial tensions as a principal "American" category. His early film *Home of the*

Brave (1949) was adapted from a stage play by Arthur Laurents, in which the main character was a Jew who encountered anti-Semitism in the military. Kramer (himself Jewish) changed the plot to make the hero a black man, experiencing racial prejudice in the army in Japan in World War II. (The displacement and erasure of Jewishness here, a typical "liberal" move of the time, would come back to haunt the Left in its later confrontations with Christian fundamentalism.) Kramer's *The Member of the Wedding* (1952) was a film version of Carson McCullers's play, starring the redoubtable Ethel Waters in a major screen role. In *The Defiant Ones* (1958), the white Tony Curtis and the black Sidney Poitier star as escaped convicts chained together: an American allegory transparent enough for its own, or any, time. *Inherit the Wind* (1960) was followed by *Pressure Point* (1962), a film about a black prison psychiatrist (Poitier again) and a bigoted white prisoner (Bobby Darin). Ultimately, *Guess Who's Coming to Dinner* (1967) brought director Kramer and actor Poitier together once more in a film often ridiculed as the high- (or low-) water mark of white liberalism, "the last of the 1960s explicitly integrationist message pictures."[27] (Critic Anthony Appiah mildly and devastatingly describes it as "quaint."[28]) The elegant and unexceptionable Poitier is cast as a doctor, "good-looking, educated, mannerly, and downright brilliant." As Donald Bogle notes with gentle irony, "How could anyone refuse him for a son-in-law?"[29]

Why does Kramer—a liberal, a man apparently deeply concerned with issues of black and white, and indeed of education and tolerance, leave race out?

In his study of the antithetical sense of primal words, Sigmund Freud cites a statement from his *Interpretation of Dreams* that comments on a related phenomenon:

The way in which dreams treat the category of contraries and contradictions is highly remarkable. It is simply disregarded. "No"

27. Donald Bogle, *Blacks in American Film and Television: An Illustrated Encyclopedia* (New York: Simon and Schuster, 1988), 101.

28. K. Anthony Appiah, "'No Bad Nigger': Blacks as the Ethical Principle in the Movies," in *Media Spectacles*, ed. Marjorie Garber, Jann Matlock, and Rebecca L. Walkowitz (New York: Routledge, 1993), 84. As a leading video guide properly notes, however, the film was considered "quite daring at the time of its original release." Mick Martin and Marsha Porter, *Video Movie Guide 1995* (New York: Ballantine, 1995), 534.

29. Bogle, *Blacks in American Film*, 101.

seems not to exist so far as dreams are concerned. They show a particular preference for combining contraries into a unity or for representing them as the same thing. Dreams feel themselves at liberty, moreover, to represent any element by its wishful contrary; so that there is no way of deciding at a first glance whether any element that admits of a contrary is present in the dream-thoughts or as a negative.[30]

If we posit, just for convenience's sake here, the analogy that many film critics have made between film and the unconscious, the "screen" and the "screen memory," the dark, dimly lit movie theater and the sleeping or dreaming mind; if we do this, we can, perhaps, begin to see how contraries work in a film like Stanley Kramer's *Inherit the Wind.* Is the film talking about race and rights by leaving them out? Is there no "no" in the cinema?

Not for the first time, a blind spot marks the spot; where there is resistance, there is meaning; and what seems to be left out, or coded negatively, may turn out to carry a whole collection of meanings, some of them quite antithetical.

There are no black actors in Kramer's *Inherit the Wind,* but there is nonetheless a lone and symptomatic black voice: the voice of Leslie Uggams on the soundtrack, singing "Give Me That Old Time Religion" during the opening titles and "The Battle Hymn of the Republic" during the closing credits.

Leslie Uggams was a black child star of the 1950s and 1960s—"discovered" by Mitch Miller after a 1958 appearance on "Name That Tune." From 1961 to 1966 she was a regular on his weekly TV show, "Sing Along with Mitch." One critic called her, in phrase meant to indicate high praise, "a sepia-toned Shirley Temple."[31] Ultimately Uggams disappeared from television, reappearing almost twenty years later with star parts in "Roots" (1977) (as Kizzy, the young mother of Chicken George) and "Backstairs at the White House" (1979), as well as a few movie roles. But in those early years, Leslie Uggams was herself produced as an anodyne cultural cliché. Though drawn to the Motown sound and other black music styles of the mid-1960s, she says she felt

---

30. Sigmund Freud, *The Interpretation of Dreams: The Standard Edition of the Complete Psychological Works of Sigmund Freud,* ed. James Strachey (London: Hogarth Press and the Institute of Psychoanalysis, 1957) 4: 318.

31. Bogle, *Blacks in American Film,* 473–74.

trapped in the persona TV and Mitch Miller had crafted for her: the public, said Uggams, "didn't want to see me grow up." (That was of course also true of Shirley Temple.)

At the time the film was made, Leslie Uggams was, in effect, white America's idea of a "good black girl," no rebel. She was, in fact, the absolute counterpart of those clean-scrubbed white youths who wait outside the Mansion House for lawyer Henry Drummond (the Clarence Darrow figure) in *Inherit the Wind*—and we might remember that Drummond and reporter Hornbeck (Gene Kelly, playing a figure closely modeled on Darrow's friend Mencken) at first found those silent, respectful young men menacing.

I want to suggest that the film of 1960, *Inherit the Wind,* may be smug about Creation and evolution, but it is deeply anxious about race. This issue is the dangerous "inheritance" that is not acknowledged, the offscreen crisis ("See no evil") that is everywhere to be glimpsed. We might contrast it with the too-overt symbolism of Hornbeck as Satan, eating an apple, an over-the-top allegorical reading that is deliberately brought to the surface and that he himself dismisses.

Although there are no blacks in the little southern town of the Kramer film, not even among the crowds or as servants in the houses, there is repeated mention of lynching and of the Ku Klux Klan. The cynical reporter Hornbeck tells Bert Cates (the Scopes figure), "The *Baltimore Herald* is with you—right up to the lynching." Later, when Cates chivalrously insists that his fiancée be allowed to leave the witness stand unchallenged after testifying about his religious doubts, Hornbeck hands him a sketch of a lynched stick-figure hanging from a tree. In the streets of the film's fictional town of "heavenly" Hillsboro, there are burning effigies. A crowd sings, "We'll hang Bert Cates to a sour apple tree." It's at this point that Hornbeck knocks on Drummond's door wearing a white hood with holes for eyes ("See no evil").

The Ku Klux Klan was founded in Pulaski, a small town 120 miles west of Dayton, Tennessee, in 1865. And in the namesake town of Dayton, Ohio, right after William Jennings Bryan's death, the KKK burned a cross in Bryan's memory, calling him "the greatest Klansman of our time."[32] Historian Larry Levine describes Bryan's "attitude toward the

---

32. Cited in Barnes, introduction to *World's Most Famous Court Trial* (1984), 5. In 1926—the year after the Scopes trial—the imperial wizard and emperor of the Klan made an impassioned speech that could, alas, have been written by an "angry white male" of today, railing about affirmative action:

Southern Negro" as "worthy of any Klan member," though Bryan rarely made his views public. In 1922 he gave it as his opinion that the passage of an antilynching bill then before the House of Representatives would be "a grave mistake." A year later he defended white supremacy as "a doctrine absolutely essential to the welfare of the south," contending that "The black people in the south have the advantage of living under a government that the white people make for themselves. The laws apply to everyone and are better laws than the black man would make for himself."[33]

Clarence Darrow was as well known for his defense of disadvantaged black clients as he was for his resistance to fundamentalism. When the Scopes case was appealed to the Supreme Court in Tennessee a year later, he arrived to offer closing arguments fresh from defending a group of black men accused of murder in Detroit (the Sweet case).[34] Darrow withdrew from the Scottsboro case when he concluded that the Communist party was using the five black men accused of rape for political purposes.[35] A member of the NAACP since its beginning, Darrow wrote articles for the black press, defended poor blacks in court, attended black churches, and lectured at Howard Law School and to organizations of black laborers, tradesmen, and educators. W. E. B. Du Bois said he was "drawn to Clarence Darrow" because "he was one of the few white folk with whom I felt quite free to discuss matters of race and class."[36] "All his life he fought for the rights of the Negro," one of his biographers observed.[37]

Nordic Americans for the last generation have found themselves increasingly uncomfortable and finally deeply distressed. There appeared first confusion in thought and opinion, a groping hesitancy about national affairs and private life alike, in sharp contrast to the clear, straightforward purposes of our earlier years. There was futility in religion, too, which was in many ways even more distressing ... Finally there came the moral breakdown that has been going on for two decades ... The sacredness of our Sabbath, of our homes, of chastity, and finally even of our right to teach our children in our own schools fundamental facts and truths were torn away from us. (Ginger, Six Days or Forever? 9)

33. Christian Science Monitor, 24 January 1922, 24 February 1923; New York Times, 18 March 1923, sec. 8; Bryan to Thomas Walsh, 30 December 1922, Bryan to Kenneth B. Griffin, 24 February 1923, Bryan Papers, Library of Congress. All of the above are cited in Lawrence W. Levine, Defender of the Faith: William Jennings Bryan, The Last Decade, 1915–1925 (New York: Oxford University Press, 1965), 257.

34. de Camp, Great Monkey Trial, 463.

35. de Camp, Great Monkey Trial, 76.

36. Quoted in Irving Stone, Clarence Darrow for the Defense (Garden City, NY: Garden City Publishing Co., 1943), 471.

37. Stone, Darrow for the Defense, 89.

Leslie Uggams; the white hood and the Klan; the overdetermined jokes about lynching; the known and contrasting views of Bryan and Darrow on race—all these are symptoms of a cultural anxiety about Darwinism and race conflict that the film declines or refuses to name. And there is one other very disturbing marker of racialism in *Inherit the Wind*, however briefly glimpsed and relatively glossed over by the filmmaker, and that is the scene at the fair stall in the town square, in the carnival atmosphere surrounding the trial, the scene in which a satiric exhibit of the wonders of "devolution" is accompanied by "exhibit A": a chimpanzee dressed like a man, in overalls, a hat, a plaid shirt—the obverse—or is he?—of the biological chart displayed in Bertram Cates's classroom, the anatomical drawing of the musculature of a male gorilla, his arm menacingly upraised. In a trial that became derisively known as the "monkey trial," what does this monkey signify?[38]

Was *monkey* in Dayton, Tennessee, a racialized code word for "Negro" or "African"? It's disturbing to think so. Many of Dayton's citizens were descended from men who had fought on the Union side in the Civil War. Catholicism was as much, or more, a perceived threat as race struggle: the local Anti-Evolution League, which rented an entire storefront for the display and sale of its books, included works like *Romanism versus Americanism* on the shelf with *Evolution or Christ, Hell and the High Schools,* and *God—or Gorilla?*[39] But thirty-seven antievolution bills were introduced into twenty state legislatures between 1921 and 1929, though only one (in Mississippi) was passed.[40] And as these so-called "monkey bills" were introduced into the legislatures—twelve of them in the two years after Scopes, the height of antievolution sentiment in this country—the Arkansas-based American Anti-Evolution Association declared itself open to membership to all except "Negroes and persons of African descent, Atheists, Infidels, Agnostics, such persons as hold to the theory of Evolution, habitual drunkards, gamblers, profane swearers, despoilers of the domestic life of others, desecrators

---

38. "The ironic reversal of a received racist image of the black as simianlike, the Signifying Monkey, he who dwells at the margins of discourse, ever punning, ever troping, ever embodying the ambiguities of language," notes Henry Louis Gates, Jr., "is our trope for repetition and revision, indeed our trope of chiasmus, repeating and reversing simultaneously as he does in one deft discursive act." Henry Louis Gates Jr., *The Signifying Monkey* (New York: Oxford, 1988), 52.

39. T. T. Martin, *Evolution or Christ* and *Hell in the High Schools;* Alfred McCann, *God—or Gorilla?* (New York: Devin-Adair Co, 1922).

40. Willard H. Smith, *The Social and Religious Thought of William Jennings Bryan* (Lawrence, KS: Coronado Press, 1975).

of the Lord's Day and those who would depreciate feminine virtue by vulgarly discussing [the] sex relationship."[41] As Frederick Douglass had long ago testified, blacks so often saw themselves "described and painted as monkeys" that, in Douglass's words, they "think it a great piece of fortune to find an exception to this general rule."[42]

The potential for justifying racism has always already been present in the development of evolutionary theory. Describing the racial discourse of the eighteenth-century French naturalist Buffon, a precursor of Lamarck and Darwin, Sander Gilman quotes Buffon's apparently untroubled observation that "the interval which separates the monkey from the Negro is hard to understand."[43] Black psychiatrist and anticolonial theorist Frantz Fanon, educated in Buffon's France two centuries later, would write in *Black Skin, White Masks*, "A Negro behaves differently with a white man and with another Negro. That this self-division is a direct result of colonialist subjugation is beyond question. . . . No one would dream of doubting that its major artery is fed from the heart of those various theories that have tried to prove that the Negro is a stage in the slow evolution of monkey into man."[44] And again, "It has been said that the Negro is the link between monkey and man—meaning, of course, white man" (30). For Fanon, *evolution* was a key—and contestatory—term. The French language refers to blacks who want to assimilate to European culture as *evolués*. "In response to a profound desire they sought to change, to 'evolve.' This right was denied them. At any rate, it was challenged" (59). As Fanon wrote with bitter irony, "Black magic, primitive mentality, animism, animal eroticism, it all floods over me. All of it is typical of peoples that have not kept pace with the evolution of the human race" (126).

"In the history of the life sciences," notes biologist and cultural analyst Donna Haraway, "the great chain of being leading from 'lower'

---

41. R. Halliburton Jr., "The Adoption of Arkansas' Anti-Evolution Law," *Arkansas Historical Quarterly* (autumn 1964), 280.

42. Frederick Douglass, cited in Dinita Smith, "Reconstruction's Deep Imprint," *New York Times*, 18 June 1997, B2.

43. Sander Gilman, *Sexuality: An Illustrated History: Representing the Sexual in Medicine and Culture from the Middle Ages to the Age of AIDS* (New York: John Wiley, 1989), 101–2.

44. Frantz Fanon, *Black Skin, White Masks*, trans. Charles Lam Markmann (New York: Grove Weidenfeld, 1967), 17. Originally published as *Peau Noire, Masques Blancs* (Paris: Editions du Seuil, 1952).

to 'higher' life forms has played a crucial part in the discursive construction of race as an object of knowledge and of racism as a living
force. After World War II and the partial removal of explicit racism from
evolutionary biology and physical anthropology, a good deal of racist
and colonial discourse remained projected onto the screen of 'man's
closest relatives,' the anthropoid apes."[45] If the monkey dressed like a
farmer in Kramer's film was merely a memorial quotation of the more
elegant Joe Mendl, he nonetheless conjures up, in the context of a discourse of Klan hoods and lynching, an all-too-familiar rhetoric of racial
disparagement—one that, as Fanon bitterly noted, was directly and
"scientifically" linked to a theory of evolution.

   Black Skin, White Masks was published in 1952. In 1951, four years
before the stage play of *Inherit the Wind* and nine years prior to the film
version, another Hollywood film took on the tangled question of genetics, heredity, and environment with specific reference to Darwin's evolutionary theory. The film could, indeed, have itself been called "The
Monkey Trial," since it centers on an experiment performed by a psychology professor on a chimpanzee. In the event, it was given a different title: *Bedtime for Bonzo. Bonzo* uses a Darwinian frame to make a
counter-Darwinian argument. Its plot involves the attempt of a young
professor of psychology, played by Ronald Reagan, to demonstrate the
importance of environment over heredity. The professor, Peter Boyd,
has a personal stake in the matter: his father (also known—to the
police—as "The Professor") had been a habitual criminal who died
behind bars, and the dean of the faculty of Sheridan College, learning of
this family taint, demands that Boyd break off his engagement to the
dean's daughter. "You forget that I was a professor of genetics myself,"
says the dean, repressively. But Boyd, the author of a work called *The
Power of Environment*, is determined to prove his case, with the aid of
Bonzo, a chimpanzee recently acquired by the psychology department,
and Jane, a young woman who answers his ad for a housekeeper.

   Soon Peter and Jane are calling each other Poppa and Momma for
the benefit of the impressionable young Bonzo and simulating family
values: a peck on the cheek before departing for work, a hot meal on the
table at night (Bonzo, fully dressed, eats decorously with a cup and
spoon), and lessons in "moral reasoning." Predictable events ensue:

45. Donna Haraway, "The Promise of Monsters: A Regenerative Politics for Inap-
propriate/d Others." in *Cultural Studies*, ed. Lawrence Grossberg, Cary Nelson, and
Paula Triecher (New York: Routledge, 1992), 308.

Bonzo runs away, is recovered, and is threatened with a fate worse than death in the Yale University Animal Research lab; Boyd's snobbish, highborn fiancée (herself a Ph.D.—*not* an asset in this 1950s family saga) suspects hanky-panky, and the simulated family values of low-born Jane and Peter, ultimately captured in a series of Bonzo-centered home movies shown on screen, begin to take hold for real. The (faux?) naïveté of the film's race consciousness is such that when Boyd needs to use a a code phrase to describe the missing chimpanzee to his colleague, he calls him "the young man who's visiting here from Africa." Bonzo's environmentally developed moral sense leads him to return a stolen necklace to a jewelry store as the amazed police look on (exonerating Boyd of the suspicion that he has followed in his father's footsteps as a criminal), the dean realizes that "Operation Bonzo" has been good publicity for the college, and the bumbling Boyd finally notices that Jane has fallen in love with him. As they drive away for their honeymoon in his convertible, Bonzo riding in the back seat, they are the perfect American family. Environment counts for everything, as Peter Boyd had vowed to prove; genetics counts for nothing.

Yet in some ways, despite its comic tone and its aura of innocence, *Bedtime for Bonzo* is the *same* film as *Inherit the Wind*. In both, a censorious blocking father intervenes between the feckless young academic and his fiancée. (Scopes in fact was not engaged to anyone at the time of the trial and was regarded in Dayton as a bit of a playboy. The film's faithful fiancée is dramatic license, emotional punctuation.) Both films depict coming-of-age fables in which the monkey is at once catalyst and matchmaker, for both of these films are about family values. The perky Reagan and the blond, vapid Diana Lynn as Poppa and Mamma need Bonzo to construct the family unit backward; in this case, the child is father to the man, or at least to the father, reconfiguring a personal genealogy or family tree backward from the chimp-as-child, himself briefly up a tree in the film's most comic sequence, luring his frantic "parents" there in quest of him. In *Inherit the Wind*, the nuclear family discourse is also firmly in place, but in a significantly different place. There "Mother" is the Bryan character Brady's wife, Sarah, and he is, explicitly and frequently, her whining and dependent (and beloved) "Baby." "Mother, they laughed at me," Frederic March-as-Bryan wails, and she comforts him: "It's all right, baby . . . baby . . . baby." This is the patriarch as helpless and narcissistic infant, Freud's "His majesty the baby."

The exposure of Bryan's human weaknesses also played into another story detectable beneath the surface of *Inherit the Wind*, another political allegory readily apprehensible to contemporary viewers. For the play, and later the film, were produced at the crossroads of not one but *two* key cultural events in American history, both of them made into media spectacles: the civil rights movement and the Army-McCarthy hearings.

In the 1920s, the time of the Scopes trial, the Red Scare and Darwinism were linked in the popular imagination. The North had its Red hunts and Palmer raids, the South had the demon Darwin. A writer in the journal *Christian Fundamentals* claimed that almost the only believers in evolution were "the university crowd and the social Reds."[46] (Huey Long, a Forrest Gump for his time, found it good politics to declare on the floor of the Senate that he was ignorant.[47]) Thirty years later, the Red scare was back again, with a vengeance. Not only back, but back on prime-time TV.

The Army-McCarthy hearings of 1954, televised at the express desire of Senator Joseph McCarthy, proved—in a way almost Shakespearean—to be his undoing. The unraveling of the heretofore impervious demagogue, self-righteous and bullying by turns, proved an irresistible draw to at least a segment of the nascent television audience. Balding, paunchy, jowly, and prolix, McCarthy was not the revered figure Bryan had been at the end of *his* career, and the resounding mot juste of attorney Joseph N. Welch—"Have you no sense of decency, sir, at long last? Have you left no sense of decency?"—fit the scoundrel in a way that it could never touch the fundamentalist saint. But what the two scenes had indelibly in common was the stage effect of cultural schadenfreude, the modern twist on tragedy: a great man goes too far in the public eye, he overreaches himself, and he falls. Thus McCarthy, trying to exert patronage control over the U.S. armed services; thus also Bryan, seeking to outwit and outgrandstand Clarence Darrow, assum-

---

46. Ginger, *Six Days or Forever?* 15.

47. Ibid., 15. Mencken, as we have already noted, excoriated the Fundamentalist Christian colleges for their resistance to learning: "Certainly Fundamentalism should not be hard to understand when its sources are inspected. How can the teacher teach when his own head is empty? . . . Of the arts he knows absolutely nothing; of the sciences he has never so much as heard. No good book ever penetrates to those remote 'colleges,' nor does any graduate ever take away a desire to read one. He has been warned, indeed, against their blandishments." H. L. Mencken, editorial in *American Mercury,* November 1925, 287.

ing that his encyclopedic grasp of Scripture would suffice to make—dare we say it?—a monkey of his interlocutor. Anyone who remembers the Army-McCarthy hearings or who has seen the documentary *Point of Order* will recognize in the weakly grinning figure of the discomfited Bryan in Kramer's film the long-awaited public humiliation of Joseph McCarthy.[48] It is symptomatic both of the intrinsically theatrical nature of the Army-McCarthy hearings, and of the constant crossover between the purportedly fictive and the purportedly real, that Joseph Welch went on to become a movie star in his own right, starring as the judge in the 1959 courtroom thriller *Anatomy of a Murder*.

Inherit the Wind, which came to Broadway just two years after Arthur Miller's *The Crucible*, might—like that play—be understood as an allegory of McCarthyism. Its plot drew attention to the stifling of intellectual freedom under political pressure, and in the spectacle of the discomfited and disoriented Bryan it restaged McCarthyism's self-subversion through narcissistic excess. But between the writing of the play and the making of the film, public attention began to be drawn to another developing political crisis: the rise of the civil rights movement in the American South. 1960, the date of *Inherit the Wind*'s release, was a year of sit-down strikes; in subsequent years the visibility of the move-

---

48. The analogy between Red-hunting and religious fundamentalism or antievolution sentiment is far from far-fetched, historically speaking. T. T. Martin, the author of *Hell in the High Schools,* one of the books prominently on display at the Anti-Evolution book stall in Dayton, who had attended the Scopes trial, offered this exhortation to the Mississippi legislature when it was considering an antievolution bill a year later, in 1926: "Go back to the fathers and mothers of Mississippi and tell them because you could not face the ridicule and scorn and abuse of Bolsheviks and Anarchists and Atheists and Agnostics and their co-workers, you turned over their children to a teaching that God's Word is a tissue of lies and that the Saviour who said it was God's word was only the illegitimate son of a Jewish fallen woman"(T. T. Martin, quoted in Furniss, *Fundamentalist Controversy,* 34). The journal *Christian Fundamentals* asserted that virtually the only believers in evolution were "the university crowd and the social Reds." (Ginger, *Six Days or Forever?* 15). In 1925, the year of the Scopes trial, a writer for the British *Observer* took cognizance of the American tendency to cultural paranoia: "America since the War," he wrote, "has been the prey of multiple terror: fear of the European alien, the Negro, the Asiatic; of Radicalism, Labor, Bolshevism. Harassed by the prophets of woe, scared by the hundred-headed demon of Propaganda, the good American conceives a dread of every sort of modernism. And in Tennessee, particularly, he is at the moment taking it out of an English avatar of Anti-christ—Charles Darwin." As a commentator on the "Monkey trial" noted in 1968, "the same practice [of labeling any unwelcome change as "Red"] featured the McCarthy agitation of the late 1940s and early 50s and features the 'radical right' agitation of today" (de Camp, *Great Monkey Trial,* 17). "Today" then was almost thirty years ago—but it is still, or again, true "today."

ment gathered strength nationwide. The tensions highlighted by *Brown v. Board of Education* and the order to desegregate schools in seventeen states and the Distinct of Columbia generated resistance, lawsuits, and violence. The Montgomery bus boycott of 1955–56 was followed by other challenges to segregation. Northern lawyers and others committed to changing the old ways descended on southern cities and towns.

And here, too, *Inherit the Wind* would offer resonances with current events, resonances both familiar and disquieting. The arrival of Henry Drummond and his panel of experts from northern universities, the generational conflict between the idealistic young teacher and the insult-hurling townspeople of "heavenly Hillsboro," might well strike an audience as similar to what was going on in some southern communities. The picket-wielding, hymn-singing marchers depicting their struggle as one of preserving traditional values against the incursions of outsiders bent on troublemaking fit the scenario of the early 1960s as well as the 1920s. My argument here, it is important to say, is not one of directorial "intention" but rather of interpretative adjacency. Entering a movie theater—or *any* theater, for that matter—an audience brings its own world to match with the screen's fictions. The question I want to pose, again, is, "Which film do we see?"

To an audience watching Kramer's film more than forty years after its release, moreover, the associations with current events might be even more uncanny. The scenes of protesters with contorted faces, intemperate signs, and biblical quotations borne on high could call to mind another crusade: that of the antiabortion demonstrators who proclaim themselves "pro life" and whose tactics include "blocking access to the clinics, thrusting disgusting posters, shouting threats and hounding clinic employees," as columnist A. M. Rosenthal wrote scathingly in the *New York Times*. "Have we forgotten when blockage, vilification and harassment were the weapons of the left, particularly in the universities? They brought the same result the pro-lifers now bestow upon the country—contempt for law, hatred as a substitute for civil discourse and ugliness, mean indelible ugliness."[49] Rosenthal associates such tactics with the bad Left rather than with the bad Right. He is not thinking of the civil rights struggle of the 1950s and early 1960s but rather of the Vietnam War protest later in the decade. His analogy is between the antiabortion movement of the 1990s and student strikes of the 1960s, of

---

49. A. M. Rosenthal, "On My Mind," *New York Times,* 14 February 1995, A19.

the violent encounters between police and demonstrators on college campuses and in the streets of Chicago. But the grimacing faces of Kramer's antievolution picketers revisited today might well be snapshots of Florida or Brookline antiabortion demonstrators, replete with signage: "Read Your Bible."

We have already asked "which Bible" was the infallible Word of the fundamentalists' God. We need now to ask "which evolution" and "which Darwinism" are at stake in the modern story of the Scopes trial. Kramer's film seemed to align the views of the Right with a die-hard creationism and the views of the Left with the progressive belief in Darwin's theory of evolution. But like all binaries, this one is hardly clearcut. For social Darwinism (the "survival of the fittest," in stark economic terms) emerged in late-nineteenth-century culture as a justification for imperialism abroad and unbridled capitalism at home: the rich were rich because they deserved to be so. Thus scholars and politicians on the Left have been attacking attempts to apply Darwinism to current human behavior for generations, while defending non-Biblical accounts of human evolution and animal behavior against right-wing fundamentalist attacks. In a modern-day Scopes trial, a figure like Stephen J. Gould, who has contested the claims of creationists, might well be called to testify in defense of evolutionist science.

But the persistence of Darwinism and an escalating debate about it is today being critiqued from *within* the ranks of evolutionists. Claims for the centrality of evolutionary theory in determining human traits and choices have raised new concerns for progressives about the implications of this view of "human nature." The debate is now often couched in moral rather than economic terms, but scientific proofs are now being brought forward by evolutionary biologists and psychologists to explain (though not necessarily to justify) certain gender and racial stereotypes. The manifest liberal bias of Stanley Kramer's film *Inherit the Wind* (1960) ridicules those who resist Darwin and the theory of evolution as "bigots" (to use reporter Hornbeck's term). But the label of bigotry has lately sometimes been applied to those who *cite* Darwin, Darwinism.

In a book called *The Moral Animal: Evolutionary Psychology and Everyday Life,* Robert Wright described a "new, improved, Darwinian theory [applied] to the human species"—a theory that would, he said, avoid the excesses of so-called social Darwinism and the "simplistic ideas about the hereditary basis of behavior" that "played into the hands of racists, fascists, and the most heartless sort of capitalists" but would nonetheless explain the "deeper unity within the species."[50] Wright argues, using Darwin as his authority, that both "many of our moral sentiments" and our gendered behavior are based in biology.

A more overt claim about the "evolutionary" nature of gender roles is offered by David Buss, an evolutionary psychologist at the University of Michigan, in a book called *The Evolution of Desire*. "In evolutionary terms," asserts Buss, "the payoff for each sex in parental involvement differs: to produce a child a woman has an obligatory nine-month commitment, while for a man it's just one sexual act."[51] "For men in evolutionary terms what pays is sexual access to a wide variety of women, who will commit time and resources to helping raise children."[52] When this kind of "knowledge" trickles down, or up, the evolutionary scale of public influence, the results can be both striking and risible, as for example when Speaker of the House Newt Gingrich observed that women were clearly not meant for military combat since "females have biological problems staying in a ditch for 30 days because they get infections," while "males are biologically driven to go out and hunt giraffes."[53]

Another, even more controversial symptom of this "evolutionary" thinking is the kind of "scientific reasoning" presented in a book like *The Bell Curve*, subtitled *Intelligence and Class Structure in American Life*, which declares in the opening sentence of its preface (and in bold print on the back of the dust jacket), "This book is about differences in intellectual capacity among people and groups, and what those differences mean for America's future." Notoriously, the "groups" turned out to be racial and ethnic. Phrases like "genetic cognitive differences between the races" and "racial differences in intelligence"[54] mark the bias toward what is called "heritability" ("Inherit the wind"). And for this

50. Robert Wright, *The Moral Animal: Evolutionary Psychology and Everyday Life* (New York: Pantheon Books, 1994), 7, 9.

51. David Buss, *The Evolution of Desire* (New York: Basic Books, 1994).

52. David Buss, quoted in Daniel Goleman, "For Man and Beast, Language of Love Shares Many Traits," *New York Times*, 14 February 1995, C9.

53. Gingrich, lecture on "Renewing American Civilization" at Reinhardt College in Georgia, reported in the *Chicago Tribune*, 19 January 1995; Pat Schroeder's commentary on these remarks in the House of Representatives, reported in the *New York Times*, 19 January 1995, A20.

54. Richard J. Herrnstein and Charles Murray, *The Bell Curve: Intelligence and Class Structure in American Life* (New York: Free Press, 1994), 297.

insight into the inherited intellectual capacity of the races, page one of the book, the first page of the introduction, credits—or blames— Charles Darwin.

"Variations in intelligence," write the authors, "became the subject of productive scientific study in the last half of the nineteenth century, stimulated, like so many other intellectual developments of that era, by Charles Darwin's theory of evolution. Darwin had asserted that the transmission of inherited intelligence was a key step in human evolution, driving our simian ancestors apart from the apes."[55] When Charles Murray, one of the *Bell Curve* authors, appeared at a Harvard University forum to defend his book, Stephen J. Gould (who had authored a devastating review in the *New Yorker*) offered a stinging rebuttal. "It's an old argument," Gould observed about the book's genetic intelligence thesis. "What was called social Darwinism in the 19th century."[56] Social Darwinism is, of course, something different from Darwinism; but then, as we have already seen, Darwinism appears to have become, increasingly, self-different, different from itself. If "Darwin" to Stanley Kramer meant a Darrow-like liberality of social, political, and religious views, "Darwin" to Murray seemed to mean something more like the inescapable determinism of genetic— and racial—inheritance.

The theory of evolution is represented in *Inherit the Wind* as manifestly progressive, not regressive. Writing in 1955, playwrights Lawrence and Lee could "assume that audiences share their Darwinism," making "much sport of attempts to defend the belief that the world was created at 9 A.M. on October 23, 4004 B.C."[57] Five years later Stanley Kramer produced a confidently serious film in the clear expectation that audiences would cheer the freethinking Spencer Tracy and be irritated by the pious pomposities of Frederic March.

For much of the country, though indeed never for all of it, the idea that evolution could *not* be taught in the public schools was as unthinkable

---

55. Ibid., 1. *The Bell Curve*'s other citation of Darwin by name tells us that "Darwin himself had noted that, even within the lower classes, the smaller families had the brighter, the more 'prudent,' people in them" (343).

56. Cited in Anthony Flint, "'Bell Curve' Book on Race and Intelligence Debated," *Boston Globe*, 15 February 1095, 23.

57. Vincent Canby, "Of Monkeys, Reason and the Creation" (review of a production of *Inherit the Wind* at the National Actors Theater in Manhattan), *New York Times*, 5 April 1996, C21.

as the idea that something called "creation science" or "creationism" *could* be taught there. How shortsighted that was, and, indeed, how presumptuous and parochial, has amply been demonstrated by a new tide of court cases and proposed legislation.

Speak No Evil: The Politics of Academic Freedom

The star of the collection was undoubtedly a large bespectacled baboon, standing upright, dressed in wing-collar, morning-coat and tie, and carrying under its arm the manuscript of a lecture on *The Origin of Species.* . . . Labelled Professor Fiske after a prominent Darwinian academic, Madame Blavatsky's baboon signalled her own posture in this debate as an adamant anti-Darwinian.
　　　　—Peter Washington, *Madame Blavatsky's Baboon*[58]

Oh, what's the use? Even if Bonzo gave a lecture on Darwin, it wouldn't do any good.
　　　　—Ronald Reagan as psychology professor Peter Boyd in *Bedtime for Bonzo* (1951)

Seventy years after the Scopes trial, Vanderbilt University staged a symposium to commemorate the event. A few months later, in Vanderbilt's home city of Nashville, Tennessee, the state legislature considered a bill that would allow school boards to dismiss teachers who present evolution as a fact, rather than just a theory. "Many teachers won't teach evolution at all because of the stigma and the controversy," reported a Nashville high school biology teacher, whose last class of thirty students included only three who had studied evolution.[59] "I see this as a political power play to insert Bible Belt beliefs into our educational system," said another teacher in the same city. "The other day I went into my classroom and I said, 'Evolution, evolution, evolution, evolution,' and then told my students that I was saying it now because I might not be able to say it anymore."[60]

In January 1995 the pastor of the Merrimack, New Hampshire, Baptist Temple appeared before the school board to urge that creationism and evolution be treated equally in classrooms. "I can't prove my model, and they can't prove their model," declared the Reverend Paul

---

58. Peter Washington, *Madame Blavatsky's Baboon* (New York: Schocken Books, 1995), 44–45.

59. Wesley Roberts, quoted in Applebome, "Creationism Fight Returns," 22.

60. Pamela Messick, quoted in Applebome, "Creationism Fight Returns, 22.

Norwalt to the board. One of the two newly elected members of the school board explained that she supports his request "based on my belief in academic freedom." "I've been sitting here listening to all these evolutionists speak and speak and they get up and tell us evolution is an absolute fact," said board member Virginia Twardowsky. "I'm more convinced than ever before that creation science has got to be taught in the schools." "Creation science" is the new and preferred term: the chair of the New Hampshire State Board of Education said he wouldn't object to a local district "teaching about creation science as an alternative to evolution" and that, in his opinion, the Bible could be used as "anecdotal evidence" to support the lesson.[61]

The key points here seemed to be two: "academic freedom" (à la Twardowsky) and local control (New Hampshire's motto is "Live Free or Die"). Thus the governor, a Republican, weighed in with his own views ("There are worse things taught in our schools, and I will continue to support local control of education"), while a state senator who was chair of the Education Committee confessed that there were "a lot of things I don't understand about both theories. Why, let's remember the creation theory says God made the world in six days and rested on the seventh. I accept that as a Bible-believing Christian. I say students should be taught both theories in school. If I was on the local school board, I would want it taught in school. I would vote for it. I say even Darwin himself would vote for it."[62]

That "creationism" had (re)emerged as a tenet of some factions within the New Right was exemplified by a letter of protest published in the *Boston Globe*.

> The recent "revival" of debate about creationism misses the mark and is a disservice to everyone on both sides of the issue. This is not about "truth" but about venue.
>
> Creationism is not a scientific theory. Its foundation is faith, not scientific evidence. It is not subject to the kinds of tests and scrutiny that we apply to scientific theories.
>
> As a nonscientific theory, creationism belongs in Sunday school.

---

61. "Town Divided Over Whether to Teach Creationism in Schools," *New York Times*, 13 February 1995, A13.
62. Ibid.

It has no place being discussed in science classes, which ought to limit themselves to science, not English literature, modern art or religious faith.

In contrast, evolution is a scientific theory. Like all good scientific theories, evolution itself has evolved over the years as information has become available. It is proper to teach it in science classes. I thought this was settled by the First Amendment and the Scopes trial. It would seem that the Christian right is trying to resurrect an old fossil.[63]

"I thought this was settled by the First Amendment and the Scopes trial." So, apparently, did the National Academy of Sciences, when it declared in 1981, "Religion and science are separate and mutually exclusive realms of human thought whose presentation in the same context leads to a misunderstanding of both scientific and religious belief."[64] But this "misunderstanding" is increasingly widely held.

According to a 1993 Gallup Poll, 47 percent of Americans believe that God created human beings pretty much in their present form sometime during the past ten thousand years. Only 46 percent believe that humans evolved from less advanced forms of life over millions of years. Ten years earlier the figures were reversed; believing creationists are now a majority. So reported the *Boston Globe*'s science reporter, Chet Raymo, in March of this year, responding to the story of the Merrimack school. "I grew up in the Bible Belt," writes Raymo, "not far from Dayton, Tenn., the site of the famous Scopes Monkey Trial. Early on I came to New England so that my children could be raised in the thoughtful tradition of the Adamses, Emerson, Thoreau, Agassiz and Gray. Now the Bible Belt has been loosened to encompass the expanding girth of fundamentalism, just in time for my grandchildren to hear in science class that the world is 10,000 years old." Lamenting the fact that "school boards are taken over by folks who learned their science from supermarket tabloids and radio talk shows" and that textbook publishers now "back away from teaching evolution and human pre-history for fear of losing sales," Raymo urges "enlightened communities" to "con-

---

63. Letter to the editor from Daniel Kurtz, "Creationism Doesn't Belong in Classroom," *Boston Globe*, 31 March 1995, 18.

64. Cited in Peter Steinfels, "Beliefs," *New York Times*, 2 December 1995, 12.

tinue to fight the constitutional battle in the courts." If the battle is lost, he says, "all of America may become the Dayton, Tenn., of the 21st century."[65]

He may be right. Revisitations of the Scopes trial and the antievolution movement have been popping up all over. In 1996 one Georgia school district endorsed the teaching of creationism. In Alabama in the same year, it was decided that biology textbooks were henceforth to contain a disclaimer, in which evolution was described as "a controversial theory some scientists present as a scientific explanation for the origin of living things." The state's reasoning was empirical. "No one was present when life first appeared on earth. Therefore any statement about life's origins should be considered as theory, not fact."[66]

Despite this absence of an on-site observer, some creationists have come to a firm decision. At a meeting of three thousand members of the Christian Coalition in Washington in September 1994, a video booth sold a tape called "Evolution: Hoax of the Century?"[67] In August of the same year, what was called a "latter-day Scopes trial" in Georgia pitted schoolteacher Brian Bown against the Georgia state legislature on the question of the "moment of silence" mandated for all students in Georgia's public schools. The *Palm Beach Post* drew attention to the analogy: "In another time, before television besieged us with constant news from all over the globe, Brian Bown would have achieved the fame and notoriety of John Scopes. Mr. Bown, like John Scopes, is a schoolteacher. And like Mr. Scopes—who defied the neanderthals of Tennessee on the teaching of evolution—Mr. Bown is a man of principle and quiet courage."[68]

A 1988 revival of *Inherit the Wind* for a television movie starring Kirk Douglas as Matthew Harrison Brady and Jason Robards as Henry Drummond was hailed by all participants as "timely." Douglas explained that he "fashioned [his] character after the televangelists of today. . . . like Pat Robertson, charming and softspoken, like Jimmy Swaggart with more flair and drama."[69] When the cast went to the

65. Chet Raymo, "The Real Battle Over Creationism," *Boston Globe*, 6 March 1995, 26.

66. Applebome, "Creationism Fight Returns," *New York Times*, 10 March 1996, 1, 22.

67. Kim Masters, *Washington Post*, 19 September 1994, D1.

68. George McEvoy, "Georgia's Latter-Day Scopes Trial," *Palm Beach Post*, 29 August 1994, 9A.

69. Merrill Schindler, "Kirk Douglas Inherits a Role Still Valid Today," *Chicago Tribune*, 20 March 1988, "TV Week" section, 3.

small Oregon town of Medford to film a schoolroom scene in which the young teacher is talking to his students about Darwin's theory of evolution, the school officials gave them their money back and threw them out. "We don't teach that here," representatives of the school, a Catholic institution, explained.[70] "They don't teach evolution, they only teach the Bible. In this day and age!" exclaimed Douglas with astonishment.

He need not have been so surprised. A Supreme Court ruling in 1987 striking down a Louisiana state law that mandated the teaching of creationism along with the teaching of evolution in the public schools met with a strong response from conservative Christian forces. The law, the Balanced Treatment for Creation-Science and Evolution-Science in Public School Instruction Act, did not require that either evolution or creationism be taught, but rather that if one was, the other should be given equal time. Both the majority and the dissenters, perhaps inevitably, cited Scopes.

Justice Antonin Scalia, in a long dissent joined by Chief Justice Rehnquist, termed the decision "repressive" and "illiberal." In what looks like a mirror image of the Scopes defense, several experts— "whose academic credentials are rather impressive," according to Scalia—cast doubt on the science of evolution and alleged that creationism was a believable alternative. Scalia insisted in his dissent that the law (which had never been enacted) was intended to promote the "academic freedom" of schoolchildren who were being "indoctrinated" in the false belief that evolution was a proven fact. "The evidence for evolution is far less compelling than we have been led to believe," wrote Scalia. "Teachers have been brainwashed by an entrenched scientific establishment."[71] The reversal seemed to him to be clear: "In this case," the justice wrote, "it seems to me that the court's position is the repressive one. That illiberal judgment, that Scopes-in-reverse, is ultimately the axis on which the court's facile rejection of the Louisiana legislature's purpose must rest."[72]

In their opinions in the case (*Edwards v. Aguillard*) two justices had disputed both the claims to science and the claims of academic freedom: "The tenets of creation science parallel the Genesis story of

70. *Los Angeles Times*, 18 March 1988.

71. Stuart Taylor Jr., "High Court Voids Curb on Teaching Evolution Theory," *New York Times*, 20 June 1987, sec. 1, p. 1.

72. Al Kamen, "Supreme Court Voids Creationism Law; 7–2 Ruling Deals Blow to Fundamentalists," *Washington Post*, 20 June 1987, A1.

creation, and this is a religious belief," wrote Justice Lewis Powell, and the majority opinion by Justice William Brennan declared, "The preeminent purpose [of the Louisiana law] was clearly to advance the religious viewpoint that a supernatural being created humankind." It thus endorsed religion, in violation of the First Amendment.[73] The law, he said, "does not serve to protect academic freedom, but has the distinctly different purpose of discrediting evolution by requiring it to be counterbalanced at every turn with the teaching of creation science."[74]

Religious broadcaster and incipient presidential candidate Pat Robertson, predictably, announced himself "outraged." In fact, he predicted that his outrage would become general. Here is Robertson's statement in response to the Supreme Court's ruling in the Louisiana case:

> Everyone in America who believes that he or she has been created by God will be outraged by this decision. The interpretation by the Supreme Court of the establishment of religion clause is an intellectual scandal. By this decision the U.S. Supreme Court has effectively repudiated the Declaration of Independence, which declares that our rights as Americans are endowed by our creator. The Supreme Court has written into the Constitution a questionable scientific theory of the origin of life. This decision will accelerate the exodus of the children of America into private and parochial schools. This decision strengthens my resolve to be elected president of the United States.[75]

No cloud, apparently, however dark, is without its silver lining.

The most striking result of the Supreme Court ruling in the Louisiana case, however, beyond propelling Pat Robertson with even more zeal into the presidential fray, was a shift in the strategy of the opposition forces. To counter the court's claim that teaching creationism was teaching religion, the Institute for Creation Research in El Cajon, California, produced a document that offered to distinguish

---

73. Bruce Buursma, "New Creationist Strategy May Evolve from Ruling," *Chicago Tribune*, 21 June 1987, 1.

74. Kamen, "Court Voids Law."

75. PR (Pat Robertson) Newswire, "Robertson Responds to Supreme Court Decision on Creation Science," 19 June 1987.

"scientific creationism" from "Biblical creationism" by omitting the names of the principals. "Biblical creationism," says the ICR, holds that "The first human beings, Adam and Eve, were specially created by God, and all other men and women are their descendants." By contrast, "scientific creationism" teaches that "The first human beings did not evolve from an animal ancestry but were specially created in fully human form from the start" and that "the 'spiritual' nature of man (self-image, moral consciousness, abstract reasoning, language, will, religious nature, etc.) is itself a supernaturally created entity distinct from mere biological life."[76]

The chair of the Midwest Creation Fellowship, an organization based in suburban Wheaton, near Chicago, predicted that the result would be a refocused emphasis on academic freedom: "We anticipate that the evolutionary activists may feel free now to discriminate against the creation position. So legislation to protect teachers and students who may teach or espouse the scientific evidence that supports creationism could and should be quickly passed." Atlanta attorney Wendell Bird suggested that the decision would be "interpreted to restrict student rights, student academic freedom to hear all the information on the subject."[77] Meanwhile, in Louisiana, creation surfaced again as an "alternative": "All we're saying," said one parent in Livingston Parish who signed a petition in March 1995, "is give them both sides of the story, and let [the students] decide."[78] The "major defeat for religious fundamentalists" trumpeted by the *Washington Post* in 1987 had turned into a live issue once again.

When English professor Gerald Graff concluded that in the matter of the so-called culture wars, combatants should "teach the debate," he might not have had creationism in mind, but he was nonetheless prescient. As an article in the *Chapel Hill Herald* of May 1994, would note, "In the 1920s, creationists in the United States tried to ban the teaching of evolution in the public schools. Now they're just trying to get equal time."[79]

---

76. Institute for Creation Research, El Cajon, California, quoted in *New York Times*, 10 March 1996, 22.

77. Buursma, "New Creationist Strategy," 1.

78. Mary Broussard, "Livingston Eyes Creationism as School Course," *(Baton Rouge) State-Times/Morning Advocate*, 25 March 1995, 3B, 4B.

79. See Gerald Graff, *Professing Literature* (Chicago: University of Chicago Press, 1987); Karen Lange, "Advocate Showing Resilience," *Chapel Hill Herald*, 1 May 1994, 1.

Thus "creation science," having achieved with the stroke of an oxymoron the status of intellectual legitimacy, laid claim to exactly the space of academic freedom that evolution had previously asserted. Was this an evolution—or a revolution?

"Academic freedom" had originally been claimed by the *evolutionists*, the pro-Scopes forces in the "monkey trial," as justification for teaching the theory of evolution in the public schools. Indeed, in the courtroom the question of academic freedom became quite heated, when William Jennings Bryan attempted to use Darrow's own words in the Leopold and Loeb case against him in the Scopes trial—much as Darrow had used Bryan as a witness for *his* own argument about the interpretation of the Bible.

Nathan Leopold and Richard Loeb, two wealthy New York schoolboys, had been charged in the brutal "thrill-murder" of another boy, Bobby Franks. Bryan quoted Darrow's court argument, alleging that he had said that it was "Nietszche's philosophy of the superman," studied in the classrooms of the University of Chicago, that was to blame for the notorious crime—that "the teachings of Nietzsche made Leopold a murderer." "Your honor," Darrow had said, "it is hardly fair to hang a 19-year-old boy for the philosophy that was taught him at the university." Darrow bitterly objected to this quotation out of context, reading into the court record his own subsequent words on that occasion: "[Y]ou cannot destroy thought because, forsooth, some brain may be deranged by thought. It is the duty of the university, as I conceive it, to be the great storehouse of the wisdom of the ages, and to let students go there, and learn, and choose."[80]

But it was Bryan's intention—in that closing statement he never got to deliver—to return to Darrow's words, this time from Darrow's defense of Richard ("Dicky") Loeb: "I know that one of two things happened to this boy; that this terrible crime was inherent in his organism, and came from some ancestor, or that it came through his education and his training after he was born."[81] In the written text of his speech, Bryan seizes on the first option, to condemn the theory of evolution. "Evolutionists say that back in the twilight of life a beast, name and nature unknown, planted a murderous seed and that the impulse that

---

80. *World's Greatest Court Trial,* 178–79, 182.
81. Ibid., 332.

originated in that seed throbs forever in the blood of the brute's descendants, inspiring killings innumerable, for which the murderers are not responsible because coerced by a fate fixed by the laws of heredity! It is an insult to reason and shocks the heart." Bryan urges "responsibility," accountability, and morality; he wants to be able to punish the murderer and not absolve him. But he sees it as an impediment to social progress, and to individual betterment. Evolution "discourages those who labor for the improvement of man's condition."[82]

Bryan thus hoped to turn the tables on Darrow, who had used *Bryan's* words on the stand to support his own case for the teaching of evolution. Which is the "conservative" position here and which the "liberal"? Which kind of "evolution" is evolving here?

Consider this little story from the 1994 autobiography of a scientist[83] who, as it happened, in 1950 found himself in graduate school at the University of Tennessee (in Knoxville):

> The academic challenge was not great at the University of Tennessee, and I grew restive. Out of boredom I also became a bit reckless. I was intrigued by the fact that a statute was still on the books forbidding the teaching of evolution in the state. In 1925 the Tennessee legislature had declared unlawful any doctrine that questioned the divine origin of man.
>
> [Here he tells the story of the Scopes trial, and then continues.]
>
> The law stayed in place and was still untested in the higher courts when I came to Knoxville.
>
> In the fall of that year, while teaching laboratory sessions in the general biology course at the University of Tennessee, I learned about the extraordinary discovery of the first of the South African man-apes. . . . They were the key missing links between remote apelike ancestors and the most primitive humans of the genus *Homo* known at the time of the Scopes trial . . .
>
> Here, I thought, was one of the most important scientific discoveries of the century: Eden revealed in Africa by the lights of Darwin!

---

82. Ibid., 179.
83. Edward O. Wilson, *Naturalist* (Washington, DC: Island Press, 1994), 130–32. The extracted quotation and the quotations in the following four paragraphs are from this source.

The young scientist, prompted by a "mischievous itch to shake things up" and by his conviction that "the evidence was so much more solid— I felt sure—and the faculty would support me—I hoped," determined to give "a lecture on the subject to the elementary biology class. I told them the matter was settled: we *did* descend from apes, or a close approximation thereof. . . . Eden was no garden. The students, some my own age, were mostly Protestants, and many had been raised in fundamentalist families. Some, I am sure, had been taught that Darwin was the devil's parson, the spokesman of evil heresy. They scribbled notes; some glanced at the clock."

Finally the class was over, and the young teacher waited, nervously, for a a reaction. One large blond boy did approach him, and looked him in the eye: "Will this be on the final exam?" he asked. No, said the teacher. "He seemed relieved; one less thing to memorize. Nothing more was heard of my lecture."

Seventeen years later, in 1967, the state legislature of Tennessee finally repealed the antievolution law. But the young teacher, or, as he calls himself in his autobiography, *Naturalist,* had learned, he said, "a lesson of my own in Tennessee: the greater problems of history are not solved; they are merely forgotten."

The young teacher was E. O. Wilson, the father of sociobiology, and the teacher, as it happens, of many of the scientists and social scientists of the next generation who would invent, and defend, evolutionary psychology (including David Buss, the author of *The Evolution of Desire*). "By early 1951 I had decided to move on to Harvard University. It was my destiny," he writes in his autobiography. And not only his.

Wilson thus uncannily fulfills and trumps the half-ironic fantasy of H. L. Mencken, who had seen in the shirt-sleeved John T. Scopes an academic who "would fit into any college campus in America save that of Harvard alone." Yet the genial "father of sociobiology" has found it not so easy to protect the reputation of his own intellectual family tree. "Sociobiology," notes Robert Wright, "drew so much fire, provoked so many charges of malign political intent, so much caricature of sociobiology's substance, that the word became tainted. Most practitioners of the field he defined now try to avoid his label . . . they go by different names: behavioral ecologists, Darwinian anthropologists, evolutionary psychologists, evolutionary psychiatrists. People sometimes ask: What ever happened to sociobiology? The answer is that it went underground, where it has been eating away at the foundations of academic orthodoxy."[84]

Academic freedom, local option, religion in the schools, prayer in the courtroom. The events of 1925 seem uncannily familiar to denizens of the last decade of the twentieth century. Are these "liberal" or "conservative" issues? What I want to stress is the fact that the political valence of an incident or an argument cannot be detached from its cultural context—that ideas and events are read differently in different cultural domains. What may seem an incontrovertibly Left position in one moment may uncannily pop up fifty years later as a basic tenet of the Right; what appears to be a conservative position, indeed one absolutely foundational to conservatism, may reappear as a recognizably liberal idea. This is a "knowledge" that many people would prefer not to know, since it creates crises of alliance and epistemology, especially that mode of autoepistemology we have tended of late to call "identity politics." My argument, then, is neither about political correctness nor about political incorrectness, but rather about something that might perhaps be called political incorrigibility.

"Now it's the left that's trying to restrict free speech," wrote Stanford law professor Charles Lawrence III in an essay on campus regulation of racist hate speech. "Though the political labels have shifted, the rationale is the same: Our adversaries are dangerous and therefore should not be allowed to speak."[85] "Have we forgotten when blockage, vilification and harassment were the weapons of the left, particularly in the universities?" asked moderate columnist A. M. Rosenthal in a description of the antiabortion movement we have already noted.

Or consider Bill Clinton's impassioned response to the Oklahoma City bombing. "Those who trouble their own house will inherit the wind," declared the president, pledging to ask Congress for broad new powers to combat terrorism.[86] Clinton's call for enhanced surveillance

---

84. Wright, *Moral Animal*, 6–7.
85. Charles R. Lawrence III, "If He Hollers, Let Him Go: Regulating Racist Speech on Campus," in *Words That Wound: Critical Race Theory, Assaultive Speech, and the First Amendment*, ed. Mari J. Matsuda et al. (Boulder, CO: Westview Press, 1993), 55.
86. Todd S. Purdum, "Clinton Seeks Broad Powers in Battle Against Terrorism," *New York Times*, 24 April 1995, A1.

of potential terrorist groups was met by a cautious response from the ACLU and the the *New York Times,* which reminded readers of a time when dissidents on the Left were the targets: "Exploiting precisely the kind of enforcement latitude Mr. Clinton would re-establish, the F.B.I. and C.I.A. illegally harassed Americans who opposed the Vietnam War. The F.B.I. burglarized the offices of suspect groups, bugged Martin Luther King Jr. and used infiltrators to provoke illegal activities. Even noble goals, like the control of Ku Klux Klan violence, were tainted by needlessly excessive tactics."[87] The president's own history of war resistance, often thrown in his face by political opponents, was reconsidered by some columnists in the wake of former Secretary of Defense Robert McNamara's startling and belated apologia, *In Retrospect: The Tragedy and Lessons of Vietnam.*[88] One commentator suggested that if he had the courage, Clinton would now speak out in moral support of draft resisters. The *New York Times,* in a brilliant editorial, noted that "another set of heroes—the thousands of students who returned the nation to sanity by chanting, 'Hell, no, we won't go'—is under renewed attack from a band of politicians who sat out the war on student or family deferments. In that sense we are still living in the wreckage created by the Cabinet on which McNamara served."[89]

In the days following the bombing in Oklahoma City, it was disclosed that the architects who designed federal building number 22 previously were "asked to toss in some extra concrete to reinforce it against possible terrorist attack"—which they did. "The perceived threat then," writes *Boston Globe* columnist David Nyhan, "was from the left: anarchistic Vietnam War protesters, who'd torched or bombed some lightly guarded government installations and college ROTC buildings." As Nyhan noted, "The worm has turned."[90]

Repetition and repression are the twin mechanisms by which a culture processes and comes to terms with its intolerable history. The inevitability and linkage of these processes, repetition and repression, makes it impossible to secure the historical moment politically or ideologically in a single place. Neither the Left nor the Right can be securely

---

87. "Don't Legislate in Haste," editorial, *New York Times,* 25 April 1995, A22.

88. Robert S. McNamara and Brian Vandemark, *In Retrospect: The Tragedy and Lessons of Vietnam* (New York: Vintage Press, 1996).

89. "Mr. McNamara's War," editorial, *New York Times,* 12 April 1995, A24.

90. David Nyhan, "Assessing the Threat Within," *Boston Globe,* 28 April 1995, 10.

in possession of the sense of its own primal words: when the repressed returns, it may well turn out to be on the other side.

Which is the Left position, and which is the Right? Which is the liberal move, and which the conservative? What are the "weapons of the Left"—and of the Right? Who pickets? Who prohibits? Who blocks? Who bombs? We may think we know the answers to these questions. But history sometimes answers them differently. As the overdetermined example of creationism and evolution suggests, there can be more than one way to stage a primal scene.

Clint Eastwood and Equity: Popular Culture's Theory of Revenge

William Ian Miller

Revenge is not a publicly admissible motive for individual action. Church, state, and reason all line up against it. Officially revenge is thus sinful to the theologian, illegal to the prince, and irrational to the economist (it defies the rule of sunk costs). Order and peace depend upon its extirpation; salvation and rational political and economic arrangements on its denial. The official antivengeance discourse has a long history even preceding the Stoics, taken up and elaborated by medieval churchmen and later by the architects of state building.

The state builders constructed two basic antirevenge accounts. One was given its final form by legal historians of the nineteenth century. They told an evolutionary story that saw blood revenge replaced by compensation payment and then compensation by the rule of law. For them revenge died naturally, suffering from obsolescence and inadaptability. The other main account is from contractarian political theory. Like the legal historical one, it supposes a vengeful world in times long past, but it departs from the legal historical model by seeing revenge not as disappearing by some inevitable force of human progress, but rather as something that must be continually overcome by acts of will, conscious political commitment, and wise social planning. If for the legal historian the order-threatening nature of honor and revenge doomed them by natural selection to extinction, then for Hobbes honor and revenge doomed humanity unless one worked to devise institutions to suppress them, for Hobbes knew that honor and glory were as much a temptation as they were a terror. Revenge still plays the role of the *éminence grise,* the defining Other, in classic texts of liberal moral and political philosophy.

In contrast to a blood-feuding honor-based society in which revenge and honor are the center of one's public and psychic life, revenge for us operates mostly on the fantastic periphery. Among one repressed segment of us, for instance, revenges go on inside as fantasies of getting even, of dominating, of discomfiting those we envy, fantasies that are what Nietzsche supposed were the substance of *ressentiment.* And in another less repressed segment, revenge still thrives, but it is understood that that very thriving is the determinative characteristic of the ineffable vulgarity of young lower-class males.[1] In our world revenge becomes either small-minded or vulgarly loud and adolescent.

So revenge has died a death after a fashion. That is, the ruling elites officially gave up on it, substituting reason and cost-benefit analysis instead. But if the upper classes learned to walk away from fights with each other, the lower classes, whom by aristocratic ideology were denied the very capacity for honor, kept it alive in barrooms and in back alleys; even the children of the elite still cared about these things on the playground. Unofficially, of course, the upper classes still cared to get even, held grudges, and behaved like normally vengeful human beings, but their revenges were transmuted and took place in economic arenas and in routine social activities like gossip and slighting rather than in face-to-face confrontation. Honor and revenge did not disappear so much as become vulgar and unfashionable, a source of embarrassment to the refined and civilized that needed to be glossed over and carried out in disguise, if carried out at all.

No small part of the antihonor, antirevenge political and moral discourse was to distinguish revenge (bad) from retribution (justifiable). Retribution can still be mentioned in polite company and only with minor apology offered as a respectable reason for punishment of wrongs, administered as it must be by the state in a controlled, proportional fashion. Revenge, in contrast, is portrayed as crazed, uncontrolled, subjective, individual, admitting no reason, no rule of limita-

---

1. I here make the obligatory move of noting that the judgment of vulgarity is an imposition of one class's view on another. That is obvious, yet I wonder if there isn't truly a Platonic form of vulgarity that allows the category to be serviceable for description. If we define the vulgar as a form of aggressive self-assertion, assertion that must recognize its own success solely by the fact that it disgusts the other, then we have liberated the notion of vulgarity from such easy relativistic dismissal.

tion. It is conceived of not only as lawless, but as unruled and ruleless. Revenge, so understood, is anathema to the rule of law. Criminal law books quote passages like this: "Vengeance is self-serving since it is arbitrarily (by its own authority) taken by anyone who feels injured and wishes to retaliate. Vengeance is not defined by preexisting rules nor proportioned to the injury avenged." That quote comes from a dedicated proponent of capital punishment eager to deny that capital punishment is merely revenge.[2]

Consider how Robert Nozick distinguishes revenge from retribution, turning revenge by definitional fiat into a pathology rather than a behavior upon which many societies we still think of as rather glorious based their moral and social order. (I take his distinction here as representative of the general antirevenge tradition of political, moral, and legal philosophy.)

1. Revenge is for an injury, retribution for a wrong.
2. Retribution sets an internal limit to the amount of the punishment, according to the seriousness of the wrong.
3. Revenge is personal; the agent of retribution need have no special or personal tie to the victim of the wrong for which he exacts retribution.
4. Revenge involves a particular emotional tone, pleasure in the suffering of another, while retribution need involve no emotional tone.
5. There need be no generality in revenge. Not only is the avenger not committed to revenging any similar act done to anyone; he is not committed to avenging all done to himself.[3]

Some might wonder whether retribution is preferable to revenge, even to a revenge so unfavorably defined. One might wonder whether a serious commitment to restoring the victim's dignity, rather than worrying more about how the victimizer might not be deprived of his, might lead us to prefer revenge to retribution in point 3. As to point 4, what do we suppose retribution without the accompaniment of emo-

---

2. Ernest van den Haag, *Punishing Criminals* (New York: Basic Books, 1975), 10, quoted in John Kaplan and Robert Weisberg, *Criminal Law,* 2d ed. (Boston: Little, Brown, 1991), 29.

3. Robert Nozick, *Philosophical Explanations* (Cambridge: Harvard University Press, 1982), 366–68.

tions—like a sense of duty, indignation, disapproval, or outrage—
would look like? How could retribution possibly be justified without
an emotional accompaniment? Unemotional bureaucratic implementa-
tion of punishment looks much like law according to Kafka. The anti-
revenger's problem more correctly must not be with emotions themselves so much as with particular emotions, namely *Schadenfreude*. (One
might reasonably wonder whether *Schadenfreude* is in some real sense a
necessary feature of corrective justice.) Point 5 prefers generality in the
application of sanction, and there is much to recommend this position,
but it comes at a cost: it rejects mercy in favor of dreary bureaucratic
uniformity.

Let's put all this aside as raising issues both too complex and too
divisive for quick disposition. What is clear is that revenge in the eyes
of this tradition is merely a stand-in for anarchy and anomie. It is an
uninteresting straw man. Of course no one wants to live around people
carrying out revenge without measure for any imagined slight. Honor-
based vengeance cultures found such people no less troublesome than
bureaucratized societies fear them likely to be. And honor cultures
knew how to handle such misfits with more than a slap on the wrist.
The Norse called them berserks or *ójafnaðarmenn* (men of no measure)
and found ways of rudely disposing of them. Revenge cultures don't
dignify this straw man with the honorific of revenge, and neither, it
turns out, do Clint Eastwood movies. There is, in other words, no
meaningful distinction between retribution and revenge outside the
confines of the antihonor discourse.[4]

One cannot help but notice that in American culture at least, in
spite of more than a millennium of the antihonor discourse, revenge
retains its allure. It still motivates more of our action than we like to
admit, but that is nothing compared to how it motivates the plots of the
movies we pay to see. We still hunger for revenge in one way or

---

4. Robert C. Solomon (*Passion for Justice: Emotions and the Origins of the Social Contract* [Reading, MA: Addison Wesley, 1990]) is much kinder to the passion of vengeance:
"[Vengeance] is a primal sense of the moral self and its boundaries. By denying the reality or the legitimacy of vengeance we deny this sense of the moral self and moralize away
those boundaries of the self without which it makes no sense to talk about dignity or
integrity. But these boundaries do not define just the individual. To the contrary, they for
the most part enclose one's family and friends and the world that one cares about. . . . Not
to feel vengeance may therefore be not a sign of virtue but a symptom of callousness and
withdrawal . . ." (41). See also Susan Jacoby, *Wild Justice: The Evolution of Revenge* (New
York: Harper and Row, 1983).

another. If we can't take it ourselves because the law and other competing internal inhibitions won't let us, we still thrill to fantasies constructed around it. Even the authorities, the guardians and purveyors
of the official discourse, are ambivalent about revenge. The very polity
that will not allow its citizens to claim revenge as justification in its
courts of law sees nothing strange about telling its people that revenge
and honor are good reasons for invading another state. When God
claimed vengeance to himself—"vengeance is mine, saith the Lord"—
one senses he is not taking upon himself a burden but rather selfishly
reserving to himself a pleasure, too good to share with mere mortals. It
was because revenge was so alluring that barriers of sinfulness, crimi-
nality, and other forms of taxing it were felt to be necessary.

I do not mean to suggest that revenge is subject to a law of conservation. I do not believe that if you repress it here, it will pop up there,
either as acne or as fiction. Or that the authorities will become more violent to the extent it is disallowed to the people. It is not, in other words,
that the cultural fascination with vengeance stories is merely compen-
sating us with fantasy for the loss of the reality. Real vengeance cultures
couldn't get enough of these stories either. No conservation there. As an
aside: The literature of revenge served more than just to amuse the
denizens of heroic culture; it gave them heroic models to imitate. Fantasy also could be educative and aspirational. After all, vengeance taking was risky business, and not a few people would avoid it if they
could. Conventional wisdom conceives of vengeance cultures as barely
cultured at all, all id and no superego: big dumb brutes looking for
excuses to kill. But it may be that we are less naturally *homo lupus* than
homo pullus, not man the wolf so much as man the chicken. Prudence
just may be more natural than foolhardiness. There is good reason to
believe that it takes much more socialization labor to produce blood
feuders than accountants.[5] Honor cultures assumed risk-averse man as
the given. They thus developed elaborate means of goading, shaming,
and humiliating to get people to do their dangerous duty.

Revenge and honor are not part of some presocial, precultural,

---

5. See William Ian Miller, *Humiliation* (Ithaca, NY: Cornell University Press, 1993), 5;
and Gilbert Herdt, "Sambia Nosebleeding Rites and Male Proximity to Women," in *Cultural Psychology: Essays on Comparative Human Development,* ed. James W. Stigler, Richard
A. Shweder, and Gilbert Herdt (Cambridge: Cambridge University Press, 1990), 366–400.
Herdt demonstrates the extraordinarily intense and intrusive socialization work that
must be engaged in to maintain a culture of violence in the face of fear, risk aversion, prudence, and desires for ease and relaxation.

wolfish human nature. The story is more complex. We might reasonably assume that a desire for justice and the capacity for experiencing something like indignation at injustice are near universal features of human affective life, but we are not entitled to assume that the desire for justice will be played out in the same way cross-culturally. If we take revenge to stand for the extreme instance of killing those who dishonor us, then some cultures go in for it more than others. If we take revenge as a more generalized concept of simply meaning to pay back the wrongs done us, then we may be butting up against a necessary condition of human social arrangements: reciprocity and exchange.

In honor cultures, justice was inextricably tied to the notion of honor (and hence to revenge) although not entirely congruent with it. But let me put that aside as a matter to be dealt with at another time. For our present purposes it is sufficient to note that revenges were understood as ripostes to shames. Without being dishonored, there was no cause for revenge. The whole process of vengeance taking was, at least in the saga world, understood in metaphors of debt and gift exchange, of giving, owing, and paying back what you owed. You owed a man a return for the harms he inflicted on you. You were thus, strangely, considered to be in his debt for the wrong he had done you. And the cardinal rule of justice (and honor) was that debts must be reciprocated. Not to pay back is to be unmanly; it is to be perpetually the victim. The condition of owing someone is a privileging condition, for it was by paying back that you manifested your honor and revealed yourself as entitled to it.

Honor is not just about repaying harms. If someone does you a nice turn, honor also demands a return. Like a harm done you, a favor done you makes you a debtor, and you are a lesser moral being if you do not repay what you owe. In both cases, you are shameless and acting without justice. There is an elegance in this simple model of reciprocity; it is one, moreover, that still holds many of us in its grip. Notice that such a model does not allow for easy forgiveness of wrongs or harms; in fact, it makes it conceptually incoherent.[6] I can forgive what you owe me, but not what I owe you, and I owe you for what you have done to and for me. To forgive is thus to act like a coward, or a welsher.

---

6. Forgiveness of course was possible in cultures of honor, but it was an option available only to the powerful, that is, to those for whom it would look like a grand gesture precisely because they had the power to carry out a strategy of nonforgiveness if they so chose.

We too at some level accept the model of positioning the wronged person as debtor. Payback time, we say. But we also use the notion of indebtedness and repayment to describe the wrongdoer's position. We say he owes the victim or he owes a debt to society; we speak of him as having to pay for what he did, to atone for, to expiate his wrong. This paradigm competes with the one of the preceding two paragraphs. It transposes the roles of creditor and debtor. In this second paradigm the strategy of forgiveness is morally possible since it is no longer the victim who owes. This paradigm, however, tends to ignore the victim and focuses instead on the wrongdoer. It looks to what the wrongdoer must suffer, rather than to what the victim must do to even up the score. This is the notion that underlies the idea of penance, sin, and state-defined crimes. If we look only at what the wrongdoer should suffer, then it is not important that he be made to suffer by his victim just so long as he be made to suffer by some authority charged with punishing him. Although this paradigm is perfectly consistent with revenge, as a historical matter it came to be part of the justification for giving a monopoly on vengeance to the state.

In the first paradigm—victim as debtor—we speak of paying back; in the second—wrongdoer as debtor—we speak of paying for. This can mark a notable difference.[7] The notion of paying for focuses on the wrongful act, which provides the grammatical object of the verb. Lost in this grammar of payment is the idea that the act created or modified a relationship between specific people, between, that is, the wrongdoer and the victim. In the usual way "paying for" is institutionalized, one doesn't pay for the wrong one did by paying something to the victim, but by propitiation of some abstraction or fiction, like the state or God or the Furies, which then literally cash in on the discords of the society over which they claim authority. In the paying-for paradigm, the victim pretty much disappears as an object of interest. The notion of paying back, however, makes no sense unless the victim or his representative is there to hit back. Under this paradigm, it is not the wrongful act that is the focal point. The focus is rather on the victim, who now has both the right and the obligation to repay the wrong done to him by retaliating against either the wrongdoer or someone closely connected to him. In this account, creditor and debtor, wrongdoer and victim are now bound

---

7. Compare Herbert L. Packer (*The Limits of the Criminal Sanction* [Stanford: Stanford University Press, 1968], 38–39), who finds each view simply different figures of speech for the same retributive principle.

together in an exchange relationship. This is a model we recognize only too well. It may not be the criminal law's model, but it still holds us in our grip.

But the two competing paradigms, which seem utterly antithetical regarding who stands in the debtor's shoes, are not mutually exclusive. Paying back does not, for instance, preclude seeing the wrongdoer as having paid for his wrong once he has been paid back. (Even blood-feuding cultures could understand paying back someone in revenge to be not entirely inconsistent with letting the wrongdoer pay compensation to the victim to buy off vengeance.) In some respects the two models march quite well in tandem. One model sees events from the avenger's perspective, the other from the wrongdoer's.

This intermingling of idioms, however, represents more than just a simple shift in perspectives, for the shift can have substantive consequences. The first perspective, paying back, is a pure model of revenge; the second, paying for, as just indicated, although consistent with revenge, has come to undergird a retributionist model of state-delivered justice in which the victim has little or no role to play; it is a model of a neutral arbiter administering deserved punishment to the wrongdoer but undertaking no obligation to the victim, who must find solace, like any other citizen, in seeing order maintained and some kind of small justice done. Still we talk rather loosely; even when we focus on the wrongdoer's hurt at the victim's hands, we are capable of rapid alternation between the idiom of both paradigms without feeling very troubled by mixing our metaphors. We thus can say he got paid back (the victimcentric model), he got what he had coming (an expression ambivalently hovering between the two models), and he paid for what he did (the straight expiatory model) in virtually the same breath. And this kind of loose talk suggests what the representations of justice in popular culture seem to bear out: subject to a few qualifications to be adduced subsequently, we are rather indifferent as to which model governs as long as justice gets done. We would be perfectly pleased to accord to the state our right and duty to take vengeance if in fact the state did not renege on its promise to take it. The payback model remains so attractive partly because the state is not able or has not seen fit to make wrongdoers pay for their wrongs.

Whatever else revenge may be, it is a style of doing justice. The apologists for state building and the rule of law never denied that. It was not injustice, but in Bacon's formulation "a kind of wild justice."[8] But can there be justice divorced from the passions? Can justice, corrective justice at least, ever be a coldly rational process, mere deliberation, say, behind a veil of ignorance? Justice is inextricably caught up in an emotional economy whose constraints must be satisfied, or there is no satisfaction. Note that satisfaction is both an emotion and a quasi-juridical state representing the fact of justice having been done; that is, we speak of the satisfaction of a claim and the *sense* of satisfaction at having the claim rightly or justly satisfied. Without a sense of just satisfaction there is no justice. Justice, if it means anything, means having people feel the sense of it. The ultimate legitimacy of the institutions charged with administering justice depends on this sense. Without it there is demoralization, despair, and cynicism.

The sense of justice being done can be experienced in different ways: it can range from a purposeful and even grim moral sense, through various shades of *Schadenfreude,* to a triumphant ecstasy. Revenge drama depends on this sense of satisfaction, too, and within the broad category of the revenge genre we can find those that play to the grim and tragic rightness of necessary revenge (*The Iliad, Njáls saga, Hamlet, Unforgiven*) and those that elicit ecstatic triumph that usually manifests itself in the observer by an almost involuntarily uttered, "yeah, right." It is this end of the spectrum that provides the emotional and moral economy of so many classic revenge films of the last couple decades: for example, *Death Wish, Dirty Harry,* and low-budget rape-revenge films.

The modern revenge film is characterized by a specific emotional economy that marks the genre, in fact determines it. Emotion-based theories of narrative genre are as old as Aristotle.[9] Tragedy takes us through pity and fear to catharsis; the modern Eastwood-style revenge narrative takes us from indignation and outrage at a wrong, via fear and loathing of the wrongdoer, to a sense of satisfaction of having the wrong righted on the body of the wrongdoer.[10] The outrage and sense of satisfaction are crucial and definitive of the genre, but along the way

---

8. "Of Revenge," Essays.

9. See *Poetics,* chap. 13.

10. Note that this distinguishes the revenge genre from Aristotle's model of tragedy, which should leave us emptied, rather than exhilarated. For a treatment of the relation of comedy to the emotions of embarrassment and relief, see my " 'I Can Take a Hint': Social Ineptitude, Embarrassment, and *The King of Comedy," Michigan Quarterly Review* 33 (1994): 323–44.

from outrage to satisfaction we also expect to experience some mix of apprehension, hopefulness, anxiety, frustration, despair, terror, disgust, and suspense. The indignation that gets the revenge story moving is the purest of moral emotions, triggered by the experience of injustice and more often than not more readily experienced on behalf of another than on one's own behalf, where it often gets mixed up with various self-interested envies and resentments.[11]

An aside: In our time the experts at emotion-genre theory are video store managers or the people at Blockbuster who shelve the titles. They understand that people pay to see a film in the expectation of experiencing certain emotions, and the films are classified accordingly. Thus some genres even take their name from the emotion bargained for. Horror and suspense[12] are clearly referenced to emotions, but we have come to understand that comedy, drama, and action-adventure have less to do with describing the substance of the film than the range of sentiments we are paying to experience. We thus understand action-adventure, for instance, to be, in effect, an emotion term.

The modern revenge film is about justice, doing justice. It is related to action and horror films, but there are crucial differences that distinguish the genres. In the revenge genre, the hero hunts down the wrongdoer; in action-adventure or horror, the hero is usually trying to escape a wrongdoer intent on harming him or her. In that genre he is the fugi-

---

11. Hobbes, in fact, defines indignation as "anger for great hurt done to *another* when we conceive the same to be done by injury" (*Leviathan* Part I, chap. 6, emphasis added). Indignation and resentment are commonly collapsed into one moral emotion, but that may miss some important distinctions between the two. Resentment is harder to experience vicariously than indignation. Resentment seems bound up with envy; it is perhaps a kind of rightful envy. Indignation is bound up with anger. Resentments can be nursed, not indignations. Part of the confusion is that indignation has no nonobsolete verb formed from the same root, and *to resent* has come to fill the void. So we say we resent things we are indignant about; still, at the level of the noun, we discern a difference. We seem to feel the difference between indignation and resentment. See John Rawls's account of resentment and its relation to envy and distributive justice in *A Theory of Justice* (Cambridge: Harvard University Press, 1971), 531–34; for a much less sympathetic account of resentment, largely subsuming it to Nietzsche's *ressentiment*, see Robert C. Solomon, *The Passions: The Myth and Nature of Human Emotion* (Garden City, NY: Anchor Press, 1976), 352–58.

12. For one attempt to connect the horror genre with a specific emotional economy, see Noel Carroll, *The Philosophy of Horror* (New York: Routledge, 1990) and the critique of his theory of emotions by Robert Solomon, "The Philosophy of Horror, or, Why Did Godzilla Cross the Road?" in *Entertaining Ideas* (Buffalo: Prometheus Books, 1992), 119–30.

tive,[13] unjustly accused, or she, more likely, is the final girl in various slasher films[14] or big-budget action-horror films such as the *Alien* and *Terminator* movies.[15] Villains in the action-horror genre often pretend to a claim of right; they fancy themselves as avengers in their own revenge dramas. This is Max Cady in *Cape Fear* or the villains in *Patriot Games*. These are would-be avengers aspiring to the status of avenger but who are not granted it. We, the third-party observers, are the arbiters in this matter. And the chief reason we do not grant them legitimacy is that we judge them to be acting in accord with the straw man model of revenge. They are not reacting to wrongs, but either to punishments that they deserved or to imagined insults. In the hero-as-hunted genre in which they find themselves, their claims are recognizably without right, their methods of revenge pathologically disproportionate, and their motivation inappropriate. They have idiosyncratic notions of their own right, and as a result, they do not engage us sympathetically.

---

13. For an interesting instance of genre confusion, consider *The Fugitive,* which mixes and redoubles the hero-as-hunted with hero-as-hunter genres and then superimposes them on a mystery plot. The film has a hunted hero (played by Harrison Ford), who in turn must play detective and hunt for the killer of his wife so as to exculpate himself. He is a reluctant avenger, if one at all, seeking his wife's killers less for revenge than for his own exculpation. This causes some problems for the revenge aspects of the film, which get lost in the shuffle. The wrongdoer turns out to be less the killers of his wife than the inept legal system (again) that unjustly punished him. But the film also has a typical hunting hero (Tommy Lee Jones), whom the plot disables from fulfilling the expectations of that role because he is hunting an innocent man. He is only able to reclaim a kind of avenging status when his and Ford's missions coincide to apprehend the killers.

14. The term comes from Carol Clover's definitive study of the slasher genre in *Men, Women, and Chain Saws: Gender in the Modern Horror Film* (Princeton: Princeton University Press, 1992), chap. 1.

15. These genres are not rigidly bounded, however, and can flow by degrees into one another, depending, often, on certain ebbs and flows in the hero's fortunes. Dirty Harry can hunt Scorpio as Scorpio hunts him, or the hunted hero can defend herself by getting into the avenging style and mimicking it, as with Sarah Connor (Linda Hamilton) at the conclusion of *Terminator* ("You're terminated."). Genre confusion seems to confuse Quentin Tarantino, who takes great objection to the conclusion of *Patriot Games* in which the Harrison Ford hero hits the villain, who then dies by falling on an anchor. "As far as I'm concerned, if you're going to make a revenge movie, you've got to let the hero get revenge. There's a purity in that. So you set it up: the lead guy gets screwed over. And then you want to see him kill the bad guys—with his bare hands, if possible. . . . [T]he minute you kill your bad guy by having him fall on something, you should go to movie jail. You've broken the law of good cinema" (*Harper's* [August 1994, p. 22]). Tarantino is holding the hero-as-hunted to the standards of the hunting hero. The former as a reluctant and defensive avenger is granted more leeway in the lethal competence of his revenge taking. If Ford's character were a true avenger in the Dirty Harry or Charles Bronson style, the villain's death by accident would indeed be unforgivable.

Look how thoroughly we reject the straw man conception of revenge constructed by political and moral philosophers. We do not call Max Cady in *Cape Fear* or Frank Miller in *High Noon* avengers; we do not even call them evil avengers. We simply call them villains. We value the avenger status too much to accord it promiscuously to anyone with some crazed unconfirmed sense of his own wrong. The avenger status carries with it right and legitimacy, and thus we confer it on those whose claims are deserving. As in honor-based societies, revenge must be bound up with publicly sustainable claims of right. Yet in this very pretension of the villain to the avenger status, homage is paid to the virtuousness and justifying power of revenge.

In the violent real world of honor and revenge, it is not always clear who is villain and who is good guy, for each side takes its turn harming the other and each side can usually construct a story in which they are the victims who have the obligation to pay back wrongs done them; but fiction seldom fails to make that clear, even if some of our heroes and nice guys are not always the nicest of guys and by a common film cliché come to resemble their opponents. Gray as they may be, we know to root for Clint Eastwood in *Dirty Harry* and even in *Unforgiven* and Charles Bronson in the *Death Wish* movies.

We are all readily manipulated by narrative techniques that keep us partisan to the gray hero, even though that grayness must inhibit to some extent the ease with which we can be moved to support the hero's claims for revenge. The usual move, of course, is to make his point of view the controlling one. Our sympathies will tend in his direction, not so much because he is good as because he is familiar. And then our allegiance is nicely assisted by making his opponent evil, or if not uncomplicatedly evil, then an utterly unremorseful doer of an avengeable wrong. The narrative is thus bracketed in time so as not to provide us a basis for excusing or justifying the wrongs of the villain. He will be the first mover in the chunk of time deemed relevant for the narrative, the upsetter of an uneventful and moral equilibrium. The wrong must be the first act, the necessary condition to there being a story to tell at all. The hero will thus be a reactor, which is precisely the role the deliverer of corrective justice must take. He does not aggress; he responds. And our loyalties to him are locked in as long as he meets two minimal criteria: (1) getting the right guy and (2) having the right guy having the proper mental state to justify his being hit.

This second criterion means that the villain cannot experience remorse. Regret, yes, for getting caught or for having failed, but not remorse for the wrongness of his deeds. In fact, our pleasure at justice being done is not unconnected to the wrongdoer experiencing regret. His regret is the purest sign of his terror at the hero closing in for the kill. His remorse, however, would befuddle us somewhat, and so the genre obliges us by making him too hardened to feel it. The indignation of third parties that prompts the passion for revenge has a hard time sustaining itself in the face of the wrongdoer's true remorse. Revenge might still be necessary, might still be rightful, but it now changes its style. The "yeah, right," the tone of triumphant exhilaration, would be unseemly in these circumstances and is properly replaced by a sense of the tragic, a grim sense that doing right does not always mean feeling good and must even carry out its mission as our sympathy shifts from the victim to the wrongdoer. The sense of justice done is not always exhilarating; in the tragic genre, it is spiritually draining.

The revenge genre as we have come to know it in film distinguishes two broad types of avenging hero: the one is the victim who rights the wrongs done to himself. Slow to anger, uncertain about violence, he finds himself less choosing revenge than having it pushed upon him by the inability or refusal of legal institutions to give satisfaction. He is also urged on almost magically by the audience, whose sense of outrage and indignation confirms the rightness of vengeful action. Charles Bronson in *Death Wish* stands as an easy example. The other type is the quasi-professional avenger, usually a tough cop, who looks to right wrongs done to others because by some understanding that is what his job is. This is Dirty Harry, who looks to take revenge because he *knows* that legal institutions will not give satisfaction unless he controls the institution's response. The first type of hero follows the payback model; the second, because he is taking revenge on behalf of someone else and because he is often himself a state functionary, mixes an attenuated payback with making the villain pay *for* it. Like the state, he claims vengeance as his; unlike the state, he has not quite forgotten the victim's and the indignant observer's claim for justice. Like us in the audience, this type of hero is technically a third-party observer. His indignation is ours, but he insists on acting on it. He acts for us; he is the state as it would act if it were understood that justice makes certain substantive demands that are inconsistent with a narrow devotion to pure legal form.

The position of popular culture is not just that wild justice is real justice. It doesn't stop there. Implicit in stories of revenge is that revenge is a criticism of state-delivered justice. Films like *Death Wish, Dirty Harry,* and their sequels and imitations justify the private justice of revenge precisely because the law is variously inept, corrupt, or blind to the just claims of victims and of indignant observers. In these films, Miranda warnings, Fourth Amendment search-and-seizure rules, short prison terms and easy parole frustrate justice again and again. The constitution is understood to have been trivialized by the law itself, providing nothing but a bag of lawyer's tricks designed to let predators continue to prey. Good cops can't be good cops and still be legal cops. So the good cop must strike out on his own to do justice against laws that prevent justice, as is the case with Dirty Harry; or if there are no cops willing or able to protect the citizenry and bring criminals to justice, then the private citizen must undertake to do it himself as in the *Death Wish* movies.[16]

It is not just those films explicitly proclaiming the virtues of wild justice that evidence little confidence in law and legal institutions. The films that show justice being delivered by the legal system show it being delivered only by the heroic efforts of one particularly courageous or miraculously skillful player. It takes Atticus Finch, Kelly McGillis in *The Accused,* Perry Mason, Charles Laughton, Henry Fonda; it takes genius, cunning detectives, brilliant lawyers, or jurors willing to nullify or violate their oaths (as in *Suspect*) or heroically to defy group pressures (*Twelve Angry Men*). When a film uses the cliché "don't take the law into your own hands" and argues for recourse to legal process, it isn't the routine administration of legal justice that will provide relief. The just result is only available by extraordinary measure, which often involves breaking the law,[17] for the usual bureaucratic structures are inept and blind, given to form not substance, preferring smooth administration to justice. Left to its own devices, the law produces bad results. In a way, this style of film is more antilaw than the revenge and urban vigilante genres. It implies that the law always needs heroes; it requires the extraordinary, the fortuitous, the trick, to produce right results.

---

16. A movie like *Falling Down* plays off these expectations, too, but avoids difficult issues by making the protagonist manifestly crazy.

17. See Robert C. Post, "The Popular Image of the Lawyer," *California Law Review* 75 (1987): 379–89 for a discussion of the "classic American theme" of the lawyer who "must be lawless in order to uphold the law" (382).

Without heroic interposition, law and justice have at best only occasional random convergence.

The avenger's position vis-à-vis the law is less cynical about law. The avenger does not view himself as providing a complete alternative system to formal bureaucratic law. He views his role as interstitial. He comes to remedy and complete the law, not to replace it. He has no problem with the idea of legal rules when they deliver justice, with justice conceived in terms of satisfying the rightful indignation and remedying the harms of victims rather than in terms of complying with the procedures designed to protect victimizers. He gets the law to fulfill its central mission when legalism prevents it.

Dirty Harry, in other words, does equity. He is not a law unto himself. He works where the law fails to deliver justice. Like a chancellor, his right to intervene depends on the law getting a chance to get the right result; his actions are in every sense derivative of the law, secondary, complementary, and equitable. In fact, the idea of Harry would make no sense in a world of no law, for what drives his style of heroism in particular is its implicit critique of the legal system. Like the chancellor, too, he acts upon the body of the wrongdoer, the person unjustly benefiting from legal rules that are producing offensive, shocking, and unconscionable results. It takes a viewer especially unwilling to suspend prior commitments not to feel the equity of Harry grinding the loathsome Scorpio's injured leg with his foot.[18] The equity that motivates Harry does not deny the emotional economy that drives justice. Rightful indignation demands to be compensated with a sense of satisfaction. Harry would lose his moral force (and box-office allure) if he could not satisfy this most moral of emotions.

In another view, common to many Westerns and to the urban vigilante film, it is not so much that the law will get it wrong, as that the law, even when working as it was meant to, only gives second-rate or second-best justice. That is because the interposition of legal form dissipates and delays satisfaction; heroic possibility is taken from the victim or avenging cop and claimed in vitiated form by the lawyer. Fists

18. Popular culture has not yet gotten around to blaming juries for failings in the system. The failings are still a matter of corrupt and inept officialdom, not lay people who are just trying to do their best but getting it wrong. Surely one could make films blaming the five or six Menendez jurors who were willing to give credence to any claim, no matter how unsubstantiated, of child abuse, or the jurors who acquitted O. J. Simpson in the face of a mountain of evidence, but that has not happened. Rather, I suspect, the critique will continue to follow the *Dirty Harry* and *Death Wish* line.

and bullets, the ability really to terrorize the villain, are transposed into talk and the promise of prison. Law is slow, it is prudent, and, unless it ends in execution, it always leaves open the prospect for the villain to get out and get back. Carol Clover asks us to compare the knowing smile of satisfaction on the face of the avenging rape victim that closes out *I Spit on Your Grave*, a low-budget pure rape-revenge film, with the picture of a courthouse, the closing shot of *The Accused*, a big-budget softening of the rape-revenge genre.[19] She notes that too many real-world stories of convicted rapists coming back to stalk, torment, and kill the complaining victim undercut such "happy" endings in the style of *The Accused*. I would add that legal endings usually make for a distinctly weaker sense of satisfaction. Satisfied, yes, but still looking over your shoulder. The death of the wrongdoer brings serious closure to the business at hand; a guilty verdict is only a stay, a promise of closure. Imagine a tragedy in which the protagonist or the villain went off to prison rather than to death. It is comedy and romance that hold the prospect of return, rebirth, and reintegration; the formal demands of revenge stories, like tragedy, require something more than a weak climax of prison.

The notion of revenge that plays the straw man for various traditions of legal and political theory is, as indicated earlier, by definition anarchical, uncontrolled, unprincipled, unbalanced. But the revenge of movie-hero avengers is not without normative constraints. Recall first that the avenger functions in equity. He does not deny law, he improves it. And he does not improve it by some standardless personal set of rules. We as moviegoers understand precisely that he rights wrongs, wrongs that we as an audience agree are wrongs. And not just any wrongs either. Since the avenger is likely to punish the wrongdoer capitally, the wrong must be serious. He thus is not imposing a different set of rules of right and wrong than we hold ourselves. That is what villains do. In his view, as well as ours, it is thus wrong to steal, to rape, to bully, to extort, and to kill without just cause. He, in other words, accepts much of the substance of the law. Note too that the avenger must not strike us as crazy except in his willingness to take risks to get villains. This is why Martin Riggs (Mel Gibson) in *Lethal Weapon* falls on the right side of the line but the protagonist (Michael Douglas) of *Falling Down* does not. The Douglas character is just the kind of person we do not trust to get it right, and while we delight in him blasting the

---

19. Clover, *Men, Women, and Chain Saws*, 148–49. The chapter on rape-revenge films (chap. 3) is a must-read.

franchise burgers for their failure to look as good as advertised, we know we are in the world of farce and pure fantasy when he does so. Clint, Bronson, and Gibson are different. They do get it right both as to the identity of the target and the quantity of deserved punishment. The pure revenge genre makes the avenger a very morally discriminating soul. If his risk seeking seems beyond the norm, his judgments about just desert, praise and blame, are much less controversial.

Let me take a detour for a moment into how revenge might be regulated in a stateless honor-based culture. Honorable people did not undertake revenge lightly. Revenge was never properly an individual matter; people consulted with their kin and friends before taking it, thus socializing the decision-making process. It was not just up to the individual who felt himself wronged. Kin and others would let you know if you were being supersensitive, and they would goad you to do your duty if you were not being sensitive enough. What they were concerned about was the appropriateness of your response, and they were there to help you get it right. You also needed your kin and friends for more than just advice. Most likely, you needed their help in carrying out the revenge, and you would surely need their aid when it was your turn to be on the defensive. Above all you needed the audience, the public, the uninvolved, to recognize that you were behaving appropriately and not being supersensitive. For the uninvolved were the possible class of supporters of your enemy, and support him they would if you were simply being asocial. If your cause was just, you would have an easier time getting third-party support; if it wasn't, it was easier for your enemy to get that support.

Since revenge left not only you but also your kin open to reprisal, those kin had a genuine interest in your vengeance-taking designs, and you might rein in your vengeful desires to accommodate their interests. Remember that in most vengeance cultures, you were not required to kill the person who had wronged you; his brother, cousin, uncle, son, or father could serve just as well. The principle of group liability, somewhat counterintuitively, actually did much to constrain wild revenge. If you could get killed for your uncle's jokes or your cousin's womanizing, then you had a very keen interest in your uncle's sense of humor and your cousin's sex life. You policed those with whom the other side was likely to lump you.[20]

---

20. For a full discussion of these issues, see William Ian Miller, *Bloodtaking and Peacemaking* (Chicago: University of Chicago Press, 1990), chaps. 5–6.

We in more advanced cultures have somewhat different views on group liability. Officially the criminal law, except for a few strict liability offenses involving relatively minor monetary sanction, is very concerned only to punish people who have in fact done a prohibited act with a guilty mind.[21] Without any fuss or sense of frustration, our avengers accept the law's rules of liability. They will only kill wrongdoers or in self-defense. They do not kill the fathers or sons or cousins of wrongdoers unless they also are wrongdoers. The individualizing of punishment helps create a set of expectations that liberate our avengers from having to think all that precisely about members of their own party who might be put at risk by their actions. In fact, it is rather remarkable how the story line saves them the problem of having to worry about others. Either they are loners who make it a business to take risks to do justice, like Dirty Harry, Arnold, or Rambo, or, in another genre, they are peaceful men compelled to become avengers because family or friends have been victimized by the villain (*Death Wish*).

In either case, the avengers of the movies are often strangely detached from family, from friends, often having neither. They are men who are more likely to have had family than to have it. Clint is the Man with No Name; or he is Dirty Harry and William Munny, widowers, who are mostly careful to avoid sexual encounter. Harry's occasional lapses in this regard are brief and inconsequential. These are men, in other words, for whom there is little inducement to consult with others about their course of action. They might be ordered by superiors or begged by friends to desist or save themselves, but they do not consult. They are individuals, almost grotesque parodies of American commitment to the ideology of individualism. The genre compromises their isolation only to give the avenger a tiny bit of vulnerability. Harry and Riggs have partners who along with the partners' families are put at risk, and this leads to some consternation, but not to doubt or to consultation. Partners, inevitably, are there to die so as to give the professional avenger a cause in his own right rather than merely as a surrogate for incapable victims.

But even if the avenger does not consult diagetically, that is, with characters to whom they are linked in the film itself, they in fact consult with us, the audience, who must agree with their commitments to find

---

21. I wish to avoid here certain modest hedges we might have to make for doctrines of felony-murder and conspiracy.

them worth rooting for. That may not be much constraint since, by some views, the entertainment value of the form depends on a release from constraint. But the avengers do justice, and that is one very serious constraint on their action, not only as to choice of vengeance target but even as to the methods of death. Harry especially, but even Arnold, Rambo, and Steven Siegal are often more constrained than the teenage boys who make up so much of the audience would wish the heroes to be. No teenager myself, even I experience some disappointment when the good guy dispatches the most evil of villains surgically with a bullet. Too quick and easy, in my opinion, not a sufficient payback for the terror he caused and the evil he did. Shouldn't Scorpio have suffered more? But it is a hallmark of villainy to prefer slow death for one's victims. James Bond movies turned this into high comedy, but they also revealed the irrationality of the preference: it gives the victim the opportunity for rescue, the hero the opportunity for escape. The avenger does not allow us to fulfill our worst fantasies. He plays an edifying role for the teenagers and types like me in the audience. He will meet our demands for justice, but not our desires for cruelty. A little *Schadenfreude*, maybe, but no torture.

I don't wish to overstate the case. The avenger has some serious disagreements with the law. I note some of the more salient ones:

1. Avengers will hear of no insanity defense for the nonpathetic insane, that is, for those whose insanity makes them objects of fear and loathing rather than pity. In the same vein, notions of diminished capacity that concede too much to determinist models of human behavior are not acceptable. No riot syndrome, junk-food defenses, and so forth.

2. There is no presumption of innocence to people who don't deserve it. The hostility to the presumption of innocence is succinctly captured in *Unforgiven* by the tough sheriff, Little Bill, when he is accused of having "just kicked the shit out of an innocent man." Responds Bill: "Innocent? Innocent of what?" Bill's wittiness changes the meaning of innocence to guilt and makes it the condition to be accounted for, if not quite to be proven. Moreover, Bill was right. The "innocent man" had violated his firearm ordinance and had done so because he intended to kill. Innocence in this genre is a true moral and social condition, not a legal conclusion. Innocence means decent

people minding their own business; innocence is emphatically not just having the fortune of being found not guilty because of a jury's generous notion of reasonable doubt.

3. There is a general view that the law is too narrowly concerned with wrongful acts rather than with evil characters. That teeming assemblage of awful people who continually give offense without ever being sufficiently sanctionable for any particular offense, such as the bully, the pimp, and the sadist are thus justifiable targets for the avenger. And under this rubric the avenger can legitimately go after people whose wrongs are omissions in the law's eyes rather than commissions.

4. The Fifth Amendment right against self-incrimination is serviceable mostly to rogues. The case is seldom convincingly made that the right confers benefits as weighty as its costs.

5. The criminal law's notions of proportionality do not accord with the demands of justice. Not all first-degree and second-degree murders are worse than all rapes. The notion that rape could never be a capital offense unless the victim is also killed is not an acceptable ranking of wrongs, which ranking must depend not on the internal coherence of the law, but on the sense of indignation and outrage the act elicits in third parties.

What the avenger rejects are largely procedural matters; his cause must still satisfy some sense of substantive justice. If he fails in that, then he is not an avenger. He becomes the villain. Villains kill people against whom they have no claim; villains take hostages and threaten innocent dependents of their prey. It is a nice trick of the genre that if the avenger gets the wrong man, we are not in a revenge movie anymore. He then becomes a lyncher and we are in another genre when that happens. Here *The Oxbow Incident* (1943) is the classic instance. The fact that in the revenge genre there is never a doubt as to who deserves to die, of course, allows us to indulge our vengeful desires without too much worry about what it might mean to institutionalize revenge when we are not reasonably sure of who deserves to die or when we must face the reality and the smell of death rather than celluloid representations of it.

Avenging heroes are thus constrained by the formal demands of the genre to take care to kill only those who deserve it; but lest we be deprived of our own blood lust, the various revenge subgenres make sure to provide us a delightfully large number of people who deserve to die. Monstrous villains usually have a myriad of monstrous minions. Action-adventure films are notoriously overpopulated by the chief villain's aiders and abettors, flunkies and soldiers, all of whom are characterized, on the one hand, by their utter inability, no matter how many rounds they fire, ever to hit the hero and, on the other, by their serviceability in dying from whatever the hero throws in their path. We are inured to feeling anything for these stick figures, pure cannon fodder who die in a bad cause. Their deaths do nothing to assuage the indignation generated by the crimes of their superior, and their deaths give little satisfaction beyond the apprehension they may cause the chief villain and an occasional "ooh" and "aah" from the teenage boys in the audience at the comic and cartoonish grotesquerie of seeing these expendable souls blown up or shot down. In this way popular culture makes up for the narrowing constraints of its own principles of liability. If only monstrous wrongdoers and evil predatory people can rightly be killed, then what we need is to populate the film with enough of them to make up for the fact that we would find it wrong to shoot their innocent relatives.

Yet it is true that some avengers push the limits of who may serve as a proper object of revenge. If Dirty Harry only kills people for what they in fact have done or are doing, some avengers cast a wider net. This is a crucial issue that is problematized explicitly in *Unforgiven*, which we discuss in detail in the second part of this chapter. For now consider Paul Kersey (Charles Bronson) in *Death Wish*. His wife is killed and his daughter gang-raped and sodomized by three young thugs. Contrary to the usual expectations of revenge films, Kersey never finds these killers and rapists. Instead he knocks off surrogates for them. He walks the streets of New York hoping to be mugged so he can blow away the creeps. Yet it hardly matters that he fails to get the guys who killed his wife and thus transformed his life (not to mention hers). The movie demands, and only the willfully obstreperous viewer could resist, that we find his actions fully justified. Each encounter with a mugger of course justifies some recourse to self-defense, but it is not self-defense that justifies Kersey: it's his dead wife and catatonic daughter. Somehow the enormity of the wrong done them and him, the enormity of his and our outrage at the crime, means above all that something has to be done. Cursing God or collecting life insurance or hoping for the police to bring the thugs to justice are inadequate responses to the demand the outrage makes. Outrage makes a demand on us to *do* something.

The film suggests there are moral and emotional costs in letting the state act for us, even granting the state success in its action. The view is that the state's claim to a monopoly on retributive violence reduces the decent citizen to a moral shell of his or her preindustrial self. No amount of official discourse ever seems to convince us that denying our vengeful desires and letting the state act for us is *doing* something in the same way that taking revenge is *doing* something. There are, of course, obvious prudential problems with enabling revenge societywide without embedding the avengers, like their blood-feuding predecessors, in kin groups that forced them to consult and confirm the justifiability of their outrage. But the movie is more concerned with the demoralization costs borne by the sufferers of predatory wrongs than with the costs such avengers would impose on the rest of us. *Death Wish*, in fact, makes a simple utilitarian claim that avengers are cost-effective: mugging rates drop significantly in New York once the knowledge of the avenger's activities becomes general. The demand to do *something* is, however, not a demand to do *anything*. The demand is not a blank check, but is itself subject to rich normative constraints. Kersey cannot use his grief and rage to justify preying on innocent people or on someone who negligently smashed into his car.[22] The avenger can pull only those into his sights who do wrongs that are predatory and unprovoked. He cannot deem people guilty who carry no guilt, but he can augment the punishment of those guilty beyond the slap on the wrist the law provides.[23]

But for all the official hand-wringing over our delight in depictions of vengeful justice, that justice, critical as it is about the legal administration of justice, the leniency and uncertainty of punishment, the lack of concern with victims and their satisfaction, is as a matter of substance not all that opposed to the law. If the avenger's rules for establishing

---

22. These are precisely the kind of discriminations the protagonist of *Falling Down* is incapable of making and so rightfully he must die in the end.

23. He actually augments the punishment more than just by inflicting pain or death where the law would give probation or five years, for we must discount for the law's abysmal record in bringing wrongdoers to justice. The avenger gives us certain justice, and his quarry loses the benefit of the discount of simply not getting caught.

who and what are eligible for expiation are somewhat broader than the law's, they are still not all that broad. You still have to have done wrong or harmed another. You still have to convince the neutral observer that you have right. In other words, there are still rules, very strict ones. The wild justice of revenge, for all its so-called wildness, is still recognizably justice. The filmic form in which this justice is portrayed depends on winning the support of viewers to the avenger's claims. We must be indignant, we must be outraged on behalf of victims and then satisfied by justified payback. To the end the genre forces us into the responsible role of Adam Smith's impartial spectator. The avenger cannot go it alone, inventing his own rules, his own theory of offense and injury. If he does, he goes over the edge into psychopathology and then, lo and behold, we find ourselves in a different genre from the classic revenge film. Clint and Bronson are not Jake LaMotta (*Raging Bull*), Max Cady (*Cape Fear*), Michael Douglas's character in *Falling Down* or Travis Bickle (*Taxi Driver*)—"Who you lookin' at? You lookin' at me?"—who finds avengeable offense in the mere existence of others. But is it only an irresponsible fantasy to wish the avenger to settle matters on behalf of Nicole Simpson, Ron Goldman, and Mr. and Mrs. Menendez when the law fails?

Unforgiven *and Problematizing Revenge*

Clint Eastwood directed and starred in *Unforgiven*. The film won Oscars for best picture, Eastwood for best director, and Gene Hackman for best supporting actor. The film is a spectacular piece of work, subtle, self-reflective, serious without pretentiousness, witty and mature. It puts in issue and complicates the assumptions of the revenge genre by troubling itself about the fact that the demands of heroism and of being at the center of heroic narrative may put one in a position that compromises perfect justice. Yet the film makes this critique without abandoning its commitment to the revenge genre, for in the end revenge is taken, and in spite of the critique, or maybe even because of it, it remains the most satisfying outcome, surviving completely certain ambiguities of just desert. The movie reveals that justice, the satisfaction of seeing it done, can tolerate certain failings as to its substance if it is mediated properly, that is, if it adheres to the expectations of genre and narrative convention. More concretely, less-than-perfect heroes and charming villains are still heroes and villains, and the fact that these are complex characters does not undo the demand for or the delivery of heroic vengeance. Vengeance still must come, even if not without some moral ambivalence. And it still satisfies.

The film easily merits a monograph-length explication. I am not about to tax your attention for so long. I mean to confine my observations to the themes raised in the first part of this chapter. I will focus in detail on two scenes and even then not in all their suggestiveness: the killing of Davey, a cowhand, and the killing of Little Bill Daggett, the sheriff. One of the moves that *Unforgiven* makes is to test the principles of just who is legitimately eligible as a vengeance target by making the hero's victims something less than evil. Consider the case of Davey. The film begins with two cowhands from the Bar-T ranch—one, Davey, a nice young kid, the other, Quick Mike, a thick brute—taking a tumble in Greely's, the local saloon and brothel. Mike slashes the face of the whore he is with (Delilah) when she gets the giggles at his small equipage. Davey ends up inadvertently complicit. In the confusion Mike orders him to hold the whore "or I'll cut her tits off," but when Mike starts slashing, Davey releases her, desperately beseeching Mike to stop ("Don't Mike; don't; Mike, Jesus, don't Mike"). The sheriff, Little Bill (Gene Hackman), offers to whip them both, a solution unsatisfying to the other whores ("A whipping? Is that all they get after what they done?") and to Skinny, too, the proprietor who has "an investment of capital" in Delilah, having paid her way out from the East. Bill then assesses compensation, five ponies from Mike and two from Davey, to be paid over to Skinny in the spring.

The slashed woman doesn't figure in Bill's compensatory scheme; he agrees with Skinny in seeing her as property, or at least not sufficiently individualized so as to have a compensable claim in her own right. When the time comes to hand over the ponies, Davey brings an extra pony, "the best of the lot," which he offers to Delilah, a gesture which individualizes him for us. She is clearly touched, but the other whores prevent the gift by pelting him with rocks, disgusted that he could think a pony could compensate for the loss of her looks. The whores make no distinction as to the culpability of the cowhands, something that Bill was able to do, at least minimally, when he assessed Davey a lesser compensation payment than Mike. The scene of the rejected gift is a painful one, provoking the kind of discomfort and embarrassment that attends failed ritual action and "awkward situations." A rejected gift creates a kind of mini-anomie[24] and we end up blaming the unforgiving whores for making us uncomfortable. It is Davey who gets our sympathy, even if we are perfectly able to understand the women's motivation.[25]

We should not condemn too quickly the whores' refusal to make distinctions between the two cowboys. The women have interests that justify their vengefulness on behalf of Delilah. They are vulnerable and they know it. They have no interest in seeing their faces bargained for horses, and they do not want their colleague touched into forgiveness. Her forgiveness means their faces are cheap for the taking. They want blood for their sister, who herself was willing to settle for a horse.[26] Revenge is utterly rational for the uncut whores. So they gather a fund and put out the word that $1,000 is available for anyone who kills the two cowhands. There is no evidence that the whores are especially upset that the horses are paid over to Skinny rather than to Delilah. What troubles them is the type of sanction. They want blood, not money. This too is rational. The cowboys they service are largely judgment proof when it comes to monetary assets, but they are as well funded with blood as the richest man in the world. But one senses that it is more than rationality that motivates them. There is something particularly egregious about disfigurement that suspends rational calculation. A beating would not have engendered the same resolve, nor even, one suspects, a murder.

The inducement of the bounty draws bounty hunters, dangerous men and would-be dangerous men, like the Schofield Kid who seeks out William Munny (Clint Eastwood) to assist him in the enterprise. Munny is an aging and impoverished pig farmer who as a young man held to wicked ways, a drunk, a known thief and murderer, trans-

---

24. See the discussion in Miller, *Humiliation*, chap. 1.

25. Frances Fisher, who plays the vengeful prostitute, Strawberry Alice, speaks of the movie presenting different points of view neutrally: "And who is to say who is right? The sheriff? A lot of people will see the events through his eyes. Others will think the women are right" (quoted in Hilary de Vries, "Clint Eastwood," *Los Angeles Times*, 2 August 1992, cover story, "Calendar" section).

26. The whores pun on *whores* and *horses*, showing that the equation is too readily made in the culture already and they mean to resist it: "they may ride us like horses, but though we may be whores, we ain't no horses." And if the whores fear the culture's tendency to morph them into horses, horses too have to suffer for the connection. Will Munny calls his horse, when balking at letting him mount her, a whore, showing perversely that horses are whores for not being ridden, whereas women are horses for being ridden. Will apologizes to his mount.

formed and reformed into troubled decency and sobriety by his wife, who has recently died and whom we see Will burying in the credit sequence. In his prefilm life, Munny was a violent predator who is said to have killed women and children by dynamiting trains. His past is something he has rejected, although grim visions of the maimed bodies of his victims resurface and torment him around campfires at night or when sick with fever. The young Munny was, it seems, a villain who should have been dispatched by a heroic avenger had one been available. That movie, however, never got made, and the fact that it didn't get made makes Munny distrust the existence or meaning of just deserts. But it is also his past as predator that gives him the kind of steely skills he needs to jump to the other side of the fence, to play the heroic avenger.

Munny kills Davey, the remorseful cowboy, in a disturbing scene in which, due to Munny's incompetence with a rifle, death is slow and excruciating, accompanied by the boy's terror and anguish. Munny, to his credit, is clearly unhappy, even shamed by the suffering of his quarry, by the dirtiness of the business: "Give him a drink of water, Goddamn it. Will you give him a drink of water, for Christ's sake?" The scene is lingered on and is painful for the viewer.[27] The boy is decent, clearly well liked and even loved by his workmates: "You murdering bastard," shouts one, "you killed *our Davey boy.*" Davey is innocent, to all but Strawberry Alice, the most formidably vengeful of Delilah's coworkers: "He had it coming for what he done." Here, as in Adam Smith's moral philosophy, the rightness of the avenging action must depend on the degree of outrage and indignation experienced by the impartial observer. The impartial observer feels Davey an inappropriate object of lethal retribution. For the viewer, the offer of the pony to Delilah should indeed have spared him the avenger's rifle.

Dirty Harry's world is morally easier. His targets are utterly reprehensible and leave no one mourning their deaths. Munny seems unnerved by finding himself in a situation that Clint Eastwood should not be in. Heroes of a certain ilk, especially ones that Clint Eastwood plays, aren't supposed to look ashamed, and they are supposed to be good shots, like Dirty Harry, and kill scum, like Harry does. The ugliness of the business makes rooting for Munny a harder proposition than rooting for Harry, even handicapping Harry for his politically

---

27. This was the scene that led reviewers, with Clint himself joining in, to claim the movie an antiviolence film; see interview with Eastwood in de Vries, "Clint Eastwood."

incorrect commitments. Moreover, Munny's sidekick, Ned Logan (Morgan Freeman), who is a good shot with a rifle and could have killed Davey cleanly, simply cannot steel himself to kill the boy. Scruples prevent him, and that, I suppose, is why he is a sidekick. If heroes have scruples—and they do, as heroes must—they cannot be scruples that prevent heroic action. We would not forgive a hero who killed the movie by not killing men. We partially excuse Munny, in other words, because he is Clint Eastwood in a movie whose conventions require him not to be overly scrupulous about killing, at least not *before* he kills.

But Ned does not get all that much credit for his scruples. That they are a sidekick's scruples shows them, though scrupulous, to be a sign of a failure of nerve, of an incapacity for heroism. He is moved by a general reluctance to kill, not by a reluctance to kill undeserving people. He doesn't know, any more than Will does, that Davey is as undeserving of death as we know him to be. Still, Ned raises the moral stakes for Munny simply by questioning their moral authority as avengers of a wrong that only minimally concerns them, especially when money is no small part of their motivation. Munny, a hero, will kill even when he has doubts. Yet we also see that Munny has the moral issue thrust upon him by his own inner lights, not just by Ned's inability to shoot Davey. Munny has never been able to rest easy with his prior killings. The movie gives us good reason to believe that this might be the first time he has ever killed without being too drunk to remember what he's done.[28] His first sober killing is ugly business for him as well as for us.

As a general matter, agents have a more tenuous claim to rightful revenge than a principal unless the agent acquires some legitimation from another source.[29] Will's right to kill the cowboys on behalf of the whores is a weaker moral right than his own right to avenge his friend Ned. In the first case he is an agent, in the second he is the principal aggrieved party. The agent's moral authority is harder to come by. Dirty Harry, for instance, as an initial matter, legitimates his claim to act on

---

28. In fact, before Will is actually called on to kill, he first descends into a kind of private hell for three feverish days before he can be resurrected as the killer he was before his wife had reformed him. The parody of the Passion is obvious. Unlike Christ, who arises to give eternal life, Will arises to send people to eternal death: "I will see you in hell William Munny," says Little Bill, who knows quite well where Will is sending him.

29. Notice that this sentiment is deeply held, and it is part of what state justice stumbles up against when it claims that it has the *sole* right to act against the wrongdoer's body.

behalf of others by his authority as a police officer; we do not accord the bounty hunter the same moral ground. There is, nonetheless, a moral side to Munny's action. It is more than just calculating bounty hunting. He is helping the most vulnerable of people, the prostitutes, secure reasonable safety for their bodies. And this goal is in no way compromised by killing the boy along with his bad companion. He also needs the money for his children, and by chance the Schofield Kid's attempt to recruit him for the expedition coincides with a fever that is killing all his pigs.

Yet there is some indication that it is more than just money that calls him back to his killing ways. He is also motivated by a call to do justice. The account narrated to him by the Schofield Kid, the teenage would-be killer, is that a woman has had her face cut, her ears and breasts cut off, and her eyes cut out. "Jesus!" says Will.[30] What is alleged to have happened to the woman is a deed beyond the pale, admitting those who encompassed it to the class of "those who got it coming." Someone has to take it upon himself to make sure they get it. Will is merely enforcing broadly held moral and social norms of right action. And if we sense that Dirty Harry enjoys killing a little too much, that is not the case with Will Munny, who scarcely takes pleasure in anything and who had to drown out his knowledge of the deaths he caused with drink. The problem with Munny is not his cause or his motive, but his lack of knowledge regarding the extent of Davey's involvement in Delilah's disfigurement.

The scene in which Davey is killed is presented in a much more complex and nuanced fashion than can be adequately accounted for by the explanation of the preceding few paragraphs. We learn later that Munny believes in making rather precisely individualized distinctions in the distribution of punishment and retribution, as long as he is in a position and has the desire to make such individualizing distinctions. He is shocked and incredulous when he hears that Little Bill killed Ned:

---

30. The account is vastly embellished. The prostitute's face was cut, and she has disfiguring scars. When Will goes to recruit his old buddy Ned Logan to the expedition, he further embellishes the mutilation by adding fingers to the other severed body parts. A consistent theme of the movie is how stories and legends are built and altered in transmission, and the verbal dismemberment of Delilah is connected thematically to the construction of a reputation for heroism, whether it be English Bob's, Little Bill's, or William Munny's.

"So Little Bill killed him for what we done."[31] Ned is Davey's analogue; each is the least culpable member of the group he is associated with. And in each case, other commitments and imperfect knowledge prevent their being distinguished from their group. We know more than Will. We know that Davey was appalled at what happened to the girl, that he meant no harm, that he tried to make amends for himself and his violent mate, but Munny does not know that. The movie puts the avenger in an unusual situation. Dirty Harry or Charles Bronson never know less than we know when it comes to the identity of villains and their level of culpability. They only get people who deserve it, who "got it coming." But *Unforgiven* gives its hero incomplete information. This cuts two ways: if it excuses somewhat Will's not individualizing Davey, it also undercuts the justifiability of action that does not take the audience's information into account, for it is indelibly the case that the audience perceives a tragedy in Davey's and Ned's deaths. More information would surely have spared Davey and perhaps Ned. Still, we are a long way from the broad notions of liability that would have justified killing any Bar-T boy for the actions of one of its members. This is not the world of, say, the Mafia or the Icelandic sagas. The "them" subject to retaliation is a much narrower class.

The relation among the bounty hunters—Will, Ned, and the Schofield Kid—further contrives to drive the situation toward its tragic outcome. Ned's failure to kill and the Kid's impatient nearsighted doubting of the old guys' skill and resolve complicate the micropolitics that are driving their actions. Will knows that Ned feels unmanned and ashamed by his inability to kill, and that makes for an embarrassing situation, one that makes demands on Will. For one, it means he has to do the killing. Ned, the good shot, would have made it clean; now he must do it dirty. For another, he must concern himself with his friend's dis-

---

31. If Munny is unwilling to concede Little Bill the right to group Ned with him and the Kid, he himself is willing to include Ned when it comes to splitting the bounty. The dispute is thus over who gets to define group membership for what purposes. Ned, after all, shot the horse out from under Davey, which fell on him, breaking his leg and making him a sitting duck for Munny. He is legally completely complicit. Here too we see that popular culture, which is usually more bloodthirsty than the law, is also much more forgiving in certain settings. Ned's genuine rejection of the group's mission excuses him to us and to Munny and, in our minds, ought to have excused him to Little Bill had he possessed our knowledge. Like Munny, however, we are not willing to excuse Little Bill's lack of knowledge as willingly as we excused Will's. Villains seem to be held to higher standards in some respects, at least when they are sheriffs.

grace, which pains Munny not only because he empathizes with his friend's misery, but also because he can't help but feel that Ned's dishonor redounds to him in the eyes of the Kid. If Munny's motivation had heretofore been gaining lucre in a good cause, it now becomes not losing face before the Schofield Kid, who already has expressed doubts about Munny's courage and commitment. This comical nearsighted young wanna-be has manufactured a past for himself as a Dangerous Man, in which he claims to have killed five people. Neither Ned nor Munny believes his tales, but what Will cannot tolerate is that the Kid should think the reputations of these aging heroes to be as illusory as the one the Kid has constructed for himself.

Will must maintain Ned's and his own honor against an epidemic of fraudulent reputation building, against the corrosive effect of fiction on the honor of hard fact. This is an especially important matter in the world of *Unforgiven,* in which dime novelists collude with willing aspirants to Dangerousness in constructing tall self-serving tales of prior accomplishment. It is Will Munny's peculiar distinguishing trait that he never builds his reputation through his own recountings of his past. He was always too drunk to know what he did and even *whether* he did. So it is left for others to tell him of his exploits, which he hears with a kind of dim indifference, or a vaguely regretful sense of dis-ease. And what his drunkenness didn't leave him unaware of, his wife made him penitent for. The movie, as we see, makes the killing of Davey a richly motivated act.

Whatever the precise source of Munny's shame, or Ned's scruples for that matter, it is *not* a function of Davey's lack of culpability, for, as we have seen, Will and Ned have no reason not to think him culpable. His shame is at the ugliness of the business, even if it is justified. And in what precisely lies the ugliness? The lack of purity in motivation? Or just the plain ugliness of slow death? Consider in this regard that one of the few memories from his past Munny is able to recall is the grotesquerie of blowing a guy's teeth out of the back of his head; and consider *Unforgiven's* comic leitmotiv of the unreliability of 1880s lethal technology. Guns misfire, and few people, if any, can shoot them straight. Little Bill constantly holds forth on this theme, correcting the improbable view presented in dime novels (and Westerns) of the quick-draw, hipshooting marksman. The film subsidizes Little Bill's account in numerous ways: the Schofield Kid is so nearsighted that he cannot see a target more than ten feet away; and Munny is so rusty with a pistol that he must take a shotgun to the conventional tin can atop the fence post, a consciously comic parody of the preparation topos of Western movies. Here the comic funds the tragic, for it is precisely the blunderbuss nature of the weaponry, the lack of skill, the bad eyesight and what not, that helps make the killing of Davey shameful for Will and painful for us. It is slow and messy.[32] Clean and quick killing would have spared Will most of his shame. And I also think that a quick death would have done much to assuage our scruples about the injustice in Davey's death. We would surely trouble ourselves a lot less about the morality of Will's act if it went by in the flash of an eye and a quick cut to the next scene.[33]

Davey's death does not quite follow the conventions of revenge films in the style of Dirty Harry and Charles Bronson. These men do not make mistakes about whom they kill. No matter how smart their adversaries, they are smarter, gutsier, braver, and, above all, better shots. William Munny is not a man of such parts. He was never precise about his choice of victim, being too drunk really ever to fix on them, or using means of killing, like dynamite, that made distinguishing among victims impossible. He is rumored to have killed women and children. Unlike Harry, he has limited capacity for irony, and what self-consciousness he has plays itself out in tormenting visions of the mayhem he caused in the past. Taciturn in the best Eastwood style, he can only intone that he is no longer wicked and regrets that he ever was: "I ain't like that no more." Harry has a kind of gallows wit that makes him charming in spite of himself; Will Munny has none when sober, and when drunk in the final scene, even the wit of his Clintlike quotables are witty for reasons Munny seems unaware of:

> *Little Bill:* Well, sir, you are a cowardly son of a bitch. You just shot an unarmed man.

---

32. Messiness increases our sense of the violence, and thus even of the wrongfulness, of the act. See my discussion on violence and the perception of it in Miller, *Humiliation*, chap. 2.

33. When the avenger is a tough guy, a Dirty Harry or a Charles Bronson, we expect efficiency from him and he rarely disappoints. In some sense Munny's shame is the shame of someone with the expectations of having to live up to Clint Eastwood's past roles: Munny is at this moment imagining himself failing by the standards of the Man with No Name and Dirty Harry. When, however, the avenger is put to his role by having the misfortune of being preyed upon (as in the hunted-hero genre), then we tolerate more inefficiency. The rules are thus different for final girls in horror films or for accidental avengers like Harrison Ford in *Patriot Games;* see note 15.

Will: He should have armed himself if he's going to decorate his
saloon with my friend.

Or:

Will: I've always been lucky when it comes to killing folk.

Charm, it turns out, is a feature of most all the other male characters. English Bob (Richard Harris) is loaded with it in his witty flam-
boyance. And Little Bill, the sheriff, has a brutally calibrated wit best
revealed in one of the finest humiliation scenes in film, when he
deflates every pretension of English Bob, the "Duck" of Death. His
energetic wit makes him likable despite his brutality, which, even
though he enjoys inflicting pain, is never undertaken without the purpose of maintaining public order. His goal is to sit with his pipe and his
coffee on the porch of the house he is building and watch the sunset. He
is, in this frontier setting, the progenitor of the suburbanite, and he is
dedicated to providing the kind of order that will make the suburbs
possible. Consider how ultimately unvillainous a sheriff must be who
enforces a very strict gun-control ordinance with utter success. Whatever bad deeds Little Bill might do, he is a far cry from the cartoon evil
of Scorpio. If anything, he resembles Dirty Harry with the misfortune of
being cast in a movie in which he is a supporting actor and in which
Clint Eastwood is the lead and in which the plot has the lead's friend
succumb to the supporting actor's rough interrogation techniques. Little Bill is also Gene Hackman, an actor of stature whom we are used to
seeing as a hero—as, in fact, an avenging hero, like Popeye Doyle in the
French Connection films.

All these things make the final scene in which Will dispatches Little Bill, Skinny, and three others a little more problematic than the lethal
conclusions that end the *Dirty Harry* and *Death Wish* films. But somewhat perversely, *Unforgiven*'s denouement is more powerful for the
film's equivocations on the morality of revenge. Part of the satisfaction
of the conclusion comes with the resolution of that very equivocation in
favor of vengeful action. Isn't that also the case with *Hamlet*? As a
thought experiment, imagine how silly *Hamlet* would seem if all Hamlet's equivocations led to no revenge. We are in a revenge drama, after
all. We recognize its signs, its forms, and its substance. And so we thrill
to Will grabbing the whiskey bottle and taking a drink when he hears of
Ned's death and the humiliation of his corpse. With whiskey comes res-

olution and a rejection of action-numbing moralizing and self-doubt; with whiskey the prefilm William Munny returns: a consummate and unconscious killer, lucky at little else except killing. Ethics gives way to aesthetics, or, more exactly, they merge seamlessly into each other, for both the conventions of the narrative form and justice and honor demand revenge for the death of a friend and the desecration of his corpse. William Munny, not unlike Achilles, has stopped sulking in the tent, although his tent is an allegorical one woven of his wife's teetotalling and her stern moral principles. And we know what must happen, for this is one of the oldest (and best) stories ever told.

Justice is not just a set of substantive outcomes we feel naturally appropriate; it comes mediated via the expectations raised by the narrative setting detailing the occasion for it. This is a Clint Eastwood movie, and that means something for the range of expectations we consider appropriate to the story's conclusion, for actors (and directors) do not come to us without histories that influence our expectations for what we are watching no less than the conventions of plot and genre. It is also a Western of a particular sort, and a revenge story of a particular sort with rather striking parallels to *The Iliad*. We are in the world of epic, where the attractiveness of the killer of your friend cannot excuse your duty of paying him back, whether he be Hector or Hackman.

If the aesthetic constraints of the narrative form counsel revenge that does not make revenge any less a moral demand. Will's revenge is also impelled by the norms of honor, honorable justice, and the ethic of reciprocity or paying back what you owe. But I wish to construct another aesthetic argument, an argument based on poetic justice, one that the film constructs for itself independent of the aesthetic motor that drives the revenge story. To preempt myself a bit, this argument requires that a certain kind of heroism triumph against other styles of the heroic that are revealed as either fraudulent or pretentious, or simply as too self-indulgent and verbose. Clint has to win not only because he is the star and it is his movie, but because his kind of heroism has greater dignity; it is a triumph of a certain Anglo-Saxon understated style beleaguered of late by the onslaughts of a noisy self-asserting overstatement.[34]

---

34. Overstated styles have a long tradition, from the boast speeches of Beowulf, to Rap and the dozens, to Mel Gibson in the *Lethal Weapon* movies and Bruce Willis in the various incarnations of *Die Hard*. But in spite of Beowulf, Gibson, and Willis, overstatement has come to bear the marker of a certain urban black male style to which Willis (for sure), Gibson (somewhat less), and Beowulf (not at all) are indebted.

First, by the rules of honor and the ethic of reciprocity that drives it, Will is justified in killing Little Bill and Skinny and then the others who shot at him. Ned's death outrages Will, and the exposure of his body is another outrage, designed to humiliate and offend. The difference between these two uses of outrage should be clear: Will's outrage is the emotion that motivates him. We sympathize with it, and he is justified in taking action to pay it back, even though we recognize that he does not have the cleanest hands. The manner of Ned's death violates norms of propriety that excuse Will's lack of purity. Ned is tortured, whipped to death, the whipping being the only time the movie suggests that Ned's blackness is an issue at all.[35] The second outrage—the display of the corpse—is a formal ritualized act. It may or may not lead to outrage, the emotion. In fact it does just that, but it needn't have, for the ritual itself justifies the return blow for it, whether or not the payback is actually accompanied by the emotion. One does not desecrate a body lightly in vengeance narratives. And the desecration is such an egregious act that it broadens the class of possible expiators who can be made to atone for it. The owner of the saloon, a slime to begin with, thus expiates the outrage.[36] Recall the lines quoted above:

> *Little Bill:* Well, sir, you are a cowardly son of a bitch. You just shot
>   an unarmed man [Skinny].
> *Will:* He should have armed himself if he's going to decorate his
>   saloon with my friend.

Munny does not kill without indicating which corpse is to pay for what. Skinny is paid back for the desecration and Little Bill for the death of Ned: "I'm here to kill you Little Bill for what you did to Ned." The three others who go in the cause only go because they shoot at Will and his luck takes over: "I was lucky in the order, but I've always been lucky when it comes to killing." The heavens, it seems, are not quite empty; they just have a rather grim sense of humor, for luck was no less

---

35. Little Bill first suggests whipping the cowhands for cutting Delilah but desists. He may be an equal-opportunity whipper. Yet the fact remains that it means something rather different to whip a black man and a white man in 1880.

36. That Skinny owns the saloon before which Ned is on display is sufficient cause in Munny's mind for dispatching him, but it would not be sufficient cause for the audience without Skinny also being a slime. He thus becomes, even to us, an appropriate vengeance target in accordance with the revenge genre's rules making such creatures expendable in a good cause.

with him when killing as a young man without just cause. Or in Will Munny's estimation, it can only be in the very short run that there is desert, for in the long run, "deserve's got nothing to do with it," just luck.

Like so many Clint lines, "deserve's got nothing to do with it" is rather delphic. Munny has a cocked rifle to the head of Little Bill, who is already flat on his back bleeding from a wound to his chest: "I don't deserve this; to die like this. I was building a house." Munny replies, "Deserve's got nothing to do with it." In context Munny can be understood to be simply denying Little Bill's claim of unmerited death. But he chooses to cast that thought in language that detaches itself from the context and seems to reflect a kind of cynical despair regarding the justice of his own actions at the same time he is fulfilling the precise demands of the revenge genre and delivering exactly its kind of justice. Munny's self-doubts about his life of violence, the fact that no one ever brought him to justice for his past evil deeds, makes him think the delivery of justice purely random, a matter of good or bad luck. Ironically, it is the cynic and realist, Little Bill, who is expecting more from the heavens here. Any divine order worth the name would let him finish his house. But since in Munny's view "we all have it coming," no one is situated so as to be just all the time, nor the villain all the time. Only if we narrow the time frame to very particular circumstances do things sort themselves out enough so we can indicate who has the right to play the avenger in the particular story.

In this revenge narrative, however, justice and the constraints of the narrative form demand Munny kill Little Bill; and there is a third overdeterminant of the same outcome: Recall the role of W. W. Beauchamp, the biographer and dime novelist who first appears with English Bob and who is last seen looking worshipfully at William Munny as he rides out of Big Whiskey, Wyoming, in the final scene. Beauchamp puts front and center the issue of heroic style in the Wild West, its relation to fact and its relation to fiction, and its relation to some ultimate truth as evidenced by its lethal effect, its competence at killing, that is, killing so that it satisfies, so that it can actually bring closure to films like this one. The presence of Beauchamp makes the movie into something more than a revenge story. It also becomes an essay on competing heroic styles and the manner of heroic self-fashioning. The movie thus gives us English Bob, Little Bill, William Munny, and even the Schofield Kid. And inevitably, following the lead of Beauchamp, we compare and contrast their styles and decide on their authenticity. It will come as no surprise in a Clint Eastwood film that it will be his style that wins. And we know that it must.

Let me play this out quickly, much more quickly than it deserves. English Bob (Richard Harris) fashions his accounts of his own actions in the style of the dime novelist: a kind of lowbrow chivalric knight errant. Thanks to Bill's brutal deflation of Bob, we learn the way things really happened. They were neither pretty nor noble. Beauchamp is attracted to Bob's accounts because Beauchamp only knows the heroic from the books he reads and then reproduces. English Bob is no coward and he is a good shot, but he is not a hero in the romantic mold he claims for himself. Little Bill shows him in fact to be rather purely rational, something no pretender to romantic heroism can be.[37] Mr. Beauchamp abandons English Bob for Little Bill, his next true hero.

Little Bill contrasts himself in every way to English Bob. He is the realist, the antiromantic, the debunker of the exaggerated Western commonplaces of the quick draw, of pistols that work and don't seem to need reloading, of preternatural accuracy in shooting, of grand motive and frontier chivalry in white hats. Little Bill's brand of the heroic means winning, not just winning in any way, but in a willfully antiromantic way. His "realism" is ultimately parasitical on dime-novel romance. Its heart is in debunking and undoing it. His style thus becomes a kind of inverted romanticism. Unsentimentality, opportunism, ruthlessness, and sadism become as obligatory as the spurious chivalry of the dime-novel style.[38] Moreover, Bill finds himself as smitten by the opportunity to build an image for the masses as English Bob had been. What started out as a discourse on the emptiness of English Bob's pretensions designed solely to humiliate Bob ends up becoming a claim to true heroism on his own account. The existence of Beauchamp in the world is no less corrupting to realists than to senti-

---

37. I have in mind the game Bill proposes he and Bob play in which he gives Bob a gun and lets Bob make the first move. Bob assumes, knowing Little Bill's penchant for unfair play and opportunism, that the gun is not loaded. He is wrong. Little Bill guesses the way Bob would guess, and he is able thus to show Bob either risk averse or risk neutral, both traits that utterly deflate English Bob's pretensions as a devil-may-care swashbuckling hero.

38. Note that Little Bill's one great sin against true heroism might be that he is not an avenger; he does not punish to pay back, but to warn off others. He is a pure adherent to the deterrence theory of punishment, a model utilitarian.

mental romantics. The novel turns it all to fiction, to pretense, and to collusion between the media and the subjects of its attention.

We are being too hard on Bill. The movie also punishes him because he is a good storyteller, a real raconteur. It punishes him because it pairs him off against and contrasts him with the style of Will Munny, who says nearly nothing and tells no stories. We and Beauchamp see enough of Bill's actions to know he can back up his words with deeds as well as any man. His problem is that the movie favors an aesthetics of taciturnity, especially as to your own deeds and your own past. Taciturnity turns out to be a virtue of such magnitude that it overcomes all Munny's anti- and mock heroic failings: his inability to get on his horse, his wrestling in the mud with pigs, and, above all, his almost tearfully whimpered expression of his fear of dying. Until the final scene, William Munny does little to remind us he is Clint Eastwood except in his reluctance to talk. Munny never talks about his deeds. It is others who tell his tale, and this saves it from being self-serving. We get his story in bits and pieces from the Kid when he tries to get Will to confirm stories he had heard, but Will was always too drunk to remember, and what he does remember he misremembers in the direction of understatement.[39] Eventually, Munny's full story is told offstage by Ned, extracted under prolonged torture after all Ned's previous attempts to cover it up were beaten out of him. What better emblem for the tenacity with which Munny's style of heroism resists being put in words?

But can we believe a story extracted under torture? Ned in his agony promises that Munny will come and kill Little Bill, and that turns out to be true. So why not trust everything else in Ned's account? His partner is William Munny out of Missouri who killed women and children and later shot a U.S. marshal, etcetera. When Will shows up in Greely's Saloon to kill Little Bill, it is Bill who states Munny's legend to him; Munny need only repeat it back.

> *Little Bill:* You be William Munny out of Missouri that killed women and children.
> *Will:* That's right. I've killed women and children, killed just about everything that walks or crawled at one time or another and I'm here to kill you, Little Bill.

---

39. *Ned:* I remember it was three men you shot, Will, not two.

Munny, however, is not averse to telling the story others have told about him when the telling of it constitutes a threat, a threat that achieves its creditability not only because it is told right after Will has killed Little Bill and four others, but also because he never colluded in the tale's production. So when William Munny leaves the saloon, concerned that people might be waiting to shoot him as he rides out of town, he issues a threat, the substance of which is simply a retelling of what others have already told about him unassisted by his input.

> All right I am coming out. Any man I see out there I'm gonna kill him. Any son of a bitch takes a shot at me, I'm not only gonna kill him, I'll kill his wife and all his friends, burn his damn house down.

There is of course an easy deconstructionist joke here. If the duel between Little Bill and Will Munny is one concerning just how much one should be consciously involved in building one's own legend, it might be of some interest to observe that W. W. Beauchamp is a stand-in for Clint Eastwood the director. He is the one who holds the power to tell the story any way he wants to. And if Munny is above colluding with Beauchamp to manufacture a persona, he is incapable of resisting collusion with the true descendent of the dime novelist: Clint Eastwood himself.

It's time to tie up some lose ends and draw this to a close. With Little Bill, Clint Eastwood at last opposes a competent representative of state-delivered law. No Keystone Cops here, nor is Bill corrupt. He is a little exuberant and excessive in maintaining order in Little Whiskey, and that is sufficient to make him the villain whose death alone will allow the movie to end. What has happened here? We finally get a representative of the law who takes care of business and he still can't get us to root for him. We want the outlaw to shoot the sheriff. We have come a long way from *High Noon*. But Little Bill isn't law as we want it either. Not because he is brutal; we would go much further with brutality than we would probably like to admit if we could be certain that it was in the service of right and if we were sure it would be freedom enhancing societywide. His mistake was the one popular culture believes all state-delivered law makes. He doesn't care about victims. The law has other goals that preempt satisfying the righteous indignation of victims or of third parties indignant on their behalf. Had Bill assuaged the whores, he would have lived to enjoy many sunsets from his porch.

In the minimal state of Big Whiskey in 1880, the law, in the guise of Little Bill Daggett, prefers order to the satisfaction of indignation; in *Dirty Harry,* and other films like it, set in the present, the law seems to prefer itself, its own internal purity, to order in the society it supposedly is ordering, to remedying the claims of victims or satisfying the rightful indignation of third parties. Bill prefers order to justice; our law prefers to indulge in an obsessive anxiety about its relation to wrongdoers, rather than get justice for the victims of crime or preserve order. In either case, there is plenty of remedying the law needs in order that it deliver justice and be able to end narratives about justice in a satisfactory way. No wonder popular culture welcomes the avenger.

Unconcluding Postscript

It is not just that popular culture invents the avenger, that it invents a more efficient style of justice for us, frustrated as we are by our fears, our anxieties, and our perceptions of violence and crime. Popular culture is also largely responsible for creating our image of the avenger's straw men: the legal system and the styles of villainy we love loathing. There is, of course, some connection of this image to reality, but for most of us it is very hard to get at that reality unmediated by popular culture. Those who reject the construction of law as portrayed in the revenge genre can only oppose it with the law as constructed in other genres.

Even those who should know better, those, for instance, trained in law, still have a hard time not mediating at least some substantial part of their knowledge through the constructs of popular culture. It is, after all, the heroic images of law in popular culture that help motivate so many undergraduates at a loss for what to do to try their hand at law school. Law teachers play into this imagery—those that is, unlike myself, who have had practice experience. They distill, from years of routine, fifteen to twenty good stories that remarkably track the expectations for what makes a good legal story as such stories are constructed by shows like *L.A. Law*.[40] *L.A. Law* consciously turned its back on the improbabilities of Perry Mason, creating instead a glamour of real topical cases sans the drudgery of preparing them for trial and

---

40. This is more complex a story of influence and feedback than I am representing. According to a thesis advanced by Carol Clover, it is the legal form that determines the pop culture form of narration, more than the other way around. See Clover, *Trial Movies and the Adversarial Imagination* (Princeton University Press, forthcoming).

spicing the remaining drudgery with the erotic allure of beautiful people and their problems. But the most seamless merging of the law of popular culture and the "real" thing is now taking place on Court TV, where real law becomes real entertainment, just as, I might add, law was in saga Iceland.[41]

What is our stake in supporting, sometimes resisting, but mostly creating, conniving in, and re-creating a popular culture that constructs images of a largely inept law and in turn constructs a view of a society barely pacified, if at all, a society, in other words, desperately in need of efficient and effective mechanisms of maintaining social control? Just because popular culture constructs an image doesn't mean that that image must be false or wishful or exaggerated because of passions like fear, frustration, and racial hatreds. Fears are not always a product of inner demons. Sometimes popular culture might just be getting at something. A desire for avengers may be largely a fantasy to satisfy perceived failures of justice and breakdowns in public order, a fantasy easy to indulge because most of us are ignorant of death, especially violent death, and because ultimately we suspect that we can push off the responsibility for our vengeful desires on the state, which we will then come to loathe as the hangman. But is it a fantasy that our streets aren't safe, that women can't, without foolhardiness, walk home alone at night even in small towns, that we (both black and white) kill more, carry more lethal weaponry, rape more, rob more than any other industrialized nation? Popular culture just might not be all that wrong in its view of a law blind to its mission of keeping an orderly society in accordance with just principles.

It seems we must credit truth with some of the reason for our perceptions of inept legal institutions, but that is only one piece of a complex story. Popular culture's construction of law and legal institutions is driven in part by the formal demands of the various genres of narrative we listen to. We have come to feel that good stories are much harder to generate about institutions that run smoothly by simple and efficient

---

41. See Miller, *Bloodtaking and Peacemaking*, chap. 7. What effect will TV have on law? How will the public stand for excluding evidence that is clearly relevant from the jury while allowing the judge and television viewers to hear it? Will lawyers be pressed to conform more with popular images of flashy examinations at the expense of building a record? But why assume that the entertainment value has nothing to do with the intricacies of procedure? It may well be that the mysterious perversity of legal form has a kind of entertaining allure all its own. In any event, what is clear is that there is an ever smaller area of the so-called real thing that is experienceable independent of the mediation of popular culture.

bureaucratic structures. No heroes there. Heroes require a backdrop of mediocrity, of a normal world in which glitch, hitch, incompetence, and inefficiency are the norm. We thus have heroic lawyers and heroic cops who are actually within the system, but whose excellence requires them to have at least one big foot outside of it. When the official systems operate efficiently, then, strangely, they are not the objects of praise, but rather they become monstrous and villainous: evil empires, lawless intelligence agencies, totalitarian horror. It is thus in some sense that the rule of law is damned if it does, damned if it doesn't. It's either Keystone Cops or Big Brother. We are stuck with two completely inconsistent myths about state law-enforcement capability. The fantasy of the avenger assumes the problem is Keystone Cops. Against that backdrop of unindividuated government mediocrities we pose Dirty Harry. But when the backdrop is Big Brother, we experience genre bending. The avenger is metamorphosed into a hunted hero, not the hunter.

The usual evolutionary story we tell ourselves is that revenge gives way to law and is inconsistent with it. Popular culture sees revenge as a necessary supplement to law, and it might well be that popular culture is not wrong as a matter of legal history and social theory. We could lull ourselves into the belief that revenge was outmoded and that the progress of civilization and pacification were inevitable until the meteoric and geometric rise in urban homicide rates that began in the late 1960s put an end to any complacency regarding the success of the state in maintaining minimal expectations of public order.[42] (It can hardly be an accident that *Dirty Harry* and *Death Wish* are movies made in the early 1970s and that the modern revenge genre dates from that time.) The success of the antirevenge discourse depended on a pacified population. The breakdown in social control, in the view of the revenge genre, reveals the antirevenge discourse and surely the discourse of rights of the accused to be luxuries of a society already pacified for reasons that had nothing to do with its mildness toward wrongdoers. The revenge genre, however, is not irresponsible: it only urges revenge when revenge is guided by the same large principles of culpability and liability that inform the law itself. Popular culture admits the law's priority. But it also sees the law as having been captured by procedural innovations that put the law at the service of injustice. There is a sense implicit in the genre that the law and lawyers are responsible for the

---

42. Beginning roughly in 1968, urban homicide rates spiraled upward well into the 1980s before leveling out at as much as seven to ten times higher than they were in the 1950s.

breakdown in public order by making it so hard to punish manifest wrongdoers.

Yet in some ways popular culture is not all that unkind to the law. It still makes it an arena of choice for the most favorite of entertainment shows: the trial. It even has it delivering acceptable justice at times when competent lawyering and good-minded jurors combine forces; it provides the enabling conditions for making lawyers and cops heroes. Above all, it limits the role of its most antilaw fantasy, the avenger, so that he is not against law at all. Avengers, who, as we saw, only get people who deserve it, are thus distinguished from vigilantes, who never do. As I have claimed in this chapter, revenge is perceived as a reform of the law, not a revolution displacing it. It is meant to supplement and fulfill the law, not to undo it. Above all, stories of revenge are meant to give us a chance at experiencing the delicious sense of satisfaction of justice, true justice, being done. But in the meantime we, not altogether ungladly, suffer an overly formal, inept law, blind to the substantive demands of justice, because it is that very failure that enables a certain style of good story we love so much.

One final point about good stories: Love and "wild justice" (fornicating and fighting) are the two great themes of Western narrative, with stories of the former never quite breaking away from stories of the latter until the novel, as Medea, Othello, and Malvolio, among many others, bear witness. It would be interesting to track the variation in the relative popularity of stories of fighting as against stories of fornicating. Revenge stories are not always as popular at some times as at others, but they never seem to go away, either. We still reread them as classics if we happen not to be producing any of our own. And then revenge has a way of being promiscuous across a wide range of genres. It is essential to epic, the substance of much, but not all, tragedy, and stubbornly a feature of the comedic universe, too. Corrective justice (and thus revenge) is simply the stuff of good narrative, whether epic, tragic, comic, or romantic. Funny how distributive justice does not make for good stories outside of sentimental and melodramatic forms. We simply have a hard time making the themes of distributive justice the substance of the highest art. We leave these matters to political and moral philosophers instead. And most would admit they are not generally the most engaging of narrators. And why is that?

Components of
Cultural Justice

Andrew Ross

Most of us are familiar with concepts like social justice, environmental justice, economic justice, and racial justice. They spring readily to the lips of activists and reformers, even some legislators. If pushed, most of us could probably produce a thumbnail sketch or working definition of such concepts. Some are even invoked by name in attempted legislation—viz. the Racial Justice Act, attached to Clinton's first anticrime bill, which was shot down in Congress in 1994. That bill sought to address the scandal of the disproportional number of African-American males on death row. For the most part, however, liberal concepts of justice are much broader and deeper than what is ordinarily understood as the rule of law. The pursuit of justice cannot fully be accomplished through the formal work of legal process; it also involves social and cultural transformations that lie beyond the customary reach of legislation. Even in the courtroom, which is only one of the places that the law is staged, justice often means something quite different from legality. Thus, we have a courtroom category of "jury nullification" (whereby jurors vote according to their conscience and not in strict obedience to a judge's instructions about laws they may find unjust) to guarantee this distinction, and, more generally, a long tradition of civil disobedience, rooted in the Declaration of Independence, that sanctions dissent in the face of unjust or inadequate legislation.

Alternately, former legal processes are often seen to be too mechanistic in their attention to procedural rules, and not sensitive enough to the cultural security and social aspirations of citizens. Worries arise, for example, when a Supreme Court appointee is perceived to have led a sheltered, bookish life, too removed from the busy throng of the nation's complex cultural life—as was the case in the confirmation hearings for David Souter's appointment to the Court. How can legislators from a protected social and ethnic background do justice to claims that are infused with challenging assumptions about cultural difference? Or is it their explicit task to abstract the claims from all ties to the busy social world, insofar as this is possible to do? Public and legal debate about American justice is beset by contradictions like this. The national obsession with origins, foundations, and constitutionalism is always fiercely at odds with the innovative spirit of meeting modernity with cultural resources and information that were unavailable to the framers. In the case of rights' claims, the contradictions are often at their sharpest. Depending on how history has treated your kind, the initial restriction of natural rights proclamations to the population that enjoyed them—those eighteenth-century white males who alone were recognized as free, property-bearing citizens—can be viewed as a foundational guarantee of hypocrisy or a recipe for some future state of justice, always incomplete. As a result, the subsequent struggle between majoritarian interests and minority rights has been unceasing, and arguably is still one of the central tensions governing the national system of distributive justice.

My intent here is to speculate about the concept of cultural justice as well as to examine some features that make sense under such a rubric. Cultural justice is not distinct from the transformation of socioeconomic conditions—ideally they are part and parcel of the same revolution—but some of its aspects are more easily abstracted from the economic environment than others. Increasingly, respect for people's cultural identities—conventionally associated with broad categories of gender, race, sexuality, and ethnicity—has come to be seen as a major condition of equal access to income, health, education, free association, religious freedom, housing, and employment. For some, this need for respect has even attained the rank of a basic human right, as a result of the powerful petitions on behalf of what Charles Taylor has described as a modern "politics of recognition."[1]

Much energetic debate has been devoted to the capacity of liberal democracies to accommodate respect for cultural particularity without renouncing their procedural guarantees of equal respect for all citizens.

---

1. Charles Taylor, et al., *Multiculturalism: Examining the Politics of Recognition*, ed. Amy Gutmann (Princeton: Princeton University Press, 1994).

Ironically, this debate has occurred, in the United States, at a time when the legal arm of the liberal state as in wholesale retreat from programs and measures that were introduced to remedy the socioeconomic consequences of centuries of cultural injustice. It is customary for political and legal philosophers to consider the challenges of multiculturalism, broadly speaking, at a comparative distance from the ongoing political and economic perpetuation of injustice. By intellectual instinct and training, I find it more difficult to cordon off these realms, and so in the commentary that follows, readers will find more of a porous continuity between the concept of cultural justice and the social soil from which it takes its sustenance and sense of urgent flowering. Many of those who have suffered socioeconomic injustice perceive their hardship as motivated by, or indistinguishable from, cultural disrespect, even race hatred, and they are right to do so. A politics of recognition must recognize these perceptions *in addition* to recognizing the identities that spring from the ensuing claims for just remedies. Otherwise, it will be as culturally insensitive as the "blind" justice of liberal respect that it seeks to supplant.

In addition, if we are at all interested in the larger social transformations that redistributive justice can effect, we must be committed to believing that cultural justice is not simply a temporary and convenient vehicle for remedial legislation, to be dispensed with on the realization of a level playing field, or to be hardened around new forms of bureaucratic containment. It would be better if we were to view cultural justice as in for the long haul, as an integral part of a permanent social revolution.

As Nancy Fraser has argued, there are some forms of symbolic redress—establishing respect for marginalized identities—that might be viewed as the cultural equivalent of the liberal welfare state. They promote surface reallocations of distributive shares among recognized groups but do little to restructure the underlying principles that generate injustices, both economic and cultural. In general, I am in agreement with Fraser's partiality for "transformative" over "affirmative" justice. The former involves a deep restructuring of the relations of production, in the economic sphere, and the relations of recognition, in the cultural sphere. The latter involves the strengthening of group identities in their claims upon resources and respect. As Fraser notes, however, the transformative option is further removed from the comfort levels of most people because it is the more destabilizing and radical alternative.[2] It is also the most remote horizon in our current political reality because it involves explicitly socialist and utopian measures. At a time when state programs of affirmative justice are being decimated, we cannot remove ourselves, in tone and in political persuasion, from that sphere of justice where people feel they are most immediately being punished and further disadvantaged. Moreover, it is important to remember that affirmative action policies, in particular, were conceived as a first, and not the last, step toward solving the problems of cultural and social injustice. The liberal retreat from affirmative justice ought to provide opportunities to "seed" the debate with more radical, transformative alternatives while standing firm on support for policies that have worked well to break the occupational caste system.

The immediate impulse for my speculation about cultural justice arises then from the imbroglios over affirmative action programs, against a backdrop in which identity politics, or the politics of recognition, is often cynically opposed to the politics of class. In this controversy, the conflict between procedural liberalism and contextual justice has been most pronounced. Proponents of affirmative action have been at pains to show that the arguments for specific cultural rights are inseparable from the context of economic and social inequality, and yet there is no simple legal basis, in a liberal democracy, for recognizing this relationship.

Legal consideration of the cultural rights of social or ethnic groups are barely developed. Typically such rights have been legally extended to national minorities, whose traditional culture and material existence is threatened with extinction by majoritarian forces. Indigenous cultural rights—over language, religion, and traditional practices (smoking peyote, animal sacrifice), including Native jurisprudence—have become a powerful instrument for negotiating with, and establishing moral authority over, the rule of majoritarian institutions. In the new landscape of globalization, such rights have begun to be claimed by entire nation states and regional blocs as a legal tool for resisting the sway of foreign influence, especially in the realm of the cultural marketplace where Euro-American goods and values circulate most freely. Intellectual and cultural property rights are increasingly a feature of

---

2. Nancy Fraser, "From Redistribution to Recognition: Dilemmas of Justice in a "Postsocialist Age," in *Justice Interruptus: Critical Reflections on the "Postsocialist" Condition* (New York: Routledge, 1997), 11–40.

NGO consensus, in accord with the International Covenant on Economic, Social, and Cultural Rights (ICESCR). Within the United States itself, concepts of cultural equity are habitually used to underpin interpretations of minority civil rights. They have even been claimed by white supremacist groups who submit that the survival of "white" cultural traditions is endangered by creeping multiculturalism. While the mechanics of formal entitlement is the neolegal model for such claims, and while the nature of protection sought for such rights ranges from civil tolerance to institutional empowerment, the components of cultural justice are more often informal in nature. Perhaps this is how it should be. As Homi Bhabha astutely reminded us, there are cultural rights and cultural wrongs, and legal formalism—in the practical grip of the powerful, and in a system so devoted to individualism—may be ill-equipped to deliver the appropriate quotient of justice. But the history of cultural injustice is too profound and cruel for us to evade the challenge.

Extensive Justice

Take the rallying cry of "No Justice, No Peace," which emerged in response to the first Rodney King verdict. It was not simply a demand for a retrial that would fairly allocate culpability to members of the Los Angeles Police Department. It was an implicit challenge to the idea that African-Americans have ever expected, and can ever expect, constitutional protection under the laws of the land, given (1) the legacy of legal denial and the growth of a penitentiary system that is almost as effective in its de facto racial demarcation as Jim Crow and (2) the aborted commitment to race-conscious legislation ushered in after the Civil Rights Act. There is no question that the latter development signals the collapse and retreat of liberalism from its agenda for a racially just society, that is, a society without the existing racial division of labor, housing, education, income, and health. While "No Justice, No Peace" resonates, rhetorically, with the anticolonial spirit of "No Taxation without Representation," its challenge stands in historical judgment over the failures not only of liberal rights discourse, but also of the form of representative democracy ushered in by American republicanism. Just as the demand for popular representation did not end with, but was foreclosed by, the Constitutional Convention, the call for racial justice is unlikely to be satisfied by the limited legislation that majoritarian elites occasionally grant under pressure from mass movements.[3] The history of civil rights has shown that the attainment of formal citizenship in the fullest sense, while a crucial symbolic victory for all involved, often has little long-term effect upon the materially disadvantaged if unaccompanied by structural change, while it encourages the popular bromide that, officially, "racism no longer exists." Doing justice to cultural and to economic rights involves a permanent revolution in which people's identities well as their socioeconomic circumstances are continually transformed. Ultimately, this means transforming the identities associated with white heterosexual males *along with* the identities associated with women, lesbians and gays, and ethnic and racial groups.[4]

Formal equality is only one component of that revolution, although, given the strong historical link between rights discourse and American institutions, it is impossible to launch a public debate about the shape of the national culture without raising foundational questions about rights and citizenship. Even at that formal level, as Patricia Williams has argued, it will be necessary to expand our understanding of what rights entail: "The task is to expand property rights into a conception of civil rights, into the right to expect civility from others."[5] The larger task involves translating this principle into a respect for different cultural practices, where respect is normalized in the daily life not only of institutions but also of public and popular culture. But deep civility and respect demands more than simply majoritarian concessions to the

---

3. Stephen Steinberg, *Turning Back: The Retreat from Racial Justice in American Thought and Policy* (Boston: Beacon Press, 1995).

4. The growing scholarship on "whiteness," some calling for its "abolition," is a relevant body of literature: Toni Morrison, *Playing In the Dark: Whiteness in the Literary Imagination* (Cambridge: Harvard University Press, 1992); David Roediger, *Towards the Abolition of Whiteness* (New York: Verso, 1994); Noel Ignatiev and John Garvey, eds., *Race Traitor* (New York: Routledge, 1996); Theodore Allen, *The Invention of the White Race* (New York: Verso, 1994); Ruth Frankenberg, *White Women, Race Matters; The Social Construction of Whiteness* (Minneapolis: University of Minnesota Press, 1993); Shelley Fisher Fishkin, *Was Huck Black? Mark Twain and African-American Voices* (New York: Oxford University Press, 1993); (Alexander Saxton, *The Rise and Fall of the White Republic* (New York: Verso, 1992); Michael Rogin, *Blackface, White Noise: Jewish Immigrants in the Hollywood Melting Pot* (Berkeley: University of California Press, 1996); Melvin Oliver and Thomas Shapiro, *Black Wealth/White Wealth: A New Perspective on Racial Inequality* (New York: Routledge, 1995); Cheryl Harris, "Whiteness as Property," *Harvard Law Review* 106 (June 1993); George Lipsitz, "The Possessive Investment in Whiteness," [and other essays in the same issue] *American Quarterly* 47, no. 3 (September 1995): 369–87.

5. Patricia Williams, *The Alchemy of Race and Rights* (Cambridge: Harvard University Press, 1991), 165.

cultural distinctions of others. It also requires a complete overhaul of those distinctive forms of cultural identity that arise from white skin privilege, empowered masculinity, and the heteronormative presumption. Without this overhaul, where the V-8 engines of our dominant cultural identities are stripped down and retrofitted for a more sustainable social ecology, we will still be traveling at different speeds on the same highway.

The intractability of this sphere of cultural relations might be measured by the ugly reaction to the informal proscription of racist, sexist, and homophobic jokes cast, in recent years, as the "imposition" of "political correctness." Such humor is not exactly illegal (although its contextualization in the workplace and elsewhere can count as harassment), but its degree of prevalence speaks volumes about the current progress of cultural justice in any society. No one wants a humorless culture—a plague too long associated with leftists—but the freedom to utter speech like this is informally perceived as a cultural right, or wrong, on the speaker's part. Comics, professional and amateur, who joke about Jewish or African-American mothers or who use recognizably ethnic speech patterns, usually have supporting ethnic credentials, while those who cross ethnic boundaries, in the tradition of Lenny Bruce, have a clear political point to make. Black speech and Yiddish locutions are unconsciously used in daily life by most Americans, indeed most English speakers, and yet people feel defamed if and when these speakers draw inappropriate attention to their use of this speech. There is often a subtle line between these speech acts and more overt hate speech, which has been on the rise in public discourse for some time, much of it directed, again, at single African-American mothers, proverbially always on welfare. There is a much greater gulf between the tolerance, say, for vernacular black usage by whites, most notably in sports and music cultures, and contempt for official language claims for Black Speech, as exemplified by the recent furor over the Ebonics proposals on the part of Oakland educators seeking to instil cultural self-esteem among underprivileged black students.

Any such considerations of self-esteem disappear entirely when American language use passes beyond English. The constitutional battle over making English the official language of the United States ("English Only" laws have been passed in over two dozen states in the last decade) has been one of the many ugly elements of the anti-immigrant backlash directed mostly at Spanish speakers. It has also boosted the membership of the bizarre U.S. English movement to over one million members. Is there is a continuum that links the constitutionality of English Only—an issue consistently evaded by the current Supreme Court—with the demeaning impact of daily speech acts? If so, it is part of the extensive realm of cultural justice that I am trying to delineate, one in which respect for difference might be viewed as a durable principle of civility, rather than a temporary bureaucratic form of historical restitution.

To make a fine, but telling, distinction, we might compare this concept of extensive justice with the conservative legal use of "fairness" as currently applied to race-conscious programs and affirmative action laws. The backlash against such programs and laws, led by members of the Supreme Court such as Antonin Scalia and Clarence Thomas, is based on the argument that they are "unfair" to minorities and nonminorities alike. With recent cases regarding affirmative action, the Supreme Court has decided that "benign" preferential treatment on the basis of race and in the name of equality is morally and constitutionally equivalent to laws designed to subjugate a race. For Thomas (in *Adarand Constructors v. Peña*), "government cannot make us equal: it can only recognize, respect and protect us as equal before the law." For Scalia, in the same decision, there "can be no such thing as either a creditor or debtor race. To pursue the concept of racial entitlement even for the most admirable and benign of purposes is to reinforce and preserve for future mischief the way of thinking that produced race slavery, race privilege, and race hatred. In the eyes of Government, we are just one race here. It is American."[6]

This is surely the worst kind of analytic jurisprudence in action, flaunting its blindness to every last shred of cultural justice. On the other hand, we can expect that the willful retreat from race-conscious legislation as a medium for redistributive justice will only go so far. The self-esteem of the white majority depends upon a show of benevolence in allocating a limited share of the resources under its control to minorities. As Girardeau Spann has argued, the good cop–bad cop routine staged between congressional legislation and Supreme Court judicial review has proved effective in managing the process by which the bare minimum of redistributive justice is permitted. Because affirmative action programs tend to be centralized, and recognized primarily at the federal

---

6. Adarand Constructors v. Peña.

level, minorities are obliged to compete for resources on a national scale rather than a local one, where regional power and political self-determination is easier to achieve. Majoritarian preferences and assumptions are more easily enacted and absorbed into the formal writing of decisions in the highly centralized forum of the Supreme Court.[7]

The Clinton administration's policy of "mend it, don't end it" is a classically mindful expression of the prohibitive costs to the white majority when it is seen to renounce all responsibility for remedying those racial inequities that it created. Any abdication of political will that is too visible is likely to incite civil disorder and urban revolt. Nonetheless, the plurality decisions of the Supreme Court and state legislation like the California Civil Rights Initiative have accelerated the tendency to forbid any race-conscious remedial acts and to recognize only overtly intentional discrimination as a constitutional violation. Demonstrating racial disparities or institutional racism is no longer recognized as proof of unequal protection under the Fourteenth Amendment. Legal conservatives would have us believe that twenty-five years of remedial legislation have eradicated, or compensated for, all such constitutional violations and that it is near time to return to business as usual: in Scalia's words, "we must soon revert to the ordinary principles of our law, of our democratic heritage, and of our educational tradition."[8] For Scalia and his sympathizers, the period of temporary unfairness is almost over. The Constitution will once again be "color-blind." The legal culture of rights will be returned to its assumed default condition of neutrality, uniformity, and universality; the ground rules will be back in effect. Fair play will resume.

This fair-play scenario, which threatens an outcome similar to the regressive period following Reconstruction, must stand in stark contrast to any principle of justice for which overcoming racism involves taking race into account on a permanent, rather than simply a remedial, basis en route to improving the lives of all citizens. Effective principles of justice must confront the present and future legacy of the racial formation of a state in which African-Americans in particular were included (not excluded) as nonparticipants and where their chattel labor was a condition of freedom for the white majority to assert its natural rights and its monopoly of wealth and property. Only in this his-

---

7. Freeman v. Pitts, 112 S. Ct. 1430 (1992).
8. Giradeau Spann, *Race Against the Court: The Supreme Court and Minorities in Contemporary America* (New York University Press, 1993), chapter 8.

torical light can we rightfully understand Scalia's "ordinary principles of our law" to be nothing ordinary at all, but, rather, the result of the economic and social history of this nation-state and therefore an embodiment of the inequalities of majoritarian interests in their very ground rules. As for Scalia's disingenuous reference to "our educational tradition," he is referring to precisely the sector of social opportunity where African-Americans, Hispanics, and American Indians are most disadvantaged, since they fare worse than Anglos when placed in a "meritocratic" system of standardized testing. In the face of today's debates about multicultural education, moreover, anyone who knows the least thing about the historical record of religious battles over school curricula, more fractious in periods of the nineteenth century than today, will recognize these appeals to some common educational tradition as a ludicrous fiction.

And what of the Supreme Court's record on reviewing the nation's "democratic heritage"? Do we need to be reminded of the rank arrogance of these high judges in the annals of constitutional history, who, under the pressure of what Madison referred to as "the iron law of oligarchy," have boosted their own power to protect and enrich business moguls; routinely voided acts of Congress; discouraged the application of the Bill of Rights to the states (until 1933); dismissed the notion of women as "persons" at the same time as corporations were designated as such, and under the Fourteenth Amendment at that; nullified the status of American Indian nations in spite of long-standing international treaties; sanctioned the use of eugenics laws to restrict immigration; repressed, imprisoned, and deported political dissidents and labor reformers; and awarded the U.S. president almost total and unconstitutional control over foreign policy, including, most notoriously, the power to wage war. It does not go without saying that these legal habits, among many others, of serving the wealthy and the powerful, and the racial majority, belong to Scalia's "democratic heritage" in which "the ordinary principles of our law" must once again prevail.

The principles of affirmative action—designed to bring racial minorities into the mainstream of public life—have always inspired some ambivalence, even among their advocates, but the 1994 congressional election was the event that elevated racial preference into a political "wedge." Suddenly affirmative action, with AFDC running a close second, was proclaimed to be a leading cause of injustice in the nation, and popular sentiment was held to be running against it. Statistical revelations about the existence of a "glass ceiling" for women and minorities were brushed aside in the Republican stampede to embrace the newly salient "rights" of economically depressed white males. Within six months, affirmative action had been catapulted into the gladiators' ring reserved for the two or three issues that the pundits designate, at any one time, as eligible for the public spectacle of high political consumption.

How did that happen? The depressed economic condition of white workers is only one part of the story and is hardly divorced from racial sentiment, given that they continue to enjoy the psychological "wages of whiteness" that David Roediger has described as the birthright of the white working poor in the United States.[9] Making a political idea into "common sense," even among a relatively homogeneous group, is a complex cultural process in which changes in the law do not simply emerge as more-or-less final outcomes, elevated above the fray: the law is a real cultural agent, however provisional, in this process. For one thing, the law exudes an air of neutral commonality that makes all other claims seem, by comparison, exceptional and interested. But there were also other factors at work in the sphere of public opinion, no less committed to paying lip service to the creed of fairness, no less bent on trampling on cultural justice.

Cultural Politics and the Culture Wars

In the case of the affirmative action backlash, the vehicle for this process had been a fractious public debate about cultural values, or, more specifically, the values of an assumed "common culture" in a nation-state whose history has been marked by an extraordinary degree of multilingualism, a plurality of religious traditions, and a variety of diverse regional and ethnic subcultures. Indeed it is more accurate to observe that this debate has been over the shape of the dominant culture in the United States rather than over a patently false consensus about common culture. In a general vein, the prosecutor's case against multicultural challenges to the dominance of white, Christian, Anglo-European values might be summarized in a way that echoes Judge Scalia's comments about the law. *It is time to revert to the ordinary princi-*

---

9. David Roediger, *The Wages of Whiteness: Race and the Making of the American Working Class* (London: Verso, 1991).

ples of our culture, whose fundamental values are not perceived as political. Neutral principles of excellence, as embodied in the ground rules of the common cultural heritage, must once again prevail.

Whether it is the ground rules of a culture or those of the law, a neutral environment is one in which dominant interests are able to masquerade informally as a background, default condition. Dominant cultural groups always fare best under the rule of the gender-free, color-blind, heteronormative "common culture." (The *general public,* for example, is a term that excludes the *majority* of citizens: minorities, recent immigrants, youth, the intelligentsia, the institutionalized, radicals, religious fundamentalists, etc.). It is such a "common culture" that traditionally operates as affirmative action for privileged white males. In the same way, the rules of property, contract, and tort law make the vast inequalities in our society seem like part of nature or, at least, like factory settings. Attempts to change the settings are thus seen as aggressively unfair alterations of a commonly recognized norm in order to meet the needs of those with "special interests."

It is not my purpose here to take issue with what is fair and what is not—the proverbial level field of play is much too corrupt to honor such a discussion. Nor do I believe it is necessary to prove that the forms of cultural politics that have provoked so much conflict in the last thirty years are real modes of political engagement and not mere diversions from the struggle for improvements in the material conditions of people's lives. Proprietary struggles over culture have proven to be one of the fiercest sites of entrenched resistance to change in the post-CRA era. The vast amounts of funding and media persuasion devoted by conservatives to the Culture Wars are ample evidence of the high stakes and passions invested in monoculturalism. Right wing foundations and their hired mouthpieces have elevated "paid speech" into the dominant public force in these debates, reinforcing the majoritarian perception that powerful white males have proprietary rights over the history and culture of the country. Nor is there any evidence that these conflicts are subsiding. The avalanche of official political attention to cultural issues has only swelled in recent years, barely missing a beat after Clinton's accession in 1992, when neoconservatives like Irving Kristol declared that the Culture Wars were over, and that his side had lost.

At the time of writing, the stage set aside for public controversy is occupied by the debate over Ebonics, the National History Standards, the future of the NEA and the NEH, same-sex marriage, and the regulating of Internet speech. The vestiges of previous conflicts are still active, like smoking volcanoes: "political correctness," bilingualism, hate speech, multiculturalism (and its many alternatives: multiracialism, cross-culturalism, and interculturalism), educational testing, the "inassimilable" cultures of new immigrant communities, family values, gays in the military, gangsta rap, and pornography. Interspersed between these battlefields are the megastadiums hosting the trials of the month, where many of the great cultural pathologies of national civil life are dissected for mass media consumption. Timothy McVeigh, O. J. Simpson, Colin Ferguson, and Sheik Abdel Rahman and, offstage, the memories of Lorena Bobbitt, Rodney King, Howard Beach, the Menendez brothers, Amy Fisher, Woody Allen, Mike Tyson, Baby M, Charles Stuart, William Kennedy Smith, Glen Ridge, and Central Park, not to mention the large, televised pseudotrials on Capitol Hill like the Supreme Court judge confirmations, Clarence Thomas–Anita Hill, and hearings on Iran-Contra, and the like. On Capitol Hill, the Republican class of 1994 adopted a prosecutive posture toward the alleged "cultural elite," intent on wringing out every last drop of liberal guilt from the hyperemoting anchormen and women of the TV nation. And in higher education, where the left has gained its strongest foothold in the last two decades, the sustained attack on tenured radicals continues unabated. This campaign is only the most visible feature of the drive to corporatize colleges and universities, where the low-wage revolution has penetrated so deeply that the de facto erosion of tenure has long preceded attempts, now on the horizon, to abolish this principle that is so vital to the freedom of academic speech.[10]

With this example of academic labor in mind, it is tempting to consider that the furor over Great Books, cultural studies, multiculturalism, and political correctness in the academy is simply a diversionary smokescreen for advancing the real economic interests of managerial elites and trustees. This is a callous misrecognition of the powerful attempts to fuel the race fires in education that began in the battles over school integration after *Brown v. Board of Education* and that continue today in curricular moves to teach the history of women and people of color. It also ignores the fact that education and cultural products in general are a vast economic sphere in their own right. American gradu-

---

10. See Cary Nelson, ed., *Will Teach For Food* (Minneapolis: University of Minnesota Press, 1997), and *Manifesto of a Tenured Radical* (New York: New York University Press, 1997); and the special *Social Text* issue on Academic Labor (Summer 1997).

ate credentials are one of the most valued sources of cultural capital in the world, and the research activities conducted through the arm of higher education account for a huge portion of the information sector of the national and transnational economy. The debate about cultural values not only affects these economic sectors directly, it is part of the content of the information itself. These are much more than simply contests over national cultural symbolism; they have immense economic value within the culture and information industries themselves.

This becomes clearer if we move beyond the Great Books debate—should T. S. Eliot make room for Toni Morrison?—to the realm of raunchy popular culture, the other preferred target of conservative morality-brokers. Here, the traditional contradiction between free market conservatism and cultural conservatives is all the more apparent, with the lords of Hollywood and the moguls of multimedia foreordained to take the heat. Culture trading is a vast economy of transnational scale, and its dependence upon spectacular products puts it in direct conflict with the national moral campaigns of cultural conservatives, whether Christian, Islamic, Hindu, or Jewish, whether in France, India, or Zaire. Indeed, the new transnational trading zones are often defined by the willingness of their national clients to liberalize the circulation and reception of cultural and information products. Legislation that favors the global reach of the transnational media Goliaths still vies with judicial attempts on the part of national bodies to regulate the flow of culture across their sovereign borders, attempts which themselves often appeal to a selective, moralizing definition of national, regional, or local cultures. In this global context, local cultural justice, embodied in older reformist agendas like UNESCO's New International Information Order, has long been part of the response to the perceived imperialism of Western culture industries, in a climate where the "free flow" of neoliberal markets results in a one-way flow of cultural products. Nothing appeals more powerfully to the nation-state system of world politics than the concept of a country's right to self-representation in the global field. More often than not, however, it is this "frontier justice" of nationalism that facilitates the domestic repression of minority cultures.

The new patterns of economic integration are not fully global. They have been culturally marked by regional, supranational agreements like NAFTA, G3 (Mexico, Venezuala, and Colombia), the Andean Pact, ASEAN, the EEC, and the Southern Cone (Brazil, Argentina,

Chile). Cultural brokering within and between these entities is performed on behalf of powerful producer states, or industrial blocs like Hollywood. A more critical form of brokering accepts that the new public spheres and funded networks emerging along with supranational economic integration are potential sites of visibility for groups and communities culturally or politically denied at the level of individual states. These new sites are real opportunities for cultural justice, hitherto only available in forums like the UN, to indigenous groups constituted as nations, or to international movements (women, environmentalists, political prisoners) through NGOs with access to the UN. Like organized labor, pushing now for a living wage for workers in offshore factories and free trade zones, the scope of cultural activism increasingly crosses borders.[11]

Despite their bureaucratic underpinnings, it is important to imagine these new supranational cultural formations in provisionally utopian ways. This habit has a long precedent in the syncretic traditions of music, dance, and religion of the African diaspora for which mixing and fusing cultural influences is the core principle of survival and innovation. The latest exemplars are champions of the *mestizo* aesthetic of the American borderlands, where the history and experience of cultural mingling presents itself as the crucible for a postnational future that is a hysterically modern medley of syntheses: the future is *mestizo*. Guillermo Gómez-Peña, the border performance artist and court jester of hybridity, has given the "taco-surrealist" picture of this dechauvinized culture in his prophetic vision of the "New World Border" after the "Gringostroika" of the "Free Raid Agreement":

> The monocultural territories of the disbanded United States, commonly known as Gringolandia, have become drastically impoverished, leading to massive migration of unemployed *wasp-backs* to the South. All major metropolises have been fully *borderised*. . . . They all look like downtown Tijuana on a Saturday night. . . . The legendary U.S.-Mexico borderline, affectionately known as "The Tortilla Curtain," no longer exists. Pieces of the great Tortilla are now sentimental souvenirs hanging on the bedroom walls of idiotic tourists like you. . . . The twin cities of San Dollariego and

---

11. Andrew Ross, ed., *No Sweat: Fashion, Free Trade and the Rights of Garment Workers* (London: Verso, 1997).

Tijuana have united to form the Maquiladora Republic of San Diejuana. Hong Kong relocates to Baja California to constitute the powerful Baja-Kong, the world's greatest producer of porn and tourist kitsch. The cities of Lost Angeles and Tokyo share a corporate government called Japangeles, in charge of all the financial operations of the Pacific Rim. The Republik of Berkeley is the only Marxist-Leninist nation left on the globe . . . The CIA joined forces with the DEA and moved to Hollywood to create a movie studio that specializes in producing and distributing multicultural utopias. . . . Ageing pop star Madonna has reincarnated as Saint Frida Kahlo. She roams around nasty streets in search of people who suffer from identity blisters and heals them. . . . Nearly every important city in the FUSR has a Museum of Cultimultural Art. They all feature classical shows from the '80s and before as a reminder of what culture used to be before Gringostroika destroyed all traditional borders and categories. Among the most popular travelling exhibits are "1,000 Ex-Minority Artists" . . .[12]

It is not by happenstance that this macaronic image of a hybrid near future has emerged at the same moment as a fierce rekindling of nativist sentiment into the legislative firestorm around California's Proposition 187, where welfare-bashing attitude fuels anti-immigration hysteria and vice versa.

Developments like this should remind us that it is a mistake to approach the national question as if it were removed from the supranational, especially in a nation that exports cultural values and paradigms more successfully than its manufacturing products these days (aside from weapons and civilian aircraft, software and culture are leading U.S. products) and whose recent record of immigration has exacerbated long-running nativist anxieties to the point of the current legislative backlash. Long-standing North American settler fears about the displacement of native-born labor and the nonassimilability of cultural traits have been reawakened. There is nothing new here, except for the "problem" of the acculturation of specifically non-European migrants, mostly of Latino, Afro-Caribbean, and Asian origins. What *is* different about the latest nativist revival is its backdrop of the waning of the

12. Guillermo Gómez-Peña, "The New World Border: Prophecies for the End of the Century," *Drama Review* 38 (spring 1994): 119–42.

modern nation-state, set off by the vast economic restructuring that has progressively transferred the exercise of fiscal power away from the centralized national bureaucracies into the quasi-sovereign fiefdoms of the corporate transstate. That the state bureaucracy can still be invoked as a resisting bulwark against this transfer of power offshore has made the state's capacity to function as a coherent expression of national cultural identity all the more of a problem and subject to ever-increasing public attention. This, then, is the context of the heated debate about multiculturalism, framed, on the right, by race-based phobias about the advent of anything approaching cultural equity, in the center, by fears about the "centrifugal" tendency of cultural "fragmentation," and, on the left, by concerns about the corporate state's management of cultural diversity or the hidebound essentialism of identity politics.

The same might be said of the current Republican crusade to dismantle the New Deal version of the welfare state. In the debates that surrounded the Constitutional Convention, radical Democrats advocated states' rights and local self-government against the centralized state favored by conservative Federalists. Today, these ideological positions, crudely sketched, appear to have been reversed, largely because of the growth, in the course of this century, of the state's powers to administer, regulate, and distribute resources. In reality, however, we find these oppositions fused in productive tension today within what many regard as the one-party state of corporate liberalism. Nominally conservative attacks on the progressive, or redistributive, character of the state coexist with the neoliberal need to retain the monopoly of central authority to make laws that will enrich national and transnational capital. (The most recent example is the deregulatory rewriting of the sixty-year-old telecommunication law, intended to smooth the way for the monopoly mergers that will facilitate the information superhighway and its would-be governorship by the media-entertainment/information leviathans). Thus are the contradictions of the corporate state resolved, largely through the symbolic staging of political conflict.

A similar argument applies to the history of debates about pluralism and national identity, staged in the tension between techniques of Americanization explicitly intended to purge preindustrial cultural traits and labor habits, and the national celebration of ethnic pluralism that came to incorporate the unofficial persistence of these distinctive identities. Glossed over in that tension is the story of the racial formation of the state, specifically in relation to native genocide, African slavery, and Chicano criminalization. Unlike in other postcolonial "settler" states like Australia and Canada, multiculturalism is not official, top-down, national policy in the United States. (The more instructive comparison would be with Brazil, which shares more structural history with the United States as a slavery society. In Brazil, the chief democratic myth is that of a "raceless" society, and so political controversy centers on class. The U.S. equivalent is that of a "classless" society, in which politics, consequently, is insistently displaced onto questions of race.) And yet, the emergent dogma of multiculturalism has already threatened to displace the demands for *multiracialism* and to obliterate public recognition of the power dynamic that exists between dominant and subordinate cultures. In addition, and because this dogma is so tied to the cult of ethnicity, its increasing centrality has also displaced the associated critiques of the gender-based and heteronormative state. Among non-European populations, the persistence of racial stratification and prejudice—in labor, income, health, housing, and civic respect—appears to be more fundamental in its hold upon the national political economy. The deep racialization of these inequities is not likely to be remedied by pretty-ing-up corporate diversity statistics (while leaving corporate culture unaltered) or by injecting some color into school curricula.

The Numbers Game

Struggles for cultural equity may begin and end with deep alterations of civil society, but they cannot afford to ignore numerical assessments of recognition and redistribution—not in a nation so devoted to statistical forms of expression in government and in economic life. Because of the representative nature of North American democracy, movements for cultural equity are not only concerned with the securing of rights, but are also directed at the visible attainment of representation in public service and professional life. A typical outcome of such movements can be summed up in Bill Clinton's promise to make his 1992 administration "look more like America" by deferring to ethnic and gender demographics in making government appointments, a procedure adopted, before and since, by many nonfederal institutions and encouraged by affirmative action policies. These policies have been largely successful, even in blue-collar and public employment, but they have arguably worked best at the managerial levels. The successes have also been accompanied by new kinds of class polarization within minority communities because the racial division of labor have remained relatively untouched, relegating workers of color to the least desirable jobs or excluding them from legitimate job markets that carry health benefits and social security. So, too, the habitual price of representation in the middle-class professions is acceptance of the restrictive codes of bourgeois Anglo civility; precisely those ground rules that have, in the past, guaranteed racial exclusivity. The result is a growing divide between the sufficiently empowered, in a position to broker the redistribution of resources for those caught in the poverty trap, and the disadvantaged, from whom the former are culturally detached. In Jefferson's day, as now, the system of representative government was intended candidly as insurance for republican elites against popular democracy. There was no truly democratic argument against popular democracy, except that it was unworkable in a large and populous society. Nonetheless, the institution of the North American system of checks and balances was not so much a protection of minorities and individuals against majoritarian rule as an explicit acceptance of the permanence of class inequalities, inscribed henceforth into the ground rules of representative government.

Even more decisive was the establishment of representation by population, entailing a rigorous census taking that has come to pervade the administration of national life with the cult of statistics and demographics. Majority and minority are more than just a numbers game, but they are also precisely that, and all the more so since the Office of Management and Budget's Statistical Directive 15 of 1977, which created what David Hollinger has called the "ethno-racial pentagon" of national bureaucratic life: African American, Asian American, Hispanic (or Latino), Indigenous (or Native American), and European American.[13] While these categories are highly contingent, they are impressively resilient once put in place, and very quickly attain the air of natural, normalized facts, creating expectations in others' minds about how to treat members of each category. They make very little sense as categories linked by some common culture—what does such a culture mean, for example, to those of Vietnamese, Chinese, Korean, Japanese, Thai, Filipino, Samoan, and South Asian descent who are identified as Asian/Pacific Americans? Over time,

---

13. David Hollinger, *Post-Ethnic America: Beyond Multiculturalism* (New York, 1995).

however, these categories exert a cohesive cultural influence upon those obliged to share group membership.

With the bureaucratic creation of such broad, multiethnic categories, census classification has continued to boost numbers of whites. Most Mexican-Americans are primarily from native stock and yet many are now classed as whites. The blood quantum for American Indians has long been used as a means of depleting Indian numbers as part of a genocidal federal policy implemented by laws that took advantage of the sovereign status of Indian nations to systematically marginalize their populations from Euro-American society. The resulting legal history, from the frontier to the courtroom, ran from the Doctrine of Discovery and Rights of Conquest, to the restriction of trading rights, the breakup of traditional land tenure, and federal incorporation of land into domestic assets, the destruction of traditional jurisprudence and religious observance, the brutal policy of the Indian Wars, the termination of sovereign nations (109 nations were terminated between 1953 and 1958), massive urban relocation of half the Indian population under the Relocation Act of 1956, the counterinsurgency assassination of indigenous leaders in the AIM, and the radioactive colonialism of military policy around the tribal lands of the West and Southwest. While statistical demography has played a pernicious role in this history, it has also become an important tool for legal opposition. Estimates of precolonial urban Indian populations have been used (1) to contest the legality, partially based on the thesis of "vacant lands," of conquest and discovery, (2) to strengthen the case for remedial legislation and for reclaiming the land base, and (3) to generally challenge the cultural mythology of the vanishing Indian.

A different form of demographic mentality has governed the color line in North America, most notably in the administration of the one-drop rule and in its legacy—the persistence of bichromatic public consciousness about two nations, black and white, that excludes any accounting for the multiracial mixtures that make up the emerging majority of Americans. This color line, which once separated what neoconservatives used to call "unmeltable ethnics" in the black nation from assimilable ethnics in the white nation, remains very much in effect, mostly because of institutional racism and partly because empowered blacks have often been constrained to use it, in a fiscal climate where limited resources are made available for competing minorities, to advance their interests over those of other nonwhite minorities.[14] In an age of social austerity, or more accurately, proscarcity politics, targeted at the working poor and unemployed, the competition for resources and low-wage jobs is sharpened. The contest is not just among minorities, but also between native born and immigrants. Lobbying for a share of shrinking resources is difficult enough. Campaigning for rights and resources on the basis of restitution or ancestral reparations, is even tighter. These are the circumstances under which the politics of ethnoracial tradition come to be appraised in transactional terms. Not surprisingly, a cultural calculus comes into play. Purist appeals to blood identity and undiluted heritage are important cards to be played in the game of distributive politics. Claims for cultural justice are reduced to fiscal assessments; authenticity and racial essence figure as blue-chip collateral. Such conditions of enforced scarcity discourage any acknowledgment of cultural mixing, let alone the development of a multiracial society. Under such circumstances, the recognition of mixed-race hybridity weakens and undermines the legitimacy of entitlement claims. In addition, these conditions lend themselves to the process by which cultural essentialism assumes a commodity value that is difficult to renounce in hard times.

As some level minority demographics, however undercounted from census to census, get their share of recognition from the system of state apportionment. Given the history of denial and exclusion, and the abdication of any political will to confront racism, cultural justice is unlikely to be served any other way soon. But there is a high price for any society to pay in accepting a cultural politics that takes its cue from such census classifications. Culturally, it closes off the often vast differences in values, beliefs, and practices espoused by members within these group identifications. Sometimes, these differences are the result of multiple ethnic traditions—Cuban, Mexican, Iberian, Puerto Rican, Central and South American, in the case of Latinos. Sometimes, they are the result of divergent social identities, relating to sexuality, gender, and religion, within these subethnic groupings themselves. Ultimately, the language of collective identity, whether encouraged by the state's bureaucratic categories or by cultural nationalism, cannot fully satisfy

---

14. Jorge Klor de Alva makes this argument in "Beyond Black, Brown or White: Cultural Diversity, Strategic Hybridity, and the Future of Democracy" (Bohen Foundation Lecture Series on Cultural Diversity, March 1994, unpublished).

the need for autonomous action and self-organization that radical democracy lives by.[15]

Generic Justice

Consider also the unequal treatment of cultural practices in the public eye. Hard-core rap, especially in the gangsta genre, draws the full repressive attention of state agents—the ostensible aim of this attention being to expunge uncivil speech from the public sphere. But it amounts to outlawing the only form of cultural expression with experiential links to the life of poor minorities, and in the name of penalizing quite possibly the most *powerless* manifestations of the masculine legacies of misogyny and homophobia. By contrast, consider the degree to which a relentlessly racist and misogynistic film like 1994's summer Schwartzenegger vehicle, *True Lies,* was not only smiled upon by a militarized public consciousness basking in the rays of post–cold war triumphalism but also, and quite inexplicably, praised by Bob Dole on the 1996 campaign trail as a film with his kind of family values. On the one hand, we have, in gangsta rap, an attempt to represent the antisocial desperation of the economically denied black male; on the other hand, in *True Lies,* a postheroic representation of the sadistic swagger of Homo Pentagonus. To take another example, consider how avant-garde artists exploring the full realm of homosexual expression have attracted widespread public censure and often been denied access to performance venues where, in the same communities, and sometimes in the same spaces, the heterosexual pornography business is booming. The differing treatments accorded these casual indicators of cultural diversity is stark evidence of cultural injustice at the level of public representation.

To turn to representation *within* a cultural practice is to encounter a different kind of cultural justice—respect for the rules and laws of the genre. In the examples I have just mentioned, that would involve taking into account the generic conventions of ghettocentric rap, the action-adventure blockbuster, body-based performance art, and popular pornography. For the cultural critic, verdicts passed upon the controversial or prejudicial content of cultural forms are usually qualified

---

15. See Anthony Appiah, "Identity, Authenticity, Survival: Multicultural Societies and Social Reproduction," in Gutmann, ed., *Multiculturalism,* 149–64.

by some knowledge about the genre—its dominant formulas, its history of formalistic self-consciousness, its determination by the demands of culture industries and cultural institutions, its contract with audience expectations, its social origins and uses, its deep political structure, and so on. Some genres, of course, are stronger in their formation than others, but most are highly evolved and ever maturing arrangements that nonetheless preserve a strict core of regulations over time. Any lay user or aficionado knows that the conventional rules exercise a kind of quasi-legal sway over what is possible to say and do within the limits of the genre; generically speaking, characters don't suffer gory deaths in TV sitcoms any more than they can be reincarnated without the help of advanced technology in science fiction novels. The "laws" of a genre are therefore a complex form of legislation, both formal *and* social, since their mature shape only comes into being in a particular time and place. I would go so far as to say that they are the ground rules, however hidden, for any discussion of cultural material. All too often, however, generic conventions are habitually neglected, to the detriment of all, when charges of sexism, racism, or homophobia are brought to bear against a film, a song, or a custom. Aficionados of the genre will have a different judgment to make; an insider's assessment of the text's adherence to or interpretation of the rules.

Yet another kind of cultural justice comes into play when considering the realm of everyday creative activities. These are informal practices that, however rigorously organized, do not usually evolve into a stable generic form. The most inventive examples can be found in youth culture, where commercial cultural products are often consumed and used in unforeseen and yet inspired ways, and where cultural materials are generally treated as a catalyst rather than as a settled destination for communication between individuals and groups. It is in this informal sphere that social identities are provisionally tried on and tried out, sometimes leading to, but more often challenging those usually associated with the prevailing definitions of behavior appropriate to gender, race, class, and sexuality. And it is here that youth culture in particular provides a crucible for experimenting with old and new, outside of the constraints of formally established genres and customs. The location of this informal sphere is often given the shorthand designation of "the street" (still a site where males are most comfortable), but the creativity is just as likely to be found on the suburban walls of a teenage girl's bedroom, or in front of her wardrobe mirror. To speak of cultural justice here is to refer to an intricate system of peer innovation and emulation, where generational respect for inventive interpretations of style, language, and self-expression establishes the informal logic of youth taste. Respect for this logic conventionally includes the complaint that commercial popular culture does not do justice to the fluidity and vibrancy of informal or street cultures when it tries to represent the latest thing. Moving up the food chain dilutes and drains the street version of its protein-rich roots. Responding to pressure from above, each community tries to retain control over its distinctive forms. There are true practitioners, and there are sellouts, rather like the distinction within the hard-core rap audience between performers who "front" and those who "represent" (represent the true hip-hop spirit).

Conclusion

It may be a far cry from the concept of the hip-hop nation (or queer nation, or any other alternative version of nationality) to the concept of the national culture that has recently been subject to such heated scrutiny. But there are links between these spheres, and I have tried to follow some of them by examining the quasi-legal basis of representation in each sphere.

The phenomenon of conservative, even racist, multiculturalism has demonstrated the dangers of doing otherwise. Consider the version proposed by Charles Murray and Richard Herrnstein, authors of *The Bell Curve*. They call it "wise ethnocentrism," and it appeals cynically to the virtues of cultural difference. Ethnic minority groups, Murray and Herrnstein argue, should be released from the injunction to assimilate and should be encouraged to protect and sustain their "clannish" self-esteem. Cultures are different, they should remain so, and there is no need to compare one with another. Best not to mix at all, really. In their version, a prescription for segregationism masquerades as tolerance for human variation.[16]

Etienne Balibar has most forcefully argued that the new racism proceeds not from older myths of superiority about "biological heredity" but rather from nominally antiracist beliefs about the harmfulness of abolishing "cultural differences." Culturalism, he argues, has come

---

16. The most succinct formulation can be found in Charles Murray and Richard Herrnstein, "Race, Genes and I.Q.—An Apologia," *New Republic*, 31 October 1994, 27–37.

to replace biologism as the basis for a racism without race.[17] It may be that this is more true of the insurgent European racism than of North America, but, at the very least, it seems to me that Balibar is a little premature in declaring the death of biological racism. To see why, one need look no further than *The Bell Curve*. But beyond the hue and cry raised by that book, there lies a host of other social Darwinist tracts bristling with biological determinism.[18] While cultural racism is still relatively weak, hereditarianism is always at the ready, with trumped-up statistics and pseudoscience, to prove that redistributive politics, in whatever form, is wasted on the "cognitively disabled" poor.

At least one lesson can be drawn from this. Science, and not cultural values, is the common language in liberal democracies. By that I do not, however, mean to suggest that science is not shaped by cultural values, nor that everyone has equal access to the authority that science confers on truth claims. On the contrary, any movement for cultural justice has to address the way in which science both meets social and cultural demands, and fashions these demands in turn. With the new eugenics, biotech-style, waiting in the wings, and the legacy of nineteenth-century scientific racism still dormant and festering in the public mind, there is no defensible alternative.

As for the liberal Left, claims for cultural justice, insofar as they go beyond the limited domain of representation, must be tied to criteria that the actually existing state does not satisfy. Why? Because, unlike the rule of law, which derives its authority from the state's appeal to precedent, substantive justice ultimately derives its authority from what is radically lacking in the state. To succeed, the conditions of cultural injustice have to be historically explicable, and their resolution has to be seen to lie in a realizable future. There is a liberal version of this notion called the "promise of America" in which the eternally young nation (despite being much older than most of the world's sovereign states) serves justice upon all of her children in some future, ideal state of the union. Liberation politics, most notably in the form of the civil rights movement, partially appealed to such a narrative; the state, once transformed, will be coterminous with the transformation of its citi-

---

17. Etienne Balibar, "Is There a 'Neo-Racism'?" in Etienne Balibar and Immanuel Wallerstein, *Race, Nation, Class* (London: Verso, 1993).

18. A good example of the genre (and much more respectable than *The Bell Curve*) is Robert Wright, *The Moral Animal: Why We Are the Way We Are: The New Science of Evolutionary Psychology* (New York: Pantheon, 1994).

zens. Identity politics, in many ways its successor, assumes that its constituents are already transformed, and it demands not only their recognition as women, gays, Latinos, but also their right to representation and their empowerment within the state and civil society on the basis of these identities. Yet another branch of movement politics seeks to expose the state's protection of special interests under the guise of neutrality; for example, it challenges how the state promotes heterosexuality in its assumptions about the heteronormativity of all aspects of citizenship.[19] This last initiative, associated with queer theory, is also consonant with a race politics aimed at the "abolition of whiteness," and a gender politics that challenges the masculine proprietary identity of the public (as opposed to the private) sphere.

We cannot afford to abandon any of these three strategies; claims for cultural justice must be able to draw upon liberation politics, upon identity politics, and upon a politics that interrogates state neutrality.

Flexible communication between generations and communities demands it, no less than the long overdue rapprochement between the cultural and social justice wings of left-liberal thought. For too long there has been a division between those concerned with justice claims relating primarily to gender, race, and sexuality, and those concerned with economic issues. Class politics must thrive alongside group-differentiated politics in a broad coalition. Cultural politics can no longer be trivialized as a colorful sideshow, just as political economy can no longer be regarded as the sole preserve of unreconstructed Marxists. The managers of the United States's representative institutions have always been more willing to grant political democracy than economic democracy on the basis that symbolic reform is less of a concession than the redistribution of material wealth. On the other hand, people increasingly feel their right to respect for their cultural identities almost as strongly as they feel the benefits of the social wage. To recognize this is to insist that the exercise of citizenship is a cultural achievement just as much as it is a socioeconomic prerogative. It takes a great deal of effort to separate the one from the other—effort that is surely better spent in the common pursuit of goals.

---

19. See Lisa Duggan, "Queering the State," *Social Text* 39 (summer 1994): 1–14.

Contributors

Carol J. Clover is Professor of Rhetoric at the University of California–Berkeley.

Rosemary J. Coombe is Professor of Law at the University of Toronto.

Marjorie Garber is Professor of English at Harvard University and Director of the Harvard Center for Literary and Cultural Studies.

Thomas R. Kearns is William Hastie Professor of Philosophy and Professor of Law, Jurisprudence, and Social Thought at Amherst College.

William Ian Miller is Professor of Law at the University of Michigan.

Andrew Ross is Professor of Comparative Literature and Director of the American Studies Program at New York University.

Austin Sarat is William Nelson Cromwell Professor of Jurisprudence and Political Science and Professor of Law, Jurisprudence, and Social Thought at Amherst College. He is President-elect of the Law and Society Association.

Martha Woodmansee is Professor of English and Comparative Literature at Case Western Reserve University and Director of the Society for Critical Exchange.

Index